RICOEUR AS ANOTHER

SUNY series in the Philosophy of the Social Sciences

Lenore Langsdorf, editor

RICOEUR AS ANOTHER

The Ethics of Subjectivity

Edited by
Richard A. Cohen
James L. Marsh

State University of New York Press

Published by
State University of New York Press, Albany

© 2002 State University of New York

All rights reserved

Printed in the United States of America

No part of this book may be used or reproduced in any manner whatsoever without written permission. No part of this book may be stored in a retrieval system or transmitted in any form or by any means including electronic, electrostatic, magnetic tape, mechanical, photocopying, recording, or otherwise without the prior permission in writing of the publisher.

For information, address State University of New York Press,
90 State Street, Suite 700, Albany, NY 12207

Production by Judith Block
Marketing by Anne Valentine

Library of Congress Cataloging-in-Publication Data

Ricoeur as another : the ethics of subjectivity / edited by Richard A. Cohen, James L. Marsh.
    p. cm. — (SUNY series in the philosophy of the social sciences)
    Includes bibliographical references and index.
    ISBN 0-7914-5189-5 (alk. paper)—ISBN 0-7914-5190-9 (pbk. : alk. paper)
    1. Ricoeur, Paul. 2. Ethics. 3. Subjectivity. I. Cohen, Richard A. II. Marsh, James L. III. Series.

B2430.R554 R53 2002
194—dc21
                                                                                                                    2001031188

10 9 8 7 6 5 4 3 2 1

Contents

Introduction by James L. Marsh	vii
Sigla	xv
PART ONE. RICOEUR IN HIMSELF	1
1. Personal Identity *Charles E. Reagan*	3
2. The Doubleness of Subjectivity: Regenerating the Phenomenology of Intentionality *Lenore Langsdorf*	33
3. Rethinking Subjectivity: Narrative Identity and the Self *David Rasmussen*	57
4. Can There Be a Science of Action? *John van den Hengel*	71
5. Literary and Science Fictions: Philosophers and Technomyths *Don Ihde*	93
PART TWO. RICOEUR IN RELATION TO OTHERS	107
6. Ricoeur and Levinas: Solicitude in Reciprocity and Solitude in Existence *Patrick L. Bourgeois*	109
7. Moral Selfhood: A Levinasian Response to Ricoeur on Levinas *Richard A. Cohen*	127

8. Between Conviction and Critique: Reflexive
   Philosophy, Testimony, and Pneumatology
   Eric Crump   161

9. At the Limit of Practical Wisdom: Moral Blindness
   David Pellauer   187

10. Response to Rawls
    Bernard P. Dauenhauer   203

11. The Right and the Good: A Solution to the
    Communicative Ethics Controversy
    James L. Marsh   223

About the Contributors   235

Index   237

Introduction

After an initial reading of Ricoeur's *Oneself as Another*, we have the impression of a very significant work. One may or may not go all the way with Charles Reagan, one of the contributors to this volume, when he says that this is "Ricoeur's most elegantly written, clearly organized, and closely argued work" (2), or, later in his essay, that the book is "the very model of his philosophical style" (33). But we do have a sense nonetheless that the work brings to a tentative conclusion, always open to further development, a series of different but related inquiries carried out over the course of a lifetime into the self, freedom, interpretation, narrative, and critique.

One relatively new aspect of the work is that the last four chapters represent Ricoeur's first fully systematic and sustained statement of his ethics and its ontological implications. Ethics is not a fully new concern of Ricoeur's, but his reflections in the past have been more momentary and episodic and most often in the context of pursuing something else. This relatively new ethical aspect of his work is related to other kinds of inquiry that have been typical Ricoeurian themes, such as action theory, the semantics and pragmatics of language, and narrative theory. All of the themes in this new book, however, are unified by the theme of the self as another and as related to the other.

One of Ricoeur's early works, *Freedom and Nature*, was a sustained phenomenological inquiry into the nature and limits of freedom. We are left at the end of that work, however, with a question about the ethical implications of his inquiry into freedom. *Oneself as Another* can be taken as his most mature answer to that question.

Much, of course, intervenes in the time between *Freedom and Nature* and *Oneself as Another*. Soon after writing that first book, Ricoeur in *Symbolism of Evil* begins to take his famous hermeneutical turn, moving from direct phenomenological description of human experience to interpretation of that experience. I read such a turn to interpretation as complementing rather than replacing direct description, which Ricoeur continues to employ through the rest of his career. Such a turn continues in subsequent works such as *Freud and Philosophy*, *The Conflict of Interpretations*, *The Life of Metaphor*, *Interpretation Theory: Discourse and the Surplus of Meaning*, and *Time and Narrative*. At the same time, Ricoeur is broadening his inquiry into analytic theories of action, exploring the implications for politics in *Ideology and Utopia*, and intervening in the Habermas-Gadamer debate over the relative merits of hermeneutics and critical theory.

In one sense, then, *Oneself as Another* represents a concentrated taking up and linking of previous themes in philosophy of language, action theory, and theory of narrative with the relatively new theme of ethics. In another sense the work represents the completion of a decades-long inquiry into the self in its phenomenologically accessible, linguistic, hermeneutical, and ethical aspects. Like *Freedom and Nature* in the career of early Ricoeur and *Interpretation Theory* in his early hermeneutical phase and *Time and Narrative* in the later hermeneutical phase of his work, *Oneself as Another* represents a very tightly constructed, argued synthesis of earlier, more disparate inquiries into the self, language, action, narrative, and ethics.

One senses here in this work, as in Ricoeur's other work, a dialectical interplay between particular and universal, analytic and synthetic, experiential and interpretative, hermeneutical and explanatory, disparate and synthetic lines of inquiry. *Freedom and Nature* brings to synthetic completion earlier universal, eidetic phenomenological inquiries into Husserl, Jaspers, Marcel, and other related thinkers and themes in phenomenology and existentialism. At the same time, that work opens onto more concrete reflections on existential freedom in *Fallible Man* and evil in *Symbolism of Evil*. The reflective inquiry into the hermeneutics of the symbol in *Symbolism of Evil* opens onto a series of inquiries finally completed in the much more universal and synthetic *Interpretation Theory* presented in the middle 1970s. Themes from phenomenology, analytic action theory, philosophy of language, theory of metaphor, and literary theory are integrated in the magisterial *Time and Narrative*. Again, as already stated, themes from philosophy of language, action theory, hermeneutics, and ethics are integrated into one whole in *Oneself as Another*.

Ricoeur's book, then, represents a tentative completion of earlier inquiries into the free, embodied self going back to his very earliest work. What kind of ethics is implied by his account of the free, embodied, social self, which is in the world and mediated by structures of language and by a psychological and social unconscious? The book at the same time represents a synthetic linking of earlier themes and methodologies with the method and content of ethics. At the same time, in contrast to the very comprehensive, cosmological, metaphysical orientation of *Time and Narrative*, *Oneself as Another* is a concentrated focusing of attention on the human self.

Our book is a collection of essays by North American authors, all of whom are already well known for their work in Continental philosophy and its various sub-fields of phenomenology, hermeneutics, critical theory, and postmodernism, and all of whom are animated by a sense of the importance of Ricoeur's work past and present. In contrast to some of his more flashy French counterparts, who attract because of the extremeness and colorfulness of their formulations, what Ricoeur has going for him most of the time is that he is simply right or close to being right on the issues up for discussion. I am tempted to say that, in his dialectical nuance and balance, Ricoeur is as about as Hegelian as one can be in the twentieth century while still remaining intellectually honest. This book links opposites such as sense and reference, particular and universal, interpretation and explanation, history and fiction, the right and the good, duty and happiness, justification and application, the self and the other. The contemporary ethical Humpty Dumpty, which has been split up and carved up by Aristotelians and Kantians, communitarians and Rawlsians or Habermasians, universalists and advocates of application to the particular, Ricoeur attempts to put back together again. In the opinion of at least some of the authors of this volume, contested somewhat by others, Ricoeur largely succeeds in that task. But all agree about the importance and philosophical provocativeness of what he has tried to do.

The editors have divided the volume into parts, the first dealing primarily with Ricoeur's thought itself and the second dealing with his relations to other thinkers. Charles Reagan's essay, which starts off the volume, reflects on how Ricoeur's sense of personal identity is inextricably bound up with the other; how Ricoeur's philosophical ethics is the first major statement of his ethics, a Ricoeurian groundwork for the metaphysics of morals; and how Ricoeur's style of philosophy, his dialogal and dialectical respect for other thinkers from whom he learns as well as criticizes, enacts and instantiates the relationship between self and other articulated and defended in the book.

Lenore Langsdorf's essay, following hints given by Ricoeur himself, develops a mode of intentionality correlative to Husserlian intentionality. This new mode of intentionality, generative intentionality, is characterized by a dependence on human others as helping to constitute the self, the anchoring of the self in a lived body that is agent and patient in relation to the world, and the ongoing composition of the lived body from physical constituents of other bodies during and after the process of birth. Such a conception of intentionality leaves us with a conception of self that is not vulnerable to contemporary critiques of the subject, because such a conception does not leave out the messier aspects of human existence. The self that emerges is a mediated self, multiple, mutable, and permeable, significantly fragmented in creatively powerful ways.

David Rasmussen's essay, in contrast to Langsdorf's emphasis on multiplicity, stresses the narrative identity of Ricoeur's conception of the self. Rasmussen questions whether or not it is possible to retrieve the phenomenon and concept of subjectivity under the category of the narrative unity of the self. His answer is that Ricoeur is largely successful in this project. He has narratively resolved the discontinuity between calendar time and internal time through the integration of the self in a larger temporal framework. Speech act theory, as done by Searle or Habermas, has largely undermined self-identity. Only by pushing beyond speech act theory into a conception of narrative identity more adequately relating the self to the world can one come up with a more adequate conception of personal identity.

John van den Hengel asks in his essay whether for Ricoeur there can be a science of action. He situates his question in noting the distinction and tension between *epistémé*, that which can be known with certainty, and *doxa*, which is vague opinion. This is a tension going all the way back to the Greeks. Ricoeur, steering between the Scylla of a strong foundationalism and the Charybdis of a postmodern relativism, unites understanding and explanation into one hermeneutical whole. Hermeneutics, however, leads into ethical action, which cannot be encompassed within science. Van den Hengel's answer to the question, "Can there be a science of action?" is, therefore, "yes" and "no": "yes" to the extent that explanation is essential to understanding, "no" to the extent that human action involves and implies attestation, a committed trust, a "believing" in what the self says and what it does.

Don Ihde in his essay suggests that *Oneself as Another* may be the capstone book of Ricoeur's career, because his dialectical and hermeneutical moves are "more subtly made, less visible in the foreground, and placed in the most complex and synthetic display of his philosophy to date" (97). In his essay Ihde interrogates Ricoeur's linking of analytic philosophy and hermeneutics from the perspective of his (Ihde's) own work in hermeneutics and philosophy of science. In his use of science fiction versus literary fiction to characterize the differences between analytic philosophy and hermeneutics, Ricoeur correctly criticizes science fiction's attempt to render contingent the corporeal and terrestrial condition which the hermeneutical tradition takes to be unsurmountable.

But then Ricoeur surprisingly and mistakenly identifies the science fiction version of science with technology as such. Ricoeur recognizes Parfit's technomyth, but does not recognize his own. Deepest of all, however, is another set of parallels embedded in the two technomyths, two radically different body technologies. Here Ricoeur is more insightful than analytic philosophy, and by arguing for the phenomenological sense of body as flesh shows how analytic body theory may be called a neo-Cartesianism.

Patrick Bourgeois begins Part Two with a discussion of Ricoeur and Levinas. One interesting connection in this volume is that between Bourgeois's essay, which with some qualification interprets and defends Ricoeur's critique of Levinas, Richard Cohen's essay, which is sharply critical of Ricoeur's take on Levinas, and Marsh's essay, which includes a defense of Ricoeur's critique of Levinas. While a bit too severe on Levinas, Bourgeois argues, Ricoeur's account can be altered slightly but without substantially changing his overall position. Thus, Ricoeur's nuanced position can be seen as an adequate linking of Levinasian exteriority to Husserlian intentionality analysis. Bourgeois's other main thesis is that Ricoeur, by incorporating an essential element from Levinas in a broader phenomenological and ethical account of the relationship between self and other, is a legitimate, preferable alternative to postmodern deconstruction. Thus, the issue with postmodernism is joined.

Richard Cohen's essay is a sustained critique of Ricoeur's interpretation of Levinas. As such, it represents a challenge that all defenders of Ricoeur have to meet. Responding to Ricoeur's preference in chapter 7 for a normativity based on moral solicitude over Levinas's sociality operative prior to the emergence of such normativity, Cohen argues that Levinas's stance puts into question the very Parmenidean-Hegelian model of mediation presupposed by Ricoeur. For Levinas the other qua commanding-judging other, the moral other, is the condition of the possibility for any hermeneutic of the good life. The respect for the other in the reciprocal exchange of giving and receiving cannot be called moral unless the moral dimension as such is already operative through a prior encounter with alterity as such. Moreover, the Levinasian self is not so separate as to be inviolate, closed, out of relation, simply passive as Ricoeur claims, but is more passive than any passivity, because it arises in pure subjection to the other.

Arguing further against Ricoeur's critique in chapter 10 that Levinas's self is too closed in, incapable of receiving and unable to discriminate, Cohen indicates aspects of Levinas's account of the erotic that shows it to be in relation and to be receptive, and claims that Ricoeur misses that Levinas's account works at a more radical level than Ricoeur's, forsaking epistemology altogether.

Eric Crump's essay, responding to criticisms that Ricoeur, contrary to his intentions, does not preserve philosophy's autonomy from theology, develops the often overlooked influence of Roger Mehl and Pierre Thévenaz on Ricoeur's thought. Ricoeur's philosophy of the "I am" is articulated as a reflective and deepening of the French reflexive philosophical tradition. In so doing, Crump clarifies the relationship of philosophy to theology in Ricoeur's thought, saving him from any reprehensible subordination or dependence.

David Pellauer's essay uses the issue of moral blindness to test the limits and adequacy of Ricoeur's theory of the self. Pellauer argues that Ricoeur's dialectic between ontological and teleological dimensions teaches us a kind of philosophical and moral humility and fallibilism. Our solutions to dilemmas arising on the level of practical wisdom are fragile and revisable. Experiencing their limits helps us to keep the dynamic aspect of the dialectic alive. We may not see all that there is to see, even when we trace our way back to primary ethical affirmations. Within the dialectic is also a place for reflection on evil as well as good. In the deepest sense, evil may not be an incapacity to do the good or find the just solution within some moral order, but rather a failure to see a moral problem in all of its aspects and ramifications. But because it is a failure to see for which we are responsible, we can be held accountable for it.

Bernard Dauhenauer's essay presents Ricoeur's critique of Rawls's thesis concerning the priority of the right over the good, and then assesses the strength of that critique. Dauenhauer argues that Rawls argues illegitimately for an obvious clarity to rights and duties as they are spelled out in constitutions. Because there is a necessary ambiguity and indeterminacy in constitutional law, we are inevitably forced to reflect on a people's prior sense of ethical life, in the light of which constitutions are interpreted and revised. Ricoeur's theory does more justice to this concrete historical sense of a people's ethical life, "the aiming for the good life, with and for others, in just institutions," than does Rawls. Ricoeur's understanding of ethical life better corresponds to a society's understanding that its citizens are pursuing some common good, in the light of which they become aware of complex distributional questions that call for universal norms, and hence require a constitution that rules out scapegoating. The citizenry learns that this constitutional imperative can never be definitively satisfied and hence that there is no alternative to an ongoing exercise of practical wisdom. Ricoeur thus provides a preferable alternative to Rawls's insistence on the priority of the right over the good. There is a reciprocity between right and good that Rawls does not see, as well as a rooting of abstract reflection on universal norms in a people's prior sense of the good life.

Jim Marsh's essay, in that it synthetically takes on the whole book, but especially the last four essays, touches on all or most of the themes rased in Part Two. Marsh argues that ethical theory has recently been besieged by a series of ethical antinomies between "is" and "ought," concrete individual other and reflectively justified norm, justification and application, deontology and teleology, duty and happiness, self and other. Ricoeur has taken a significant step toward putting this ethical Humpty Dumpty back together again. At the same time, Marsh does raise a few questions concerning Ricoeur's achievement. Is the ethical level prior to the moral level in the way Ricoeur claims? Is there not in our everyday experience a lived sense of deontology and right that coexists with and relates to our striving for the good? Again, does not Habermans, following Gunther, develop criteria for application of norms that Ricoeur needs to take into account? Does he not make the move too quickly to prudence and conviction?

What should be apparent in this brief summary of the essays in this volume is that *Oneself as Another* is a book rich in insights and potential consequences. As is characteristic of all of Ricoeur's works, it opens up questions for further discussion. From Part One, for example, we may ask whether Ricoeur's narrative account of the self does not give us a richer, deeper sense of self than the relatively thin accounts of thinkers such as Habermas, Rawls, or Apel. In his critique of analytic notions of literature, does not Ricoeur give in to his own technomyth, and thus inadvertently endorse an excessively negative sense of technology? Does Ricoeur's notion of the self move between the Scylla of foundationalism and the Charybdis of relativism in such a way that he provides a genuine alternative and implicit critique to postmodern claims concerning the death of the self? Is there an opening to and use of intentionality analysis in Ricoeur's work that would imply and require a more explicit thematizing of the relationship between phenomenology and hermeneutics in his work?

Part Two similarly opens up a rich vein of questioning. Three of the essays deal in whole or in part with the issue of Levinas versus Ricoeur. Does Ricoeur's judicious "yes" and "no" to Levinasian otherness and mediation with conscious, responsible selfhood work, or is such criticism and mediation open to fundamental challenge? Does Ricoeur's mediation of otherness provide an alternative to and corrective to postmodernism, or does postmodernism have resources for a reply? Is Ricoeur's rejection of the priority of the right over the good and his privileging of ethical life in community over reflective justification of ethical norms a convincing answer to thinkers such as Habermas and Rawls? Is Ricoeur's insistence on ethical universalism in form and content, at the same time recognizing the rights of particular communities and traditions, a convincing answer to communitarians such as MacIntyre and Taylor? Finally, does Ricoeur put the ethical Humpty Dumpty back together again or does he at least take significant steps toward doing so? What would or could communitarians, Kantian, Rawlsian, or Habermasian universalists, postmodernists, and Gadamerian prudentialists and traditionalists say in reply? Thus, *Oneself as Another,* the contributors to this volume think and have tried to show, is a huge step forward, not only in the questions it asks and answers, but in the questions it raises.[1]

James L. Marsh

NOTE

1. I wish to express my appreciation to Kirk Kanzelberger, my graduate assistant, for his work in scanning, word processing and editing this work. His care and competence have certainly contributed to whatever quality the work may have.

Sigla

Cc   *La Critique et la conviction*. Paris: Calmann-Lévy, 1995.

Ci   *Le Conflit des interprétations. Essais d'herméneutique*. Paris: Éditions du Seuil, 1969.

CI   *The Conflict of Interpretations: Essays in Hermeneutics*. Ed. Don Ihde. Evanston, Ill., Northwestern University Press, 1974.

DF   *De l'interpretation. Essai sur Freud*. Paris: Le Seuil, 1965.

Dta   *Du texte à l'action. Essais d'herméneutique, II*. Paris: Le Seuil, 1986.

EBI   *Essays on Biblical Interpretation*. Ed. L. Mudge. Philadelphia: Fortress Press, 1980.

FM   *Fallible Man*. Trans. Charles Kelbley. Chicago: Henry Regnery, 1965.

FN   *Freedom and Nature: The Voluntary and the Involuntary*. Trans. E. V. Kohák. Evanston, Ill.: Northwestern University Press, 1966.

FP   *Freud and Philosophy: An Essay on Interpretation*. Trans. Dennis Savage. New Haven: Yale University Press, 1970.

FS   *Figuring the Sacred: Religion, Narrative, and Imagination*. Trans. David Pellauer, ed. Mark Wallace. Minneapolis: Fortress Press, 1995.

HHS   *Hermeneutics and the Human Sciences*. Ed. and trans. John Thompson. Cambridge: Cambridge University Press, 1980.

HT   *History and Truth*. Trans. Charles Kelbley and others. Evanston, Ill.: Northwestern University Press, 1965.

IT   *Interpretation Theory: Discourse and the Surplus of Meaning*. Fort Worth: Texas Christian University Press, 1976.

L1	*Lectures 1: Autour du politique*. Paris: Éditions du Seuil, 1991.
L2	*Lectures 2: La Contrée des philosophes*. Paris: Éditions du Seuil, 1994.
L3	*Lectures 3: Aux frontièrs de la philosophie*. Paris: Éditions du Seuil, 1994.
Lf	*Finitude et culpabilité. I. L'homme faillible*. Paris: Aubier, 1960.
LJ	*Le Juste*. Paris: Éditions Esprit, 1995.
Lmv	*La métaphore vive*. Paris: Le Seuil, 1975.
LV	*La Volontaire et l'involontaire*. Paris: Aubier, 1950.
OA	*Oneself as Another*. Trans. Kathleen Blamey. Chicago: University of Chicago Press, 1992.
PA	*Platon et Aristote*. Paris: Centre de Documentation Universitaire, 1960.
RF	*Reflexions Faites. Autobiographie intellectuelle*. Paris: Éditions Esprit, 1995.
RM	*The Rule of Metaphor: Multi-Disciplinary Studies of the Creation of Meaning in Language*. Trans. R. Czerny with K. McLaughlin and J. Costello. Toronto: University of Toronto Press, 1978.
Sa	*Soi-même comme un autre*. Paris: Le Seuil, 1990.
sa	*La sémantique de l'action*. Ed. Dorian Tiffaneau. Paris: Éd. du Centre National de la Recherche Scientifique, 1977.
TA	*From Text to Action*. Trans. Kathleen Blamey and John B. Thompson. Evanston, Ill.: Northwestern University Press, 1991.
TN1	*Time and Narrative*. Vol 1. Trans. Kathleen McLaughlin and David Pellauer. Chicago: University of Chicago Press, 1984.
TN2	*Time and Narrative*. Vol 2. Trans. Kathleen McLaughlin and David Pellauer. Chicago: University of Chicago Press, 1985.
TN3	*Time and Narrative*. Vol 3. Trans. Kathleen McLaughlin and David Pellauer. Chicago: University of Chicago Press, 1988.
Tr	*Temps et Récit*. Tomes I, II, III. Paris: Le Seuil, 1983, 1984, 1985.

PART ONE

RICOEUR IN HIMSELF

ONE

Personal Identity

Charles E. Reagan

During the decade of the 1980s, Paul Ricoeur published five major works: three volumes of *Time and Narrative;*[1] *From Text to Action,*[2] an edited version of many of his articles published in English during the late 1970s and early 1980s; and, most recently, *Oneself as Another.*[3] In 1980, at the beginning of this prolific period, Ricoeur had already retired from the University of Paris-Nanterre and was thinking of reducing his teaching at the University of Chicago. Several years later, he was named the John Nuveen Professor Emeritus at the University of Chicago and limited his teaching there to one quarter per year. He was then sixty-seven years old, and, after an extraordinary intellectual career, was widely known and highly regarded both in France and in the United States. He had clearly earned his retirement.

But retirement is not his style. Rather, he began a new intellectual journey, which expanded beyond the hermeneutics he practiced in the 1970s to an understanding of the philosophical power of narratives. His three-volume work, *Time and Narrative,* excited a renewed interest in his philosophy after a ten-year, self-imposed exile from the French university scene. During this period Ricoeur lived, worked, lectured, and published primarily *outside* of France. Thus, in the mid-1980s, his French readers needed to "catch up" with the work he had been doing since the last major work he had published in France, *La métaphore vive.*[4] The articles, which are in edited and abridged form in the collection *Du texte à l'action,* were, with a few exceptions, either written and published in English, or they were written in French but published outside of France.

After finishing the third volume of *Time and Narrative,* Ricoeur began work on the Gifford Lectures, which he gave in Edinburgh in the winter of 1986. The lectures were written in French and an abridged English version was actually read. Ricoeur then revised the first version by expanding several chapters. The second edition follows closely the order and topics of the first edition. This version was first given as lectures at the University of Munich in the same year. Yet Ricoeur was not satisfied with his text and continued for two more years to work and rework it. This was time well spent: *Oneself as Another* is, in my opinion, Ricoeur's most elegantly written, clearly organized, and closely argued work. This is high praise for an author whose work as a whole exemplifies these traits.

What I intend to do here is to give a synopsis of the book in order to show what the question of personal identity is and how Ricoeur progressively argues for a concept of personal identity that is inextricably bound up with a concept of the other and the relation between the self and the other. Then, I will give a more detailed account of the three chapters on ethics. These chapters are interesting in their own right, and they come as close as anything Ricoeur has written to being a clear account of his "philosophical ethics." He has written many articles on individual moral or political concepts and concerns, but he has never written a theoretical work on ethics. These chapters serve as his "groundwork for a metaphysics of morals."

My second goal in this essay is to point out some of the things we, his students, learned about philosophy from Paul Ricoeur, as well as to comment on some of the constant features in his philosophical style. Above all, Paul Ricoeur is a *teacher* of philosophy. He taught us to do a careful reading of philosophical texts, to always give the most generous interpretation to ambiguous or obscure texts, and to give full credit to those we have read and from whom we have learned. His fundamental thesis as a philosopher is that virtually every philosopher, ancient, modern, or contemporary, has seen a piece of the truth. Now our task is to adjudicate among competing interpretations, each of which claims to be absolute.

The title itself of this book, *Oneself as Another*, indicates the three converging themes that make up this work: a reflexive meditation on the self or subject; a dialectic on the meaning of the word *même* or "same" in the sense of identical *(idem)* or in the sense of "one and the same" *(ipse)*, or selfhood; a dialectic between the self and the "other." Ricoeur's meditation takes place within the context of the history of the philosophy of the subject and, in particular, of the philosophy of Descartes and Nietzsche. For Descartes, the *cogito* is both indubitable and the ultimate foundation of all that can be known. For Nietzsche, on the contrary, the *cogito* is the name of an illusion. Ricoeur, in his typically dialectic mode, says, "the hermeneutics of the self is placed at an equal distance from the apology of the *cogito* and from its overthrow" (4).

One of the most important dialectics in Ricoeur's philosophy is between the auto-foundational claims of idealistic philosophies of the self, such as Descartes's and Husserl's, and the skeptical philosophies of the "masters of suspicion," Nietzsche, Marx, and Freud. The reflective and hermeneutic philosophy Ricoeur practices is the contrary of a philosophy of the immediate. This is why Ricoeur, the French translator of Husserl's *Ideen I*, rejected from the beginning both the transcendental *epoché* and the idealist version of Husserl's phenomenology. Ricoeur says, "The first truth—*I am, I think*—remains as abstract and empty as it is invincible; it has to be 'mediated' by the ideas, actions, works, institutions, and monuments that objectify it."[5] Thus, Ricoeur rejects the classical picture of consciousness as a veridical "mirror of nature" and says we gain self-knowledge through the long route of the interpretations of texts, monuments, and cultural forms.

Ricoeur's goal is to develop a hermeneutic of the self that bridges the gap between the *cogito* and the anti-*cogito*. He asks, "To what extent can one say that the hermeneutics of the self developed here occupies an epistemological (and ontological, as I shall state in the tenth study) place, situated beyond the alternative of the *cogito* and the anti-*cogito*?" (16).

In his preface, Ricoeur sets forth three conceptual themes that guide his study of the self: the use of "self" in natural languages, "same" in the sense of *idem* and *ipse*, and the correlation between the self and the other-than-self. "To these three grammatical features correspond the three major features of the hermeneutics of the self, namely, the detour of reflection by way of analysis, the dialectic of selfhood and sameness, and finally the dialectic of selfhood and otherness" (16). The whole hermeneutic is led by the question, who: who speaks? who acts? who tells a story? and who is the subject of moral imputation?

The first grouping (chapters 1 and 2) is based on a *philosophy of language* both as semantics and as pragmatics. This analytic stage is made necessary by the indirect status of the self. Hermeneutics is always a philosophy of detour; the hermeneutics of the self must take a detour through the analysis of the language in which we talk about the self.

The second group (chapters 3 and 4) is based on a *philosophy of action* in the sense this has taken in analytic philosophy. The interest here is in language about action and in speech acts where the agent of an action designates himself as the one who acts. "The questions 'Who is speaking?' and 'Who is acting?' appear in this way to be closely interconnected" (17). Ricoeur reminds us that these long analytic forays are "characteristic of the indirect style of a hermeneutics of self, in stark contrast to the demand for immediacy belonging to the cogito" (17).

The third grouping (chapters 5 and 6) is centered on the question of *personal identity*. This is the place of the dialectic between identity *(idem)* and identity *(ipse)* which arises from the second grammatical trait of *soi-même* (oneself) and the ambiguity of the word *même* (same). Here Ricoeur links narrative identity with the philosophy of action, since narrative is the "imitation of action" *(mimesis)*. "At the same time, and correlatively, the subject of the action recounted will begin to correspond to the broader concept of the *acting and suffering* individual, which our analytic-hermeneutical procedure is capable of eliciting" (18).

The fourth group (chapters 7, 8, and 9) makes a final detour through the ethical and moral determinations of action. "It is in the three ethical studies that the dialectic of the *same* and the *other* will find its appropriate philosophical development" (18). Ricoeur admits that his studies appear to be fragmentary and lack a unity. He says, "The fragmentary character of these studies results from the analytic-reflective structure that imposes arduous detours on our hermeneutics, beginning as early as the first study" (19). The thematic unity is found in *human action*. But human action does not serve as an ultimate foundation of some set of derived disciplines. Rather, there is an analogical unity because of the polysemy of "action" and because of "the variety and contingency of the questions that activate the analyses leading back to the reflection on the self" (19–20).

The thread that unifies Ricoeur's analyses is *description, narration, prescription*. Narrative identity serves "a transitional and relational function between the description that prevails in the analytical philosophies of action and the prescription that designates all the determinations of action by means of a generic term on the basis of the predicates 'good' and 'obligatory'" (20).

The final study (chapter 10) explores the ontological consequences of the hermeneutics of the self. Ricoeur claims that the dialectic between the "same" and the "other" will prevent an ontology of act and power from becoming encased in a tautology. "The polysemy of otherness, which I shall propose in the tenth study, will imprint upon the entire ontology of acting the seal of the diversity of sense that foils the ambition of arriving at an ultimate foundation, characteristic of the cogito philosophies" (21).

Another characteristic that distinguishes Ricoeur's hermeneutic of the self from the philosophies of the *cogito* is the type of certainty appropriate to the hermeneutics, in contradistinction to the claims of self-evidence and self-foundation of the philosophies of the *cogito*. Ricoeur uses the word *attestation* to describe the level of certitude appropriate to his hermeneutics. With respect to the "epistemological exaltation" of Descartes's *cogito* and its destruction by Nietzsche and his followers, Ricoeur claims, "Attestation may appear to require less than the one and more than the other" (21). It is opposed to the kind of certainty claims of *épistemé*, of science, "taken in the sense of ultimate and self—founding knowledge" (21). Attestation is a kind of *belief*, not in the doxic sense of "I believe that ... ," but in the sense of "I believe in. . . ." Since attestation is a much weaker claim than the foundational claims of the *cogito*, it is always vulnerable. "This vulnerability will be expressed in the permanent threat of suspicion, if we allow that suspicion is the specific contrary of attestation. The kinship between attestation and testimony is verified here: there is no 'true' testimony without 'false' testimony. But there is no recourse against false testimony than another that is more credible; and there is no recourse against suspicion but a more reliable attestation" (22). Another way Ricoeur defines attestation is as "the *assurance of being oneself acting and suffering*. This assurance remains the ultimate recourse against all suspicion" (22). He finishes laying out his thesis and his plan of study by saying, "As credence without any guarantee, but also as trust greater than any suspicion, the hermeneutics of the self can claim to hold itself at an equal distance from the cogito exalted by Descartes and from the cogito that Nietzsche proclaimed forfeit. The reader will judge whether the investigations that follow live up to this claim" (23).

The notion of "attestation" is a middle ground between apodictic certainty—which is only rarely attainable—and perpetual suspicion, and it is, he says, the level of certainty appropriate to hermeneutics. In his influential article "The Model of the Text,"[6] Ricoeur uses the analogy with judicial reasoning and discourse to show the kind of certainty appropriate to hermeneutical interpretations in literary criticism and in the social sciences. The key is the polemical character of validation. Ricoeur says,

> In front of the court, the plurivocity common to texts and to actions is exhibited in the form of a conflict of interpretations, and the final interpretation appears as a verdict to which it is possible to make appeal. Like legal utterances, all interpretations in the field of literary criticism and in the social sciences may be challenged, and the question "what can defeat a claim" is common to all argumentative situations. Only in the tribunal is there a moment when the procedures of appeal are exhausted. But it is because the decision of the judge is implemented by the force of public power. Neither in literary criticism, nor in the social sciences, is there such a last word. Or if there is any, we call that violence.[7]

In juridical arguments, we recognize levels of certainty appropriate to different situations, such as "probably cause," "preponderance of the evidence," "beyond a reasonable doubt." For Ricoeur, the task of philosophy is to avoid the skepticism that doubts everything while at the same time abandoning the ideal of total certainty.

In a special section at the end of the preface, Ricoeur explains to his readers why he omitted from this book two chapters that were originally part of the Gifford Lectures. They were called "The Self in the Mirror of the Scriptures" and "The Mandated Self." The first of these dealt with the naming of God through the Old and New Testaments. In the symbolic network of the Scriptures, we find the kerygmatic dimension distinguished from the argumentative mode of philosophy. The second lecture dealt with the narratives of "vocation," of the calling of the prophets and disciples, and the understanding of the self contained in the response to the call. "The relation between call and response was therefore the strong connection between these two lectures" (23).

Ricoeur omitted the lectures from his work for two reasons: (1) He wanted this book to be an autonomous philosophical discourse by putting into parentheses the convictions that tied him to his biblical faith. This has been a guiding principle in all of his philosophical work. (2) If Ricoeur has defended his work from becoming a "crypto-theology," he also defends biblical faith from becoming a "crypto-philosophy." In particular, he does not want biblical faith to replace the *cogito* as a form of foundation against which his hermeneutics has fought continually.

PERSONAL IDENTITY

Ricoeur begins his studies of the self by looking at the linguistic means at our disposal to identify anything, to refer to individual things and pick them out of a group of similar things. He claims that a person is, at the lowest level possible, "one of the things that we distinguish by means of identifying reference" (27). He will begin with a linguistic study of the operations of individualization found in natural languages. Definite descriptions create a class with a single member (e.g., the first man to walk on the moon), while proper names refer to a single individual without, however, giving any information about the individual (e.g., Socrates). The third category of individualizing operators is made up of pronouns (e.g., you, he) and deictics such as demonstratives (e.g., this one, that one), adverbs of time and place (e.g., now, then, here, there), and the tenses of verbs. These operators individualize with reference to the speaker. "Here" means in the proximity of the speaker, in relation to which "there" makes sense. "Now" refers to events contemporaneous with the speaking itself. At this point, none of these individualizing operations privileges the person.

In moving from the identification of any kind of particular to the identification of persons, Ricoeur follows P. F. Strawson, who in his book *Individuals*[8] claims that there are only two kinds of basic particulars, things (physical objects) and persons. Every identification refers ultimately to one of these two classes of individuals. At this point, what is important are the sets of predicates appropriate to each basic particular.

Strawson's second main thesis is that the first basic particular is the body, or physical object, because it satisfies the criterion of having a unique spatiotemporal location. Persons are also bodies, but they, unlike bodies, are a referent for two series of predicates, physical and psychological. The importance of this claim is that souls (à la Descartes), ideas, percepts, etc., are not fundamental or basic particulars. This cuts off any temptation to relapse into subjectivism or idealism. It also means that the person cannot be considered as a pure consciousness to which is added a body, as is the case in classical mind/body dualisms. The importance of this double attribution of predicates to *the same thing* is that we eliminate any double reference to body and soul by two series of predicates.

The first study follows one of the two linguistic approaches to the problem of the self, that of identifying reference. In the second chapter, Ricoeur takes up the other approach, enunciation, or speech-acts. Speech-acts immediately involve the "I" and the "you" of interlocution, whereas referential identification is centered on the "he." "The question will be finally to determine how the 'I-you' of interlocution can be externalized in a 'him' or a 'her' without losing its capacity to designate itself, and how the 'he/she' of identifying reference can be internalized in a speaking subject who designates himself or herself as an I" (41).

The theory of speech-acts, begun by Austin and perfected by Searle, is well known. A fundamental element of the theory is the distinction between performatives and constatives. The latter describe a state of affairs; the former are speech-actions, where the saying is the doing itself. Their paradigm illustration is a promise, where saying "I promise you" is to make a promise and not to describe a promise. Other examples would be rendering a verdict, making a proclamation, naming a child, etc. The importance of this is that it is a principal intersection between the theory of language and the theory of action. Secondly, reflexive speech implies both an "I" who speaks and a "you" to whom the speech is addressed. "In short, utterance equals interlocution" (44).

ACTION AND AGENT

The next two chapters link up the linguistic analysis of identifying reference and speech-acts with the philosophy of action. In chapter 3, Ricoeur deals with the concepts in the philosophy of action, devoid of reference to a particular agent. The following chapter introduces the imputation of agency. "What does action, we shall ask, teach about its agent? And to what extent can what is learned in this way contribute to clarifying the difference between *ipse* and *idem?*" (56).

At the level of identifying reference, the network of concepts with which we describe action refers to an agent as *being spoken about*. But this is far different from an explicit self-imputation of an action to an agent. Only at the end of Ricoeur's next chapter will we see the interrelationship between identifying reference and self-designation of an "acting subject."

For the purposes of this study, Ricoeur puts "in parentheses" the unifying principle of chains of actions, that is, the "practical unities of a higher order." These include techniques, skilled crafts, arts, games, all of which order chains of actions so that some actions are understood as parts of higher-order actions. This means that at this point he will set aside ethical predicates that evaluate actions, or chains of actions, as good, just, etc.

Action and agent belong to the same conceptual schema; this includes concepts such as motive, circumstance, intention, deliberation, voluntary, constraint, intended consequences, and so forth. The important thing is, they form a coherent network such that one must understand how all of them function and what they mean, in order to understand any one of them. The network as a whole determines what will "count as" an action. One way of seeing this network is that it constitutes the list of questions that can be asked of an agent about an action: when, under what circumstances, with what intention, why (what motive), what influences, and so forth.

Within the framework of identifying reference, the question "who?" can be answered with a proper name, a demonstrative, or a definite description. Ricoeur believes that analytic philosophy of action has created problems for itself by focusing its discussion on the question of what will count as an action among the *events that happen in the world*. This has led it to couple the question "what?" with the question "why?" such that distinguishing between an action and an event depends on the mode of explanation of the action (the "why?"). "The use of 'why?' in the explanation of action thus becomes the arbiter of the description of what counts as actions" (61).[9]

Ricoeur now looks at the analytic philosophy of action as it interprets the meaning of "intention." The fundamental and guiding question of this view is "what distinguishes intentional actions from unintentional ones?" Anscombe's answer is that actions are intentional if a certain sense of "because" applies to them. This sense is that the *because* gives a "reason for acting" (69). This opens a whole range of answers to "why?" that are mixed or even counterexamples. Aristotle reminds us that in some cases the question "why?" doesn't have any sense: cases where the action was the result of ignorance or of constraint. Ricoeur claims that the main victim of this kind of analysis is the dichotomy between reason for acting and cause. He says that there is a whole spectrum of answers to "why?" and only at the far extremes of the spectrum do you find a pure opposition between reason and cause. In the case of "backward-looking" motives such as vengeance, the line between cause and reason is completely erased. He concludes, "But one can see how fluid the border is between reason-for-acting, forward-looking motive, mental cause, and cause as such (a grimacing face made me jump). The criterion of the question 'why?' is therefore firm; its application surprisingly flexible" (69).

According to Ricoeur, the analytic philosophy of action has been preoccupied with the question "what-why?" to the exclusion of the question "who?". He says, "In my opinion, it is the exclusive concern with the truth of the description that tends to overshadow any interest in assigning the action to its agent" (72). This is the same reason that analytic philosophy has neglected the sense of intention as "intending-to"; the present intention to do something in the future. The dilemma is that the truth of such an intention claim rests on the nonverifiable declaration of the agent, or leads to a theory of internal mental events. For Ricoeur, only a phenomenology of attestation can account for "intending-to." The criterion of truth is not the verifiability of a description, but the confidence in a testimony. Even a declared intention belongs to the category of a shared confession and not to the category of a public description. In conclusion, the "intention-to," relegated to the third rank by conceptual analysis of the type done by Anscombe, finds itself in the first rank from the phenomenological perspective. This is because this sense of intention is very close to the act of promising.

In Ricoeur's first three chapters, the question "who?" was eclipsed by semantic considerations of the pair "what/why?". In chapter 4, he returns to the central focus of "who?", or the relation between the agent and the action. Earlier studies concentrated on distinguishing actions from events and on the relationship between intentional explanations and causal explanations. In returning to the role of the agent, Ricoeur recalls the theses of Strawson, discussed in his first chapter, and the linguistic act of *ascription*. Strawson's principal theses are that persons are "basic particulars" and all attribution of predicates is of persons or bodies; certain predicates are attributable only to persons and they are not reducible to any one or any set of predicates attributable to bodies. Secondly, we attribute both body predicates and person predicates to the *same* thing, that is, persons. Finally, mental predicates are attributable to ourselves and others without having a different meaning.

Turning his attention to contemporary theory of action, Ricoeur wants to show that ascription has a different meaning than attribution. Each term in the network of action *(what? why?)*, refers back to the *who?*. When we speak of the action, we ask who did it. When we ask for the motive, we refer directly to the agent. Ricoeur notes that these inquiries are not symmetrical: the question "who?" is answered when we name or otherwise indicate the agent; the search for motives is interminable.

Ricoeur asks why contemporary philosophy of action has resisted any kind of profound analysis of the relation between the action and the agent. He gives two reasons: Much of the discussion is dominated by an ontology of events (Davidson) and other analyses are dominated by an ontology of "things in general" (Strawson).

Ricoeur rejects, however, the claim that moral or judicial imputation of an action to an agent is merely a strong form of ascription. The first reason is that moral imputation makes no sense in cases of banal actions or simple acts disconnected from a practice or a complex human action. Secondly, imputation properly applies only in cases of actions that are praiseworthy or blamable. But to condemn an action is to submit it to an accusatory process of the "verdictive" type. The third reason is that imputation is on a different level from the self-designation of a speaker because it implies the *power to act*, including the causal efficacy—however explained—of this power.

But what does "power to act" mean? The *third problem* arises from the fact that "to say that an action depends on its agent is to say in an equivalent fashion that it is in the agent's power" (101). With an analysis of the "power to act," efficient causality, ejected from physics by Galileo, rediscovers its native land: the experience we all have of the power to act. Ricoeur claims that this experience is a "primitive fact." This does not mean it is a given or a starting point, but that it will be seen as such at the *end* of a dialectic. The dialectic will have a disjunctive phase, where efficient causality implied in the power to act is seen as different and disconnected from other forms of causality. It will have also a conjunctive phase where the primitive causality of the agent is shown to be connected with other forms of causality.

Ricoeur proposes an ontology of the *lived body (corps propre)*, "that is, of *a* body which is also *my* body and which, by its double allegiance to the order of physical bodies and to that of persons, therefore lies at the point of articulation of the power to act which is ours and of the course of things which belongs to the world order" (111). So, the power of acting is rooted in a phenomenology of the "I can" and the ontology of the "lived body."

NARRATIVE IDENTITY

Up to this point, Ricoeur limited his discussion to semantic and pragmatic considerations of the theory of language and theory of action with respect to the constitution of the self as self-designation and as agent of an action. At the end of his analyses, he reintroduced the phenomenological concept of a "lived body" as the intermediary between action and agent. All of this served as a "propadeutic to the question of selfhood *[ipséité]*" (113). In addition, the whole problematic of *personal identity* has been omitted.

To tie these two themes together, considering the contemporary debates in Anglo-American philosophy about personal identity, Ricoeur will introduce the dialectic between *sameness (mêmeté)* and *selfhood (ipséité)* and the central idea of narrative identity. Once he has been able to show the advantages of this narrative identity in resolving the paradoxes of the problem of personal identity, he can finally turn to the thesis stated in his introduction, "namely that narrative theory finds one of its major justifications in the role it plays as a middle ground between the descriptive viewpoint on action, to which we have confined ourselves until now, and the prescriptive viewpoint which will prevail in the studies that follow. A triad has thus imposed itself on my analysis: describe, narrate, prescribe—each moment of the triad implying a specific relation between the constitution of action and the constitution of the self" (114–115). Narrative already contains, even in its most descriptive mode, evaluations, estimations, and value judgments. In this sense, it serves as a preparation for ethics proper.

It is here that Ricoeur clearly lays out the two meanings of identity and begins to show their dialectical relationship. In one sense, identity means *sameness*; its other sense is *selfhood*. The context for this discussion of identity is permanence through time. What does it mean to say that someone or something is identical at two different times? On the most basic level, identity means numerical identity—there is one and the same thing, rather than two or more different things. Another sense of identity is qualitative, or the substitutability of one thing for another. Determining identity in cases separated by time, as in cases of law where we claim that the defendant is *the same person* as the person who committed the crime, can be very difficult.

This leads to a third sense of identity, that of uninterrupted continuity between two stages of development of what we take to be the same individual. This kind of identity overcomes the problem of a lack of sameness or similarity required in the qualitative sense of identity. Another sense is permanence in time represented by, say, a genetic code, or a structure, or the organization of a combinatory system. All of these meanings of identity are tied in some way to the idea of *sameness*.

The question now is whether selfhood implies a form of permanence in time that does not depend on a substratum of sameness. What we are looking for, says Ricoeur, is "a form of permanence in time that is a reply to the question 'Who am I?'" (118). His proposal is that there are two models for this kind of identity, *character* and *keeping a promise*. In the first case, identity in the sense of one's character is very close to identity in the sense of sameness, an enduring and reidentifiable substratum. In the second case, the selfhood implied in keeping promises is antithetical to sameness. For example, I say that even though I have different opinions, values, desires, inclinations, I will keep my word.

But what does "character" mean? "By 'character' I understand the set of distinctive marks which permit the reidentification of a human individual as being the same" (119). This will include all of the descriptive traits of "sameness" such as "qualitative identity, uninterrupted continuity and permanence in time" (119). Ricoeur reminds us that he has dealt at length with the concept of character in two of his previous works. In *Freedom and Nature*, character was seen as an absolutely permanent and involuntary aspect of our experience (along with our birth and our unconscious) to which we could, at most, consent.[10] It was the nonchosen perspective on our values and our capabilities. In *Fallible Man*, character represented a finite restriction on my openness to the world of things, ideas, values, and persons.[11] In the present work, Ricoeur wants to modify his view of character by situating it within the dialectic of identity. What is at issue is the immutability of character, which he took as a given in his previous works. "Character, I would say today, designates the set of lasting dispositions by which a person is recognized" (121). Here, sameness is constitutive of selfhood.

But if identity in terms of sameness and identity in terms of selfhood find convergence in the idea of character, they are seen as divergent in the analysis of a promise kept. To keep a promise is not to remain the same through time but to defy the changes wrought by time. "Even if my desire were to change, even if I were to change my opinion or my inclination, 'I will hold firm'" (124). So the dialectic of sameness and selfhood has two poles: character, where sameness and permanence of dispositions constitute selfhood; and promising, where selfhood is maintained in spite of change, or in the absence of sameness. Ricoeur thinks that narrative identity is the mediating concept.

His thesis is that the true nature of narrative identity is found only in the dialectic of sameness and selfhood, and the dialectic itself is the main contribution of the narrative theory to the constitution of the self. His arguments are in two steps: First, in an analysis of emplotment *(mise en intrigue)* along the same lines as we found in *Time and Narrative*, the construction of a narrative plot integrates diversity, variability, and discontinuity into the permanence in time. In short, it unifies elements that appear to be totally disparate. Secondly, this same emplotment, transferred from action to characters—characters in a narrative as distinct from "character" as a fundamental element of the existing individual—creates a dialectic of sameness and selfhood.

After giving a brief description of *configuration*, one of the principal concepts in *Time and Narrative*, Ricoeur undertakes to compare narrative configuration with impersonal description. He claims that narration occupies a middle place between description and prescription. He must now show its relation to both end-terms.

One touchstone of the difference between narrative and description is the role of *event*. On the one hand, an event appears to be totally contingent, and thus from the narrative point of view, a discordance. On the other hand, it advances the narrative and is seen as necessary to it. Thus, it is a concordance. The paradox of narration is that it transforms contingent events into necessary episodes by providing a context or link with other events.

Narrative identity has as its challenge to create a dynamic identity out of Locke's incompatible categories of identity and diversity. Ricoeur's thesis here is, "that the identity of the character is comprehensible through the transfer to the character of the operation of emplotment, first applied to the action recounted; characters, we will say, are themselves plots" (143). But what is the relation between character and narrated action? The personage has a unity and an identity correlative to those of the narrative itself. This is captured in the concept of a *role*. Our understanding of a narrative is that it is about agents and victims *(patients)*. Ricoeur says, "For my part, I never forget to speak of humans as acting and suffering" (144–145). This shows, I think, the close relation between narration and ethics.

What is the relation between narrative identity and ethics, between narrating and prescribing? In the first case, narration always deals with actions that are "subject to approval or disapproval and agents that are subject to praise or blame" (164). Ricoeur also says that literature is a grand laboratory of the imagination where experiments are conducted in the realm of good and evil.

In the narrative dialectic of the character, one pole is the character, a constant set of dispositions that remains the same across time. The other pole is the self-constancy represented by commitment made and kept. In the ethical version of the dialectic of identity, character is in the role of sameness: this is what is identifiable and reidentifiable in me, through time and across all of my experiences and actions. The pole of selfhood, or identity in spite of diversity, is responsibility, or acting is such a manner that others can *count* on me and thus make me *accountable* for my actions. Narrative identity is between the poles of sameness as character and selfhood as responsibility.

ETHICS AND MORALS

At this point, Ricoeur begins his extensive discussion of the moral and ethical dimension of selfhood, which is added to the linguistic, practical, and narrative aspects discussed previously. The guiding questions for these four groups of inquiries are: "Who is speaking? Who is acting? Who is telling his or her story? Who is the moral subject of imputation?" (169). The key predicates here will be "good" and "obligatory." Ricoeur says, "The ethical and moral determinations of action will be treated here as predicates of a new kind, and their relation to the subject of action as a new mediation along the return path to the self" (169).

But what is the difference between the terms *ethical* and *moral* for Ricoeur? He wants to distinguish between what is "considered to be good" and what "imposes itself as obligatory." "It is, therefore, by convention that I reserve the term 'ethics' for the *aim* of an accomplished life and the term 'morality' for the articulation of this aim in *norms* characterized at once by the claim to universality and an effect of constraint (later I shall say what links these two features together)" (170). From a historical point of view, we see the ethical concern of Aristotle in the *teleological* interest in the "good life." The moral point of view is found in Kant's *deontology*. In this chapter, Ricoeur seeks to establish the primacy of ethics over morals, the necessity for the goal of ethics to pass through the screen of norms (moral rules), and the recourse of such norms to the ethical goal. "In other words, according to the working hypothesis I am proposing, morality is held to constitute only a limited, although legitimate and even indispensable, actualization of the ethical aim, and ethics in this sense would then encompass morality" (170). But what is the relation between these terms and selfhood? Ricoeur answers, "To the ethical aim will correspond what we shall henceforth call self-esteem, and to the deontological moment, self-respect" (171).

Ricoeur argues at length for the primacy of ethics over morals. But what is the goal of ethics (*visée éthique*)? "Let us define 'ethical intention' as *aiming at the 'good life' with and for others, in just institutions*" (172). The "good life" is the aim of ethics. If we distinguish between practices and a "life-plan," the former are lower on the scale than the latter and their integration is found in the narrative unity of a life. In this discussion, which is well centered on Aristotle's *Nicomachean Ethics*, there is a hierarchy in which practices, including professions, games, and art, are subordinate to the idea of "the good life." The linkage with self-esteem is the following: Our practices are defined by constructive rules and standards of excellence. In appreciating the excellence or success in our actions, we begin to appreciate ourselves as the author of those actions. Ricoeur points out that "life" in the expression "good life" does not have a biological meaning as much as a social meaning that was familiar to the Greeks. They spoke of a "life of pleasure," a "political life," a "contemplative life," etc. For Ricoeur, "life" has this sense as well as the notion of the rootedness of our lives in the biological sense of "to live." Finally, it is in the narrative unity of a life that the estimations applied to particular actions and the evaluation of persons themselves are joined together. In fact, Ricoeur claims that there is a sort of "hermeneutical circle" between our lives as a whole under the idea of the "good life," and our most important particular choices, such as career, spouse, leisure pursuits, etc. But this is not the only hermeneutical connection. "For the agent, interpreting the text of an action is interpreting himself or herself" (179). A bit further, Ricoeur says, "On the ethical plane, self-interpretation becomes self-esteem. In return, self-esteem follows the fate of interpretation" (179).

If the "good life" is the goal of ethics, it is lived with and for others. This becomes the basis for the second part of Ricoeur's reflection on ethics. He designates this concern for the other as *solicitude*. It is not something added to self-esteem from the outside but is an internal, dialogical dimension "such that self-esteem and solicitude cannot be experienced or reflected upon one without the other" (180). Self-esteem is not founded on accomplishment, but on capacity; the ability to judge (to esteem) is based on the ability to act (*le pouvoir-faire*). "The question is then whether the mediation of the other is not required along the route from capacity to realization" (181). The importance of this question is found in certain political theories in which individuals have rights independently of any social connections and the role of the state is relegated to protecting antecedently existing rights. According to Ricoeur, this view rests on a misunderstanding of the role of the other as a mediator between capacity and effectuation. For Aristotle, friendship (*aminé*) plays a mediating role between the goal of the good life found in self-esteem, a solitary virtue, and justice, a political virtue. Friendship introduces the notion of "mutuality." "Friendship, however, is not justice, to the extent that the latter governs institutions and the former interpersonal relations" (184). Equality is presupposed in our relations of friendship, while it is a goal to be achieved in our political institutions. Ricoeur thus takes from Aristotle "the ethics of reciprocity, of sharing, of living together" (187). Self-esteem is the reflexive moment of the goal of the good life, while the relation between the self and the other is characterized by solicitude, which is based on the exchange of giving and receiving. For Ricoeur, this shows the primacy of the ethical goal of the good life, including solicitude for the other, over the moral claims of obligation. As he says, friendship involves reciprocity, while the moral injunction is asymmetrical.

The inverse of the moral injunction is *suffering*. "Suffering is not defined solely by physical pain, nor even by mental pain, but by the reduction, even the destruction, of the capacity for acting, of being-able-to-act, experienced as a violation of self-integrity" (190). Ricoeur sees this as laid out on a spectrum ranging from the injunction coming from the other ("Thou shalt not...") to the opposite end, where sympathy for the suffering other comes from the self. Friendship lies in the middle of this spectrum where the self and the other share an equality and a common wish to live together. The mutuality of friendship means that the roles are reversible, while the persons who play these roles are not substitutable. Ricoeur puts it this way: "The agents and patients of an action are caught up in relationships of exchange which, like language, join together the reversibility of roles and nonsubstitutability of persons. Solicitude adds the dimension of value, whereby each person is *irreplaceable* in our affection and our esteem" (193).

The ideas of irreplaceability and nonsubstitutability lead to the notion of *similitude*, as the result of the exchange between self-esteem and solicitude for the other. This means that, finally, I understand the other as a self, an agent and author of his actions, who has reasons for his actions, who can rank his preferences, etc. All of our ethical feelings, says Ricoeur, refer back to this phenomenology of the "you, too" and "like me." "Fundamentally equivalent are the esteem of the *other as oneself* and the esteem of *oneself as an other*" (194).

But Ricoeur wants to extend his analysis of the ethical goal of the good life from interpersonal relations to institutions, and he extends the virtue of solicitude for the other to the virtue of justice. By "institution," Ricoeur means those structures of *living together* found in historical communities, structures that extend beyond simple interpersonal relations but are bound up with the latter through their function of the distribution of roles, responsibilities, privileges, goods, and rewards. Ricoeur asks if justice is found on the level of ethics and teleology or, as Rawls and Kant would have it, only on the deontological level of morals. Ricoeur's own answer is that justice has two sides: the side of the *good* which is an extension of interpersonal relations, and the *legal* side where it implies a judicial system of coherent laws. He is concerned in this chapter with the first sense or aspect of justice.

But what is the relation between the institution, as an abstract organization of distribution of goods and burdens, and the individuals who make up social institutions? Ricoeur says, "The conception of society as a system of distribution transcends the terms of the opposition. The institution as regulation of the distribution of roles, hence as a system, is indeed something more and something other than the individuals who play those roles.... An institution considered as a rule of distribution exists only to the extent that individuals take part in it" (200). Distributive justice is not a matter of mere arithmetical equality among individuals but a *proportional* equality which relates merit to each individual. In conclusion, Ricoeur says that justice adds equality to solicitude and its range is all humanity rather than interpersonal relations. This is why he adds "in just institutions" to our ethical pursuit of the "good life" lived "with and for others."

Let us sum up the argument so far. At the beginning, Ricoeur announced three theses that he would treat in successive studies: "(1) the primacy of ethics over morality, (2) the necessity for the ethical aim to pass through the sieve of the norm, and (3) the legitimacy of recourse by the norm to the aim whenever the norm leads to impasses in practice" (170). We have just dealt with the primacy of ethics over morality. Let us now consider how Ricoeur deals with the question of the relation between the goal of ethics (teleology) and moral norms (deontology).

The criterion of universality is the hallmark of Kant's formalism. It is anticipated in Aristotle by the "golden mean," which characterizes all virtues. Aristotle's "good life" is approached by Kant's "good will, good without reservation." But the teleological character of "good" is lost when Kant adds "without reservation." What is more, for Kant it is the *will* that receives the predicate "good." As Ricoeur says, "the will, however, takes the place in Kantian morality that rational desire occupied in Aristotelian ethics; desire is recognized through its aim, will through its relation to law" (206).

Universality is the "royal road" to Kant's view of moral obligation. It is closely linked with "restraint" and through the latter with the idea of *duty*. Kant's genius was to place in the same person the power to command and the power to obey or disobey the command. The moral law is "autonomous," a universal law of reason that the autonomous subject gives himself. At the same time, his autonomy means that he can choose to obey or disobey this law. But this freedom, this autonomy, is affected by the propensity to evil. What effect does this propensity have on the status of the autonomy of the will? Ricoeur says that there are two important ideas here: (1) that evil, taken back to the origin of the maxims, should be thought of in terms of a real opposition; (2) that in radicalizing evil, Kant radicalized the idea of free will. Ricoeur concludes, "Because there is evil, the aim of the 'good life' has to be submitted to the test of moral obligation" (218).

Ricoeur has already shown how solicitude for the other was implicitly contained in the idea of self-esteem; he wants to show now that respect for others is implicit in the idea of obligation, rule, or law. His argument is that respect owed to others is tied to solicitude on the level of ethics; and, that on the level of morality, it is in the same relation to autonomy that solicitude is to the goal of the good life on the ethical level. In fact, Ricoeur claims that this relation will help us see the relation between the first formulation of the categorical imperative, in terms of obligation, and the second formulation, which tells us to respect others as ends-in-themselves. He has previously distinguished between the *power to act,* which is the capacity for an agent to be the author of his actions, and *power-in-common,* which is the capacity of the members of a community to will to live together. This latter capacity is to be distinguished from the relation of domination, which is the source of political violence. Political violence can take many forms, from constraint to torture and even to murder. In torture, it is the self-respect of the victim that is broken. Ricoeur says that all of these figures of evil are answered by the "no" of morality. This is why so many moral norms are expressed in the negative, "Thou shalt not...."

The second part of his argument concerning respect for others is to show its relation to solicitude. The Golden Rule, he says, is in an intermediary role between solicitude and Kant's second formulation of the categorical imperative in terms of respect for persons. He asks, "What, indeed, is it to treat humanity in my person and in the person of others as a *means,* if not to exert *upon* the will of others that power which, full of restraint in the case of influence, is unleashed in all forms that violence takes, culminating in torture?" (225).

Ricoeur has claimed that justice is a virtue principally of institutions. He now takes justice, in the sense of distributive justice, as the key intersection between the goal of ethics and the deontological point of view. But the very term *justice* is ambiguous. One sense emphasizes separation, in the sense of what belongs to me does not belong to you. Justice is to determine what should belong to whom. Another sense, however, puts the emphasis on cooperation and the community of interests. Related to these two senses of justice is the ambiguity between two senses of "equal": as in arithmetic, where all parts are exactly the same, and as proportional, where the parts to be distributed are proportional to some other measure such as merit, social standing, or power.

There have been many attempts to establish the principles of justice, especially on the social level. One of the most enduring is the "social contract," where justice is founded on a contract between individuals who, by this contract, create a community and establish the rules for the distribution of goods and obligations, rights and privileges, duties, and burdens. Ricoeur sees an analogy between the role of this contract on the level of institutions and the place of autonomy on the level of morality: "a freedom sufficiently disengaged from the gangue of inclinations provides a law for itself which is the very law of freedom" (229). At this point, Ricoeur turns to a long analysis of Rawls's attempt to establish the principles of justice through a theoretical and hypothetical gambit known as the "veil of ignorance." Rawls asks, what would be the principles of justice in a community if the members of the community could write those rules *not knowing what their actual lot would be?* His idea of justice as "fairness" leads, through this thought-experiment, to two general principles of justice: First, equal freedoms of citizenship, such as freedom of expression, etc.; second, a principle of difference that tells us under which circumstances inequalities are acceptable.

Ricoeur claims that what Rawls has done is to formalize a sense of justice that is already presupposed. Rawls himself agrees that he is not establishing a completely independent meaning of justice, that he relies on our precomprehension of what is just and unjust. What he does claim is that there is a "reflected equilibrium" between his theory and our "considered convictions." We do indeed have certain convictions about justice and injustice (e.g., religious intolerance, torture) that seem certain, while others such as the distribution of wealth or power seem less sure. Rawls's arguments are of the same type as those of Kant when he tries to prove the necessity for universalization of maxims. "The whole system of argumentation can therefore be seen as a progressive rationalization of these convictions, when they are affected by prejudices or weakened by doubts. This rationalization consists in a complex process of mutual adjustment between conviction and theory" (237).

At the end of his analysis of Rawls's attempt to establish a contractual basis for institutional justice, Ricoeur says that we can draw two conclusions:

(1) We can see how the attempt to give a purely procedural foundation for institutional justice takes to the maximum the ambition to free the deontological point of view of morality from the teleological perspective of ethics. (2) Yet we also see that this attempt clearly shows the limits of this ambition. In short, formalism has tried to banish inclinations from the sphere of rational will, the treatment of others as means in the interpersonal realm, and utilitarianism in the sphere of institutions. Instead, the deontological point of view insists on "autonomy in the first sphere, the person as end in himself in the second, and the social contract in the third" (238). The social contract plays the same role on the level of institutions as autonomy on the level of morality. But the social contract is a *fiction*, a "founding fiction, to be sure, but a fiction nonetheless" (239). Ricoeur criticizes social contract theories on the grounds that they are plausible only because we have forgotten our fundamental desire to live together. The foundation of deontology, in other words is, Ricoeur claims, found in *"the desire to live well with and for others in just institutions"* (239).

The third part of Ricoeur's reflections on ethics is to show how a morality of deontological norms must return to the fundamental insight of a teleological ethics in order to resolve the aporias arising in the application of the universal norms to difficult practical cases. His guiding thesis is that an ethics of obligation "produces conflictual situations where practical wisdom has no recourse, in our opinion, other than to return to the initial intuition of ethics, in the framework of moral judgment in situation; that is, to the vision or aim of the 'good life' with and for others in just institutions" (240). There are two possible misinterpretations to avoid here: First, we do not need to resort to any kind of Hegelian *Sittlichkeit,* or superior moment, which surpasses both the morality of obligation and the ethical goal of the good life. Second, the return from a morality of obligation to ethics should not be taken as a rejection of the morality of obligation. What Ricoeur is looking for, in other words, is a "practical wisdom" that allows us to decide in difficult particular cases without falling into a kind of arbitrary situationism.

At this point, Ricoeur resorts to a very unusual variation of style, reminiscent of Nietzsche, by inserting a nine-page *Interlude* called "Tragic Action." It is dedicated to his late son, Olivier, who died at the age of thirty-nine, only days after Ricoeur finished the Gifford Lectures in Edinburgh. Ricoeur takes as a case of "the tragedy of action," the moral conflict at the heart of Sophocles' *Antigone*. Antigone follows the "unwritten law" to bury her brother, Polynices, who was killed in an uprising against Thebes. She disobeys the direct order of the king, Creon, who has commanded that Polynices not be buried because he was a traitor to the city. For Creon, the moral rules are strict and easy: Only that which serves the city is good, that which harms it is evil. But Antigone is driven by the conviction that she is obliged, by unwritten laws, to provide a decent burial for her brother. Ricoeur says, "But in invoking them [the unwritten laws] to found her intimate conviction, she posited the limit that points up to human, all too human, character of every institution" (245). It is just such a limit that leads to ethics being instructed by tragedy. Once again, Ricoeur's thesis is that the dialectic of ethics and morality is played out in the moral judgment in particular situations.

Moral formalism, in Kant's sense, is forced to rely on the intuition of ethics in three areas already discussed: the universal self, the plurality of persons, and the institutional environment. Ricoeur now takes these three areas up again in reverse order, beginning with institutions. In the preceding chapter, he had already shown the possibility of conflict inherent in the idea of justice as a "just distribution." In short, it is the diversity of *contributions*, whether individual or collective, that raises the problem of a just distribution of rights, roles, responsibilities, and goods. This problem had led Aristotle to his idea of "proportional justice." The importance of institutions for this solution is clear: Referring to his seventh study, Ricoeur says, "We then admitted that it was only in a specific institutional milieu that the capacities and predispositions that distinguish human action can blossom; the individual, we said then, becomes human only under the condition of certain institutions; and we added: if this is so, the obligation to serve these institutions is itself a condition for the human agent to continue to develop" (254–255). Now, the political state is the set of practices organized around the distribution of power and domination. "Democracy," says Ricoeur, "is not a political system without conflicts but a system in which conflicts are open and negotiable in accordance with recognized rules of arbitration" (258). In response to the "crisis of legitimacy" of certain political institutions, he calls for the public recognition of traditions that make a place for tolerance and pluralism, "not out of concessions to external pressures, but out of inner conviction, even if this is late in coming" (261).

Ricoeur next considers the possibility of conflicts imbedded in the very nature of the second version of Kant's categorical imperative: the universality of humanity and the individuality of each person as an "end-in-himself." The conflict can arise between "respect for the law," which reflects universality, and "respect for persons," which reflects "the solicitude that is addressed to persons in their irreplaceable singularity" (262). Ricoeur holds that Kant does not see this possibility of conflict because he sees only the subsumption of the maxim under a rule. But it is when we consider the opposite direction, the application of the rule in concrete situations, where individuals demand to be recognized as ends-in-themselves, that we recognize the place of conflict. In the application of rules to particular situations, the rule is subject to the test of circumstances and consequences.

At this point, Ricoeur gives a summary analysis of promise making and the obligation to keep promises. He says that it is the "you can count on me" of the promise that ties selfhood with the reciprocity for the other founded in solicitude. "Not keeping one's promise is betraying both the other's expectation and the institution that mediates the mutual trust of speaking subjects" (268). What Kant failed to see is the possibility of conflict between respect for the law and respect for persons. To illustrate the kind of conflict that is possible, Ricoeur takes cases from the "end of life" and the "beginning of life." For the first, he takes the case of the obligation to tell the truth to dying persons. This obligation is tempered by compassion for certain patients who are too weak to stand the truth or those for whom the clinical truth would become simply a death sentence.

For the second kind of case, Ricoeur takes the question of abortion. While admitting that on the basis of biological criteria, the embryo is a biological individual from the moment of conception, Ricoeur asks "whether practical wisdom, without entirely losing this biologic criterion from sight, must not take into account the phenomena of thresholds and stages that put into question the simple alternative between 'person' and 'thing'" (271). Ricoeur thinks that the dialectic between sameness and selfhood leads us away from any simplistic substantialist ontology operative here. An opposite kind of thesis is that personhood is established only by well-developed capacities, such that only well-educated and autonomous adults would qualify for the status of personhood. We could decide to protect lesser beings, as we protect animals or nature, but they would have no right to be respected. Ricoeur rejects this view as well because it is an "all-or-nothing" position that does not admit degrees or stages of development. He argues for a progression of qualitatively different rights tied to a progression of biological thresholds. What is called for in these kinds of cases is "critical solicitude," where our moral judgments are the result of the good counsel of wise and competent men and women.

Ricoeur continues his argument that there are conflicts in the very heart of the claims of morality that call for a return to the most basic insight of ethics. In particular, there is the continual possibility—and reality—of conflict between the universalist claims of the rules derived from moral principles and the "recognition of positive values belonging to the *historial and communitarian contexts* of the realization of these same rules" (274). Ricoeur's claim is that there would not be a place for the tragedy of action unless there were a place for both the universalist thesis and the contextualist thesis mediated by "the practical wisdom of moral judgment in situation" (274).

In order to argue for this thesis, Ricoeur says that we must first make an extended revision to Kantian formalism that will clearly show the universalist claim and will sharpen as much as possible its conflict with contextualism. He will make this revision in three steps: (1) Question the priority Kant gives to the principle of autonomy with respect to the plurality of individuals and the principle of justice as applied to institutions. Ricoeur thinks that the principle of autonomy should be at the end of the series, not at the beginning. (2) Question the restrictive use Kant makes of the criterion of universalization. According to Ricoeur, this criterion is very impoverished since it is limited to noncontradiction and ignores the idea of the coherence of a moral system. Such a coherence shows that such a formalism is not vacuous, in the sense that a whole series of moral obligations or rules can be derived from the single principle requiring respect for others; furthermore, these moral obligations are mutually coherent and not conflictual among themselves. Finally, these rules are such that inferior rules are coherent with superior rules. (3) Finally, Kant's formalism lies on the retrospective path of *justification*, while the real conflicts arise in the prospective direction of deriving judgments from rules and rules from principles, that is, in the application of universal principles to concrete cases. In sum, Ricoeur's goal is to show both the credibility of the demand for universalization and the contextual character of the application of moral rules.

It is, he says, the job of political practice to deal with this conflict and these perplexities. He seeks moreover to underline the importance of the *historicity* of these political choices.

Next, if we move from the political level to the level of interpersonal relations, a new dichotomy or conflict arises: the otherness (*altérité*) of individuals is opposed to the unitary aspect of the concept of humanity. There is a *schism*, between respect for the law and respect for persons. In short, there is again a conflict between universalism and contextualism. If we have a concept of justice that is purely procedural, an ethics of argumentation can resolve the conflicts. But is the situation the same with the principle of respect for persons? Is resorting to developmental biology to decide whether the fetus is a person, a thing, or something intermediary not similar to looking for the best arguments in a debate over the *rights* of the fetus? Ricoeur accepts this thesis, but only to a certain point. He is in favor of contextualist explanations but objects strenuously to "an apology of difference for the sake of difference which, finally, makes all differences indifferent, to the extent that it makes all discussion useless" (286). In other words, what Ricoeur rejects in an ethics of argumentation (representing the demand for universalization) is not the taking into account of circumstances in constructing the best argument, but its attempt at *purification*. Kant wanted to purify all moral arguments from any kind of inclination, desire, pleasure, happiness, etc., and today Habermas directs his purification to anything *conventional*, in order to free moral arguments from anything having to do with tradition and authority.

Ricoeur, on the contrary, suggests a reformulation of the ethics of argumentation that integrates the objections of contextualism with the demands of universalization. He wants to call into question the conflict between argumentation and convention and substitute a dialectic between *argumentation and conviction*. He says, "what do we discuss, if not the best way for each party in the great debate to aim, beyond institutional mediations, at a complete life lived with and for others in just institutions? The articulations that we never cease to reinforce between deontology and teleology finds its highest—and most fragile—expression in *the reflective equilibrium between the ethics of argumentation and considered convictions*" (288–289). One aspect of practical wisdom is the "art of conversation, in which the ethics of argumentation is put to the test in the conflict of convictions" (290).

What is most important about Ricoeur's moral theory is that he does not accept the classical conflict between a teleological ethics and a nomological morality—to use his conventions—as an antinomy. He argues that they are poles in a dialectical relationship, each calling on the other to complete its vision of a moral universe. A teleological view of the goal of ethics needs universal moral rules as a necessary means; on the other hand, the application of these rules to difficult particular cases calls for an appeal to the ultimate *telos* of morality.

The dialectic between ethics as the teleological goal of "a good life lived with others in just institutions" and a morality of universal rules finds its mediation in "practical wisdom." This wisdom is precisely the application of moral rules to particular cases where a "conflict of convictions" is tempered by an ethics of argumentation. In his moral theory, Ricoeur replaces the "conflict of interpretations" of his hermeneutics with a conflict of convictions. In both cases, it is the task of reflective philosophy to adjudicate among the conflicting claims—each of which asserts that it is absolute.

ONTOLOGY OF THE SELF

Ricoeurs hermeneutics of the self and its relation to the other actually ends with the ninth study. Ricoeur asks, however, "What kind of being is the self?" He says that his ontology of the self will be tentative and exploratory. He reminds us that the hermeneutics of the self was based on three successive problematics: reflection by the indirect route of analysis; the determination of selfhood by its contrast with sameness; and a second determination of selfhood through its dialectic with otherness. He calls the result of this progressive study a hermeneutics of the self through a triple mediation. In the previous studies the guiding principle has been the *polysemy* of the question "who?": who speaks, who acts, who tells a story, who is responsible? But, beneath the structure organized around the question "who?" is the substructure organized around the three problematics described above. The first four studies responded to reflection through analysis; the fifth and sixth dealt with the contrast between selfhood and sameness; and the seventh, eighth, and ninth chapters focused on the dialectic between selfhood and the other.

Above all, Ricoeur wants to warn us again against any attempt to establish an epistemological—or ontological—foundation in the manner of Descartes or Husserl. Instead of any claim to absolute truth, he reminds us that attestation is a level of belief and confidence based on "testimony." It is not an attempt to create an auto-foundational certitude of a Cartesian *cogito*, and so it escapes the "humiliation of the cogito reduced to sheer illusion following the Nietzschean critique" (299). Analysis, in the sense used by analytic philosophy, *attests*, in Ricoeur's sense, to the ontological import of the self when, with Strawson, the basic individuals are bodies and persons, and, with Davidson, acts are construed as kinds of events. In these analyses, the self is that which is talked about. But hermeneutics renders a reciprocal service to analytical philosophy by showing that the self is not the result of some "linguistic mistake" or even more importantly, insisting on a referential aspect of language as a corrective for those philosophies such as French structuralism which refuse to "go outside" of language and mistrust any extralinguistic reality. Ricoeur says, "I find here again the sort of *ontological vehemence* whose advocate I have been elsewhere in the name of the conviction that—even in the uses of language that appear to be the least referential, as is the case with metaphor and narrative fiction—language expresses being, even if this ontological aim is as though postponed, deferred by the prior denial of the literal referentiality of ordinary language" (301).

An important difference between the being-true of attestation of Ricoeur and that of Aristotle is that the contrary of attestation is suspicion, while the contrary of being-true for Aristotle is being false. "Suspicion is also the path *toward and* crossing *within* attestation. It haunts attestation, as false testimony haunts true testimony. This adherence, this inherence of suspicion with respect to attestation, has marked the entire course of these studies" (302). To press on farther into the ontology of the self, Ricoeur says he must be more precise about selfhood, both in its difference from sameness and its relation to otherness.

The dialectic between selfhood and otherness is more fundamental than the relation between reflection and analysis and even the contrast between selfhood and sameness. Otherness does not come from outside selfhood, but is part of the meaning and the ontological constitution of selfhood. He says that the phenomenological response to the metacategory of otherness is "the variety of experiences of passivity, intertwined in multiple ways in human action" (318). The main point of this dialectic is to prevent the self from pretending to occupy the place of a foundation. Otherness is joined to selfhood. The passivity at the core of otherness is manifested in three ways: "First, there is the passivity represented by the experience of one's own body—or better, as we shall say later, of the flesh—as mediator between the self and a world. . . . Next, we find the passivity implied by the relation of the self to the foreign, in the precise sense of the other (than) self . . . Finally, we have the most deeply hidden passivity, that of the relation of the self to itself, which is *conscience*" (318). All three of these manifestations exhibit the complexity and density of the concept of otherness.

If, to use Strawson's terms, persons are also bodies, it is to the extent that each person is for himself his own body. The double belonging of the lived body to the order of things as well as to the self is echoed in Davidson's account of action as also an event. Ricoeur certainly includes suffering in the passivity of the body. He says, "With the variety of these degrees of passivity, one's own body is revealed to be the mediator between the intimacy of the self and the externality of the world" (322). The "flesh" is the place of the experience of passivity. Selfhood implies a "lived" otherness, of which the flesh is the foundation. In a powerful analogy, Ricoeur says,

> The problem we called the reinscription of phenomenological time in cosmological time in *Time and Narrative* finds a series of equivalences here: just as it was necessary to invent the calendar to correlate the lived now with the anonymous instant and to draw up the geographic map to correlate the charnel here with an indifferent place, and thereby to inscribe the proper name—my name—in the civil register, it is necessary, as Husserl himself states, to *make* the flesh part of the world *(mondaneiser)* if it is to appear as a body among bodies. (326)

Ricoeur goes on to speak of an otherness constitutive of the self and says that it gives full force to the paradoxical expression "oneself as another" (327).

The second category of the experience of the passivity of the self is in the "otherness" of other people. Ricoeur introduces the idea of a dialectic between self-esteem and friendship. He says that justice is generally considered in the sense of distributive justice in exchanges, but it could be rewritten in terms of a dialectic of action and affection. In the dialectic between the self and the other, it is the face of the other that appears to me and says, "Thou shalt not kill." It is the other who constitutes me as responsible, that is, capable of answering. "In this way, the word of the other comes to be placed at the origin of my acts" (336). So, self-designation which imputes moral responsibility for my acts to me has its origin outside of the self.

The next pages are a debate between Kant and Levinas. Kant puts respect for the law above respect for other persons; Levinas says that the face of the other singularizes the commandment. To be effective, however, the voice of the other must become my voice; his command must become my conviction. This dialectic between the self and the other was already anticipated in Ricoeur's discussion of promising: "If another were not counting on me, would I be capable of keeping my word, of maintaining myself?" (341).

Ricoeur says that among the most *suspect* ideas are those of the "bad" or "good" conscience. A discussion of conscience will give him, he says, a perfect opportunity to put to the test his thesis that "attestation of selfhood is inseparable from an exercise of *suspicion*" (341). Even if we overcome the distinction between "good" and "bad" conscience, we must still deal with phenomena of *injunction* and *debt* which are ingrained in the idea of conscience. There are three challenges to overcome in order to rescue the concept of conscience from Nietzsche's attack.

First challenge. The conscience is the place where illusions about oneself are mixed with the truth of attestation. After an extended discussion of Nietzsche's analyses of the concept of conscience, Ricoeur says that the force of Nietzsche's method of suspicion is that all conscience is "bad conscience." The trap, says Ricoeur, is the danger of a new dogmatism. In order to return to the idea of conscience, we must abandon the ideas of "good" and "bad" conscience and go back to a kind of nonmoral suspicion which is the other face of attestation.

Second challenge. What happens when we "de-moralize" the conscience? How do we keep from falling back into the trap of "good" and "bad" conscience? Ricoeur says, "A remark made earlier with respect to the metaphor of the *court* puts us on the right path. Is it not because the stage of morality has been dissociated from the triad ethics-morality-conviction, then hypostasized because of this dissociation, that the phenomenon of conscience has been correlatively impoverished and the revealing metaphor of the voice has been eclipsed by the stifling metaphor of the court?" (351). Ricoeur says that the first injunction is a call to live well with and for others in just institutions. It is because violence can spoil all of our interpersonal relationships that we have the law or interdiction "Thou shalt not kill." Violence causes a short circuit and the voice of conscience becomes the verdict of a court. We need to take the reverse path, from interdiction-verdict to the injunction to live well.

Third challenge. The otherness of the conscience can be found in the Freudian superego, the internalization of the ancestral voice. The otherness in the heart of the conscience is a form of the passivity of the self. The question is, if there is a *trace* of the other in conscience, is that other ancestral, or God, or "an empty place"? Ricoeur's ontological essay concludes, "With this aporia of the other, philosophical discourse comes to an end" (355).

But, of course, philosophical discourse does not come to an end, neither for Paul Ricoeur nor for us. We have taken but the first step in a careful reading of the text, lent a sympathetic ear to the arguments, reached a thorough understanding of the issues and the debates. Now, it is our time to respond, to criticize, to propose, to argue, and, finally, to advance our philosophical understanding of "oneself as another."

We can take *Oneself as Another*, the last, the most carefully constructed, and most tightly argued of Ricoeur's books, as the very model of his philosophical style. After a lifetime as a professor of philosophy, he always gives credit to other authors, and honors them by a careful and sympathetic reading of their arguments. He rejects completely any kind of foundationalism, such as those of Descartes or Husserl; but he equally rejects the nihilism and skepticism of Nietzsche. Where others see only dichotomies, Ricoeur sees dialectics. But, his dialectics never result in a "lazy eclecticism," or mere combination of elements from both poles, but rather in a "reading through" from one pole to the other in order to show their interdependence. His dialectical analyses do not result in a Hegelian "third term" that surpasses the dialectical poles and renders them useless. His "third term," such as "practical wisdom," can only be understood at the very heart of the dialectic and as completely implying both poles of the dialectic. This is a constant and essential element in his philosophical method.

Oneself as Another is not only an excellent example of Ricoeur's philosophical style, but it clearly exemplifies and continues his lifelong interest in human action and suffering. He himself has characterized his work as a "philosophical anthropology." His work is at the crossroads between "words and deeds," or a "semantics of action and desire." It is in this sense that his last book recapitulates and refines his central philosophical concerns.

NOTES

1. Paul Ricoeur, *TN*, 1, 2, 3. Translation of *TR*, I, II, III.
2. Paul Ricoeur, *TA*. Translation of *Dta*.
3. Paul Ricoeur, *OA*. Translation of *Sa*. Numbers in parentheses refer to page numbers in *OA*.

4. Paul Ricoeur, *Lmv*. Translated as *RM*.
5. Paul Ricoeur, *FP*, 43.
6. Paul Ricoeur, "The Model of the Text: Meaningful Action Considered as a Text," *Social Research* 38, no. 3 (Fall 1971): 529–562. *HHS*, 197–221.
7. Ibid., 215.
8. P. F. Strawson, *Individuals* (London: Methuen, 1959).
9. See R. S. Peters, *The Concept of Motivation* (London: Routledge and Kegan Paul, 1958).
10. Paul Ricoeur, *FN*, 355–373. Translation of *LV*.
11. Paul Ricoeur, *FM*, 77–98. Translation of *Lf*.

TWO

The Doubleness of Subjectivity
Regenerating the Phenomenology of Intentionality

Lenore Langsdorf

> ... philosophies of the past remain open to reinterpretations and reappropriations, thanks to a meaning potential left unexploited, even repressed, by the very process of systematization.... if one cannot re‑awaken and liberate those resources that the great systems of the past tend to stifle and to conceal, no innovation would be possible, and present thought would have only the choice between repetition and aimless wandering.
>
> —Paul Ricoeur, *Oneself as Another*

> The Cartesian epistemological ideals of clarity, detachment, and objectivity, although still largely unquestioned as requirements for scientific and philosophic investigation, [may be] interpreted as, serving an obsessive concern with purity and a corresponding desire to exorcise all the messier (e.g., bodily; emotional) dimensions of experience from science and philosophy...
>
> —Susan Bordo, *The Flight to Objectivity*

In this essay I develop Paul Ricoeur's suggestive comments in regard to a mode of intentionality correlative to—indeed, dialectically implicated by—the mode of intentionality that forms the core of Husserlian phenomenology. In part, my goal is to articulate an understanding of phenomenology that responds to contemporary critique of "philosophies of the subject"—within which, typically, phenomenology is located. The point of this endeavor, however, is not to immunize phenomenology against critique. Rather, my goal is to continue (and perhaps even "reawaken and liberate") the phenomenological project, now loosened (with Ricoeur's help) from presuppositions taken over from Cartesian thinking and retained within Husserl's initiating analysis of intentionality and constitution. The continuation is by way of understanding selfhood as enacting a doubled "who," intrinsically capable of articulating critique by virtue of its persistent incorporation of the other and not vulnerable to critique's dispersal of "the subject"—because not deprived of the "messier dimensions" of human experience. The invulnerability of this concept of subjectivity, therefore, does not rely on an impermeable unity. Rather, the concept of a mediated self (in contrast to a Cartesian self) that I articulate here is multiple, mutable, and permeable; loosely woven to the extent that it is fragmented in creatively powerful ways.

The exigency instigating this project is cogently and effectively expressed by contemporary theorists of decolonization (that is, of resistance to hegemonic strategies of oppression, whether that be on the grounds of nationalism, classism, sexism, or racism). These theorists struggle against a variety of voices that reject the legitimacy (or even plausibility) of their claims on the grounds that their status as subjects, capable of articulating a critical position, may be dispersed into a multiplicity of covert as well as overt positions which need hold not claim over their listeners. Philosophy's failure to supply these decolonizing theorists with useful responses to these challenges to the possibility of a critical subject can be traced to a variety of sources. Among these, contemporary deconstructive proclamations of the death of the subject are particularly loud.

Yet it seems to me that deconstructing the subject is a project that was already underway when David Hume reported on his introspective search for the self. He tells us that he found only "some particular perception" which might then be considered as part of "a bundle or collection of different perceptions," but not the "some one impression that gives rise to every real idea."[1] His conclusion—that "the self or person is not any one impression, but that to which our several impressions and ideas are suppos'd to have a reference"[2]—has been accepted as denying self-identity, rather than uncovering an alternative understanding of how the self has its being. One such alternative, which I develop here with considerable reliance upon Ricoeur's analysis in *Oneself As Another,* begins from a little-noted similarity among conceptions of self-dispersal; namely, they presuppose a particular notion of the subject as self-identical by virtue of particular qualities that it is purported to have (possess and display). They then go on to achieve their deconstructive effect by revealing the absence of those qualities. The result is to limit thinking to "the choice between repetition and aimless wandering": between repeating past and present practices despite their oppressive effect, or merely talking about those practices without any means for advocating innovative, and yet plausible, alternatives.

The alternative concept of subjectivity that I propose here relies upon phenomenological evidence of the persistence, in human conduct, of an intrinsic capacity for critique nourished by resources that are concealed, and even stifled, by systems of thinking that focus on presence or productivity. The former focus is exemplified by Hume's search for what must be present ("one impression") if there is to be a self. The latter is exemplified by Husserl's investigation of intending subjects as ceaselessly active, engaged in producing the words and actions in and through which we constitute ourselves and the objects of the environment. In contrast, Ricoeur's analysis in *Oneself as Another* uncovers concealed resources when he attends to clues-implications—that he uses as evidence for an effective and passive dimension of self.

Ricoeur has multiple goals in this analysis. First among them, I believe, is affirming "human action as a fundamental mode of being" characterized by "ipseity" (selfhood, without connotations of an identical "unchanging core of the personality," but with the character of continuity across time), rather than "identity" (sameness, as exhibited by inert matter).[3] The context for that affirmation is a hermeneutic analysis that "can stand on the authority of the resources of past ontologies that could be, as it were, reawakened, liberated, generated" so that we can understand being as "act and potentiality," despite the residue of past systems in which that sense of being was "too often sacrificed to being-as-substance."[4] I use this affirmation as a starting point in searching for phenomenological evidence of the affective/passive dimension of self that Ricoeur uncovers. That evidence is to be found, I argue, by attending to the potentiality given in specific communicative performances of others—rather than to the productivity (linguistic or otherwise) of substantive subjects.

In order to use Ricoeur's analysis to "regenerate"[5] a concept of intentionality that renders plausible an understanding of ourselves as subjects capable of critique, by virtue of particular resources given in our inherently communicative way of being, I begin by summarizing the typical characterization of Husserl's concept of intentionality. I then examine the implications of Ricoeur's name—"gnoseological"—for this concept. In the second part of the essay, I begin to "regenerate" that concept of intentionality by considering the "how" of its genesis. My goal here is to uncover an otherness concealed within subjectivity by reinterpreting deficiencies in "gnoseological intentionality" as indications of incompleteness that results from an analysis limited to but one of intentionality's functions. In other words, I work from what is absent in the familiar concept in order to uncover a "meaning potential left unexploited, even repressed" in Husserlian phenomenology as it typically is understood. I attend to historical and intellectual conditions as plausible sources for the "why" of that repression, but am primarily interested in exploring a potential that remains unexploited in the narrow conception of intentionality that is suggested by Ricoeur's naming of Husserl's concept as "gnoseological." In the concluding part of the essay, I provide phenomenological evidence for this "repressed" aspect of subjectivity.

This potential for an alternative both relies on and (I hope) demonstrates the value of the middle path that Ricoeur delineates from Husserl's starting point in the *cogito*. He describes the two divergent paths from that starting point as marked by Cartesian "certainty" or Nietzschean "humiliation," leading (respectively) to theorizing the self as a posited "self-founding" or a deposed "sheer illusion."[6] The middle path relies instead on Ricoeur's "attestation" as an alternative to a philosophy of apodicticity (as in Descartes, and to a prominent degree, also in Husserl) or a hermeneutic of suspicion (as in Nietzsche). Attesting to phenomenological evidence that eludes certainty enables us to open up both epistemological and ontological possibilities along the way of this third path. Epistemologically, we are able to appreciate contextual plausibility as an alternative that is preferable to certainty or humiliation. Ontologically, our comprehension of how oneself as another may be nonobjectively manifest in the world is strengthened by recognizing a process in which the other's communicative activity creates a noncentered subject who exemplifies "ipseity" rather than "sameness."

PART ONE

> We must now dig down to the essence of Brentano's concept of consciousness in the sense of a psychical act . . . . In perception something is perceived, in imagination, something imagined, in a statement, something stated, in love, something loved, in hate hated, in desire desired, etc. Brentano looks to what is graspably common to such instances, and says that "every mental phenomenon is characterized by what the mediaeval schoolmen called the intentional (or mental) inexistence of an object, and by what we [Brentano] call[s] the relation to a content, the direction to an object . . . or an immanent objectivity . . .
>
> —Edmund Husserl, *Logical Investigations*

It will be useful to begin by summarizing the Husserlian sense of intentionality as "consciousness of . . . " or "directedness to . . . " as he developed that basic concept from Brentano's conception. Both designations suit Husserl's starting point far better than they suit the understanding of intentionality that develops (albeit slowly and with hesitation) as he thought again and again of the deficiencies inherent in that starting point. Although Husserl attributed the concept of intentionality to Brentano, and thus to a scholastic tradition, his development of that concept in the *Logical Investigations*, *Cartesian Meditations*, and *Ideas, Book One* clearly owes a debt to the radical turn to subjectivity which we associate with Descartes's critique of the scholastic tradition. Husserl's recurrent attempts to return to that starting point in order to begin again, and hints of the distinct dimensions of intentionality identified by Ricoeur, are apparent in *The Crisis of European Sciences and Transcendental Phenomenology*. They are most evident in Husserl's only co-authored work—the *Sixth Cartesian Investigation*, which developed in both spoken and written dialogue with Eugen Fink. (That the uncovering of another dimension of intentionality occurred in the course of a collaborative effort to revise a single-authored text is not, I believe, coincidental.)

Even early on, the Cartesian debt was partial, since Husserl recognized an incompleteness in the *cogito* that escaped Descartes's attention—perhaps because the latter was eager to move deductively (and thus, with certainty) from the much-desired certain basis offered by the *cogito*. Husserl was willing to pause, however, for investigation of the phenomenon itself. Thus, he noticed that thinking need not terminate with a reflectively certain affirmation of the thinker's existence, coupled with reliance upon God's beneficence in regard to knowing (albeit indirectly) the thinker's environment. Rather, Husserl noticed that thinking opened out directly and even inevitably to termini *other than* the thinker's existence. Accordingly, phenomenology was to be the investigation of that other-than, conceptualized in terms of the objects correlative to a (Cartesian) subject's experience. By virtue of the doctrine of the epoche it was to carry out investigation without concern for existential certainty or deductive proof—yet with great concern for descriptive accuracy and analysis in terms of wholes and parts, essential structures, and transcendental conditions. The intrinsic connectedness of experiencing effort (thinking of . . . , etc.) and experienced terminus (the other-than, typically) meant that investigating any instance of intentionality means attending to both the directedness-to and directed-upon dimensions of the phenomena, which later were named "noesis" and "noema." However, this focus on intending objects did not extend to how intentionality might be operative in the constitution of the intending subject.

Paul Ricoeur's name for this conceptual structure is "gnoseological intentionality."[7] This choice of terminology should give us pause, first because of Ricoeur's abiding interest in communicating meaning through language—which suggests that this is a deliberate choice, rather than a random labeling. Even more importantly, the term deserves our attention because of Ricoeur's extensive work in biblical hermeneutics as well as his acknowledgment of the "convictions that bind [him] to biblical faith," even while he "pursue[s] . . . an autonomous, philosophical discourse."[8] Why "gnoseological," rather than (say) "epistemological," intentionality? The dictionary definition of the former term as "inquiry into the basis, nature, and limits of knowledge" could as well apply to the latter. Yet the dictionary reminds us that "gnosis," in contrast to the more familiar term *knowledge,* denotes "immediate knowledge of spiritual truth, especially such knowledge as professed by the ancient Gnostics and held to be attainable through faith alone." There are three aspects of this definition that are worth pondering: it focuses on immediate (in contrast to mediated) attainments, on spiritual (in contrast to embodied) knowledge, and on truth attained through faith (in contrast to plausibility established through consideration of competing claims).

Husserl's understanding of intentionality as the structure of directedness sustains his analysis of human inquiry as immediately directed to its surroundings, rather than limited to ideas (as it was for Locke) or to language (as for Wittgenstein and, with interesting differences, for much contemporary scholarship); or, as requiring validation through Divine mediation (as for Descartes). However, this focus on immediacy is by no means unproblematic. On the one hand, critics see Husserl's call to investigate "the things themselves"—rather than things as inherently embodying the intervention of cultural, historical, and psychological factors—as a form of realism, empiricism, or even positivism; as an insistence upon the transparency of those layers of meaningfulness that provide degrees of plausibility to multiple conflicting interpretations. As Erazim Kohak sums up that position: "Husserl is utterly committed to the primordial intelligibility of experience," and thus, to the conviction that "knowledge can be a faithful articulation grounded in immediate awareness."[9] Yet phenomenologists attempting to continue in that conviction—and, eventually, Husserl himself—discovered "dimensions of subjectivity" that resisted their epistemic efforts, and this slow recognition of "the hardness of reality"—its resistance to the gaze of immediate awareness that would render it transparent—fostered "a methodological extension of phenomenology in hermeneutics" in order to investigate those "dimensions of reality which are opaque to awareness."[10]

The evolution toward hermeneutic phenomenology, and thus perforce away from phenomenology as Husserl initially envisioned it, is in effect a ceasing to believe in "immediate knowledge" as a possible human achievement. That loss of belief can be an impetus to skepticism of various sorts. Yet it also may enable and even encourage us to acknowledge a complexity in human knowing that is obscured, if not denied, by both empiricism and skepticism. Thus, Ricoeur often speaks in terms of "an opaque subjectivity which expresses itself through the detour of countless mediations—signs, symbols, texts and human praxis itself."[11] Metaphorically speaking, this hermeneutic evolution in phenomenology resulted from Husserl's gradual (and reluctant) acknowledgment that multiple voices mediate, enrich, and often confuse, the single-minded gaze of immediate awareness that the epoche sought to establish as a standard for phenomenology. Given the complexity that results from multiplicity, "gnoseological intentionality"—the structure of experience that is knowable in "immediate awareness"—requires complementary modes of intentionality appropriate to the "opaque" dimensions of human experience, and, thus, appropriate to an alternative concept of the subject. Before turning to these possibilities, we need to consider two additional aspects of the "gnosis" implicated in "gnoseological intentionality."

The second aspect of "gnosis" worth reflecting upon is its focus on spiritual knowledge. When we speak of "spiritual" dimensions of human being, we foreground, typically, development of epistemic capacities in domains other than (say) bicycle riding, cooking, plumbing, or a variety of topics, from arithmetic to zoology, taught in secular academic settings. Although it is not the only way to distinguish knowing in those domains from that "spiritual" dimension, the degree to which we use our bodies is an especially salient distinguishing mark. The spiritual knowledge sought by the Gnostics, then, results from disembodied inquiry—precisely the form of knowing valorized by Plato, dominant in Euro-American intellectual history ever since, and insisted upon by Descartes. However, that dominance has not been unopposed. An early instance of opposition and even condemnation was the Church's identification of Gnosticism—"the thought and practice of various cults of late pre-Christian and early Christian centuries," the dictionary tells us—as a heresy. This mode of knowing (the dictionary continues) was "distinguished chiefly by pretension to mystic and esoteric religious insights, by emphasis on knowledge rather than faith, and by the conviction that matter is evil."

The third aspect of "gnosis" relevant here is its valorization of truth attained through faith, in contrast to plausibility established through consideration of competing claims. Given that valorization, Gnosticism's "emphasis on knowledge rather than faith" might seem paradoxical and even contradictory, until we recognize that what is at stake here is a conception of knowledge as the goal of methodical inquiry introduced into our history by Greek philosophy. The early Christian centuries were marked by an incorporation of this Greek conception, which remained in a rather uneasy balance with more "mystic and esoteric" focus upon faith as a Divine gift. Possession of faith could then enable a particular sort of absolute knowledge; even, knowledge of absolutes that were (so to speak) in competition with the discursively as well as empiricially affirmed results of Platonic and Aristotelian inquiry.

These aspects of a gnostic conception of knowledge gave rise to at least three reasons for the Church's condemnation of Gnosticism. First, a faith community based in affirmation that Divinity had chosen to become incarnate—that is, to take on the matter of a human body—could not accept "the conviction that matter is evil." Correlatively, given that valorization of human embodiment, the Church could not valorize a concept of knowledge that denigrated what we learn in embodied activity.[12] To do so would have meant declaring a preference for one sort of learning—"mystic and esoteric" insight—over the practice-based teachings of an incarnate Divinity who relied on listeners' drawing analogies and generalizations from their particular experiences as embodied beings living in a specific cultural and historical setting. Furthermore, those teachings offered insights to all who would listen, rather than to a select few. Gnosticism, in contrast, assumed limitations on the source and content of, as well as the audience for, knowledge. Furthermore, the logical and empirical approaches developed by Greek philosophy and incorporated into ways of thinking characteristic of early Christianity were congruent with Christian suppositions in regard to the universal accessibility and applicability of truth. Thus, the emergent Church was able to draw on an alternative understanding of knowledge that was extant in its enlarging cultural setting. The availability of this alternative doubtless encouraged the condemnation of Gnosticism.

This history enables us to appreciate the significance of Ricoeur's designation of Husserlian intentionality as "gnoseological" rather than "epistemological." It also suggests an impetus for reflecting on the limitations of that conception of intentionality—particularly when it is used as the basis for understanding the self—while retaining an appreciation for its advance over the *cogito*'s "certain" evidence of "I" as "a substance, of which the whole essence or nature consists in thinking"; even, of "I" as "a thing that thinks."[13] Ricoeur's label is justified when we recall the three aspects of "gnoseological" we pondered earlier: immediate attainment of evidence, spiritual (in contrast to embodied) knowledge, and truth attained through faith. The Husserlian concept of intentionality does enable us to expand the Cartesian "I" to include directedness-to what is other-than mental. Also, it implicitly moves away from "being-as-substance" conceptions of self that, as Ricoeur explains, rely upon criteria of "sameness" *(idem)*; and, toward an "act and potentiality" basis that relies upon "constancy" of responsibility for consequences ("ipseity").[14] But this Husserlian concept of intentionality retains Descartes's reliance upon what is immediately evident to a mind that thinks clearly and distinctly, and does not critically analyze Descartes's presupposition that embodiment can only detract from cognition. Also, this Husserlian concept retains a faith in the accessibility of truth, albeit in a secularized, Enlightenment-transformed way that places that faith in human reason's ability to discern certain truth, rather than acknowledging a more modest goal of attesting to contextually plausible claims.[15]

Ricoeur shares Husserl's willingness to remain with the phenomena themselves, rather than using them (in Cartesian fashion) as the basis for deducing apodictic truths. However, his investigation of intentionality takes us considerably farther than Husserl's, for he works within an intellectual context informed by both Husserl's investigations and his well-known frustrations in regard to the "Cartesian way," together with the subsequent findings and frustrations of the analytic and interpretive philosophers whose work instigates the "detours" characteristic of his own research. All of these factors may well contribute to Ricoeur's ability to notice what escaped Husserl's careful gaze initially and then, during the years of dialogue with Eugen Fink, came to frustrate anything less than a thorough rethinking of the Cartesian beginnings of phenomenology. The decisive difference, I believe, is that Ricoeur is as attuned to plurality, in the sense of multiple narratives that implicate what is absent, as Husserl was to unity, in the sense of an encompassing description of what is present in an experience. More specifically, Ricoeur is as open to the polysemy of the other-than, and the possibility that some kinds of experience might be structured in ways inaccessible to gnoseological intentionality, as Husserl was relentless in his efforts to ground "philosophy as a rigorous science" in (gnoseological) intentionality.[16]

Ricoeur's recognition of polysemy and his willingness to entertain the possibility of complementary models of intentionality enable an alternative to phenomenology's initial conception of intentionality. He emphasizes that the clues to this complementary mode appear despite Husserl's attempts to account for the special nature of those other-thans present in experience as fellow human beings by employing the same concept of intentionality that served him well in investigating our experience of material objects (such as the furniture of everyday life) and formal objects (such as number). That attempt—most evident in the *Cartesian Meditations*—is an understandable one: we all, when blessed with a useful way of going about things, tend to use it more and more extensively, until we are confronted with recalcitrant phenomena that resist our previously successful methods. Husserl certainly noticed that the problematic of intersubjectivity (and, even, subjectivity) resisted the methods of investigation that had been productive in other domains. We need now to reconsider his attempts to extend his method to the study of subjectivity not as failures, but as clues for resources that his way of thinking, inevitably shaped by past systems, tended "to stifle and to conceal."

PART TWO

> Up until now our meditation has taken a course... of restoring the idea of science as the grounding of knowledge of the world in regress to the apodicticity of the "I am." This whole path now seems to have been the wrong way to go.
>
> —Eugen Fink, in his draft revision of the First Cartesian Meditation
>
> So it was! A sheer muddle, and wrongheaded as a course of reflection.
>
> —Edmund Husserl, in his marginal note to the above passage

In a 1933 letter to a former student, Dietrich Mahnke, Husserl wrote that "what is immensely difficult is the doubleness of the sense of being in I, we, subjectivity," and then went on to specify that doubleness in terms of two ways of being that "belong essentially together":

1. as subjectivity for the world, in whose functioning world gains sense (the world only makes sense... for subjects that intend the world); and

2. as subjectivity that itself belongs to the world.[17]

Ronald Bruzina notes that "Husserl's words here clearly acknowledge and reflect the four years of work on his Cartesian Meditations that had... culminated in Fink's revision texts and the Sixth Meditation." What had emerged in those four years of dialogue, Bruzina goes on to say, was recognition of "the methodological question in the 'radical self-reflection' that phenomenology puts into practice" as a question of

> the nature of the move back to the beginning beyond which questioning cannot go the difference and identity between the subjectivity that lives within the world and the subjectivity that constitutes the world and all in it.[18]

The question that then arises, Bruzina notes, is how this "doubleness of subjectivity"—its being as constituted ("as subjectivity that itself belongs to the world," "that lives ... within the world") and as constituting ("as subjectivity for the world," "that constitutes the world and all in it")—"could be in any legitimate sense identical."[19]

Fink recognized that working through this question requires "a phenomenology of phenomenology" that is (as Bruzina notes) "a work of criticism: not a mere description of methods employed," but a critique that engages "the very basics of the whole enterprise of doing phenomenology, certain of which turn out to be more problematic than originally seemed."[20] The result is nothing less than a "displacement of a Cartesian-based exposition of phenomenology" in which "Husserl's ego-centrality is retained as important but ... circumscribed in a radical way" by virtue of recognizing a "necessary supposition—not a clear disclosure—of a constitutional process beyond the (or, better, my) ego's own life precisely as egoic."[21] "Such a supposition," Bruzina goes on to say, has to be justified phenomenologically;

> has to be somehow demonstratively indicated in one's own course of living experience, and this is precisely the function of empathy. Empathy has the effect of setting a limit to the efficacy of unmediated egoic self-intuiting right in the question of the most basic constitution of all, that of the world as the universal pregiven horizon for any and all subjective life whatsoever.[22]

In the concluding section of this essay, I offer a contribution to the "clear disclosure" needed to justify supposition of non-egoic constitution. What is phenomenologically disclosed there is how the Cartesian-inspired immediacy of gnoseological intentionality works to "stifle and conceal" the efficacy of communicative mediation. That disclosure is enabled by attending to what Ricoeur characterizes as Husserl's "great discovery": the "prereflexive, prepredicative operation" in which the living body *(Leib)* engages, via a "prelinguistic relation," with "a world accessible or inaccessible to the 'I can.'"[23] Before turning to that analysis, it will be helpful to identify its precedents by considering how Husserl came to that "great discovery" and how Ricoeur uses it in his analysis.

When Husserl took up the revisioning task of the *Crisis*, he recognized that he was now "asking after the how of the world's pregivenness" in a retracing of his "Cartesian way" into phenomenology, since that path "has a great shortcoming: while it leads to the transcendental ego in one leap, as it were, it brings this ego into view as apparently empty of content ... so that one is at a loss ... to know what has been gained by it."[24] The *Crisis* revisioning begins from the lifeworld and the living body *(Leib)*, and thus from the multiplicity intrinsic to lived experience, rather than from reflection by an isolated "I" whose substantial being is affirmed on the basis of monological cognition. Yet the revisioning began, in another sense, in the extended dialogue with Fink, whose "strength lay," as Bruzina notes, "in formulating comprehensive self-conception and self-criticism, rather than in producing the painstaking detail work that was Husserl's special genius."[25] The result was a "challenge to the intuitive evidential immediacy basic to Husserl's [earlier vision of] phenomenology" that is acknowledged in an interestingly understated way in Husserl's reference to the work-in-revision, in conversation with Dorion Cairns, as "quite different."[26]

From the perspective of Ricoeur's investigation of selfhood, the revisioning of the "Cartesian way" in the *Crisis* has the value of moving from substance-based responses to "What am I?" (Descartes's question) to posing questions of selfhood in terms of "How am I?" and even "Who am I?" Husserl's response to the former question would then be: I am a living body, prereflexively and even prepredicatively related with the lifeworld. This description, Ricoeur notes, enables a "detour by way of things," which is to say, "by way of objectification" in events, and has the virtue of showing that "the being of the world is the necessary correlate to the being of the self."[27] However, the preeminence of physical science within the European lifeworld works to encourage our thinking of the "what" of events in terms of the "why" of causal explanation, and so, discourages moving from "what" to "how" and then to "who" questions. Ricoeur remind us of this danger when he writes that "replies to the questions 'what' and 'why'" bring about "concealment of the question 'who'" by taking on the "perspective of semantics, heavily dominated by the way in which discourse refers to something."[28] The result is diversion from thinking of "how" we act and "who" acts; a "capture of the 'what' by the 'why'" and finally, by an "ontology of the impersonal event" that relies upon causal explanations.[29]

The path cleared by physical science, then, takes us away from discerning the possibility of a critical subject (a self capable of articulating critique, and yet not vulnerable to critique's dispersal of any claim to subjectivity that rests, directly or even indirectly, on Cartesian foundations). We can recognize that Husserl and Fink sought to resist scientistic thinking's diversion into causal thinking, despite their immersion in philosophical (and even culturally prevalent) conceptions of the subject. Then we can consider how Ricoeur's "detour of reflection by way of analysis"—even by way of the "long loops of analysis [that] are characteristic of the indirect style of a hermeneutics of the self, in stark contrast to the demand for immediacy belonging to the cogito"—furthers that effort, and so takes us a considerable way toward discerning the possibility of a critical subject.[30]

In his Translator's Introduction to the *Sixth Cartesian Mediation*, Bruzina narrates the difficult circumstances in which Husserl and Fink worked to revise the *Cartesian Meditations*. They were constrained by Husserl's heavy workload and deteriorating health, as well as by the increasingly oppressive political situation that culminated in Hitler's assumption of power in 1933. That event resulted in Husserl's dismissal from the university later that year and subsequent political and economic difficulties in regard to Fink's continued work with him through the last decade of Husserl's life.[31] The complex issues in regard to subjectivity that surface with increasing exigency in the books, manuscripts, and letters of the late 1920s and early 1930s simply were not able to benefit from the sort of systematic beginning-again that Husserl knew was necessary. The fragments and hints are more than sufficient, however, to justify Ricoeur's claim that Husserl, particularly by way of his "great discovery" of the "prelinguistic relation" between the living body *(Leib)* and "a world accessible or inaccessible to the 'I can,'" provided the vital clue that "opened the way" for an ontological investigation that asks: "What mode of being, then, belongs to the self, what sort of being or entity is it?"[32]

Ricoeur tells us at the very beginning of *Oneself as Another* that this work is situated at the "point of convergence" of "three major phenomenological intentions": "the primacy of reflective mediation over the immediate positing of the subject," sameness in contrast to selfhood, and the dialectical relationship between selfhood and the other-than-self that is not sameness.[33] This task benefits from his extraordinary patience, which enables him to resist the "leap" to a sense of ego without content which Husserl regrets in the *Crisis*. Ricoeur is prone to detours rather than leaps (as I mentioned earlier) and the terrain of his detours here, as he himself admits, is "arduous."[34] It requires a basic "challenge" to "the thesis of the indecomposable simplicity of the cogito" and of the thesis that he finds "joined to" it: the "immediacy" of the *cogito's* presence to reflection.[35] He takes up this challenge by responding to the question of the identity of self through a "hermeneutics of the self" that develops along "the detour of reflection by way of analysis, the dialectic of selfhood and sameness, and finally the dialectic of selfhood and otherness."[36] The entire analysis, then, occurs within "the primacy of reflective mediation" in contrast to the "immediate positing of the subject" characteristic of "philosophies of the subject" (equivalent, he notes, to "philosophies of the cogito"), which he rejects.[37] The alternate ontology of the self that he develops in this way is quite opposite to the "course of reflection" that Husserl came to see as "a sheer muddle, and wrongheaded."[38] In the last part of this essay, I begin from this alternative ontology in order to focus on the medium in which this mediated and multiple—even fragmented—self comes to be.

Seeking phenomenological evidence for selfhood as mediated and multiple (in contrast to the Cartesian subject's "immediacy" and "indecomposable simplicity") is difficult, because—even as reflective analysts—we typcially are preoccupied with the objects we constitute as intending subjects. This orientation to the "what" of our experience works to inhibit attention to the "how" as well as "who" of that intending. In order to learn more about the process in which the "who" comes to be, we must turn resolutely away from both mundane focus on objects (the "what") and phenomenological focus on experience (the "how"). By attending instead to a condition for that experience, we can discover phenomenological evidence for the mediacy and multiplicity that are basic to this alternative understanding of the self. This condition for experience is what Ricoeur characterizes as Husserl's "great discovery": the "prereflexive, prepredicative operation" in which the living body *(Leib)* engages, via a "prelinguistic relation," with "a world accessible or inaccessible to the 'I can.'"[39]

PART THREE

Mama's confinement took place at home. When her labor pains set in . . . an elderly midwife who had just about given up practicing had to be summoned. . . . In the bedroom she helped me and Mama to get away from each other. . . . My birth ran off smoothly. . . . I had no difficulty in freeing myself from the upside-down position so favored by mothers, embryos, and midwives. . . . I was one of those clairaudient infants whose mental development is completed at birth and after that merely needs a certain amount of filling in. The moment I was born I took a very critical attitude toward the first utterances to slip from my parents. . . . My ears were keenly alert. . . . And what my ear took in my tiny brain evaluated. After meditating at some length on what I heard, I decided to do certain things and on no account to do other things.

—Gunther Grass, *The Tin Drum*

there is a primary listening which precedes our own speech. . . . I hear the voices of others, of things, of the World long before I speak my own words. . . . Phenomenologically the "self" is modeled after the World which takes primacy in its first appearance. . . . Things, others, the gods, each have their voices to which we may listen. . . . Within auditory experience there is this primacy of listening The "prelinguistic" is the philosophical counterpart to the "pre-perceptual" bare sensation which if found at all is found by diverting one's ears and eyes from the objects.

—Don Ihde, *Listening and Voice*

The newborn listens; the philosopher speaks. The listening self, coming into the world within (and in a quite literal sense, under) the voices of others, cannot speak of that "primary listening," for it occurs at the place Ricoeur identifies as the "privileged point of perspective on the world which each speaking subject is"; a "point" at which the listener "is the limit of the world and not one of its contents."[40] However, we can extend our descriptive abilities by means of imaginative variation—and so, I detour through a novelist's first-person account of his protagonist's birth and a philosopher's reminder of the "primacy of listening," and then return to three especially salient features of Ricoeur's analysis. I do not return from phenomenological description to ontological account in order to offer a selection or summary of Ricoeur's analysis, which would, in effect, offer a shortcut around his detours. Rather, I do so in order tack back and forth between phenomenology and ontology: between the living experience of oneself as another, and Ricoeur's analysis of that doubleness of self.

The mediated "who" that Ricoeur identifies is a fragmented multiplicity; a subjectivity without a center; a self that coheres by virtue of "ipseity" rather than sameness *(idem)*. The scarcity of lexical choices here is instructive. We use "ipseity," but not "idemity." Indeed, we need "ipseity" because we have no everyday term for the coherence of oneself (self-identity) as Ricoeur discerns it; that is, as documented in the constancy of a narrative, woven from potential and actual acts within a complexity of interconnected events that he analyzes as a "dialectic of action and affection" in which the self is at times "patient" and at other times, "agent."[41] "Sameness" *(idem)*, in contrast, is documented more simply, by perseverance of the same substance.[42] Sameness, in other words, is part of our everyday experience, and so we have an everyday word for it. Ipseity, however, in forming the "who," makes that everyday experience possible and so is not named as a part of its content. With help from the novelist and the philosopher, we can now go farther in investigating the nature of the self's mediation; the conditions for its formation and the persistent efficacy of those conditions in its coherence.

The newborn listens; the philosopher speaks. We are all born listeners, and it is unlikely that we continue listening to monologue for very long after being separated from the other who delivers us (not, as in Heidegger's thinking, "throws" us) into the world. So long as it is located within the center of an other that we can identify as a mother, the fragmented multiplicity that becomes an emerging self undergoes the voices and touches of constituting others, but is able to reciprocate in only rudimentary chemical and kinesthetic ways. When this multiplicity of matter in movement is delivered from that center, it is expelled from a center of activity, volition, and affect—but that extrication is not by virtue of its own accomplishment. Typically, the literally emergent being undergoes the will, intelligence, and affect of that mother and multiple others in the process of expulsion that is also (in a paradoxically empty way) a coming into one's own. Expulsion from the center is simultaneously emergence of/as a fragmented self, enabled to continue those others' stories, but unable (for quite some time) to tell its own story.

Early on, then, the self's identity rests in narratives told by others. As such—which is to say, as listener—the self is fragmented among those narratives; dependent upon those other speakers. Gradually, however, reciprocity and reversibility of the "patient" and "agent" roles in these stories develops. Only slowly, after being separated from the primary other by being delivered into a not-yet-independent life, does this fragmented "me," persistently and necessarily acted upon by others, begin to collect or gather (in Humean fashion) experiences that, as a unifying "I," it can claim as belonging to its own self. Listening, in itself, does nothing for the coherence of that multiplicity; does nothing to solidify "the voices of others, of things, of the World" as the other-thans that surround the listener. Only as the living body begins to engage the resistance of others, and then begins to touch the resistant (other-than itself) sources of those voices, can objects be delineated. Correlatively, only by "diverting one's ears and eyes from the objects" can the reflecting philosopher rediscover this prelinguistic way of being as a particular sort of objects for others, rather than as the subject who intends others.

The particularity of this object is rooted in the fact that if this fragmented potentiality for being an intending subject is to survive, its narrative must be rooted in those of others. Very much unlike rocks and plants—and even somewhat unlike other forms of animal life—it must be the object of others' care for a long period of time. Mothers must care to feed these emerging selves, or (and in any case, eventually) other producers of the conditions of living must care to produce their own sustenance and divert some portion of their productivity to these emerging selves. By doing so, these producers keep these emerging selves enmeshed in their own narrative identities. In sum, others must be there, always and already and capable of acting in certain (caring) ways, in order that selves, fragmented among their many sources, cohere. We begin, as Ricoeur points out, in "indebtedness" to the other.[43]

This is the most basic condition for the subject's coming into being. As we consider this complex and enduring dependency, we recognize a certain polysemy of "care": it can be merely a matter of the emergent self's life mattering to others; of their not not-caring. Or, it can be a far- reaching and pervasive concern for the well-being of the emergent self. Or, and more typically, it can be an interweaving of the many variations suggested by those extremes. We all have this retrievable experience as evidence for the first salient feature that Ricoeur identifies in the mediated formation of self: a temporal multiplicity of acts that become integrated by virtue of their interconnection within a narrative, rather than by possessing the same substance. Initially, this is not the emerging self's narrative, but is the narrative of others who, by virtue of their affective, cognitive, and volitional activity, enable the emerging self to become "agent" as well as "patient."

From the perspective of Ricoeur's analysis, therefore, we can recognize the correctness, although incompleteness, of Hume's introspective report. As reflecting philosopher, he found "some particular perceptions" that might be "collected" or "bundled." But he could not find, within that introspective content, "the self or person . . . to which . . . impressions and ideas are suppos'd to have a reference."[44] The self is absent from this finding precisely because the report's narrator has not diverted himself from the objects to which he refers, in order to discover himself as the collector and teller of those diverse impressions and ideas. As I noted earlier, Hume was demonstrating Husserlian intentionality—directedness toward objects—and failed to notice the doubled nature of that activity: the self is the "privileged point of perspective" identifiable only reflectively as "the limit of the world and not one of its contents."[45] In other words, Hume's report speaks from a perspective, and so cannot report (speak about) that perspective.

As we reflect on—and in a sense, beyond—Hume's exemplification of Husserlian intentionality, however, we can focus on what Ricoeur calls the "anchoring" of that directedness in a unifying perspective. In this reflective orientation, we can discern a self in simultaneous formation with the object-directedness focused upon in Husserl's analysis. In other words, the reflective analyst can recognize what is other-than-what-is-told: the multiple and complex conditions that form a medium for emergence of the "who" hidden in every narrative as the teller who is simultaneously a listener, and who thus paradoxically receives what that teller cannot give. How shall we name this constituting of a perspective on the world that occurs simultaneously with the Humean (and Cartesian) subject's intending of objects in the world? "Generative intentionality" seems to me a fitting name for this passive constitution of a perspective (rather than an object, in any usual sense) that accompanies and provides the condition for Husserlian (gnoseological) intentionality. There are two sources for this label. Fink remarks: "This, now, belongs to the full sense of 'man': that a human stands in generative linkage to other humans, that he is dependent in being upon 'others,' that he originates from them"; to which Bruzina adds: "There appears to be some kind of necessary supposition—not a clear disclosure—of a constitutional process beyond the (or better, my) ego's own life precisely as egoic"[46] The second source is Anthony Steinbock's development of a "generative phenomenology" that begins with themes "scattered throughout Husserl's later writings and not developed systematically."[47] Generative intentionality functions in the emergent self's undergoing of the effects of other-thans, as the latter are affected by its resistance to their presence; which is to say that it occurs in the variously and persistently communicated relation between self and what is other-than self.

This mediated coherence of self, then, is continually accomplished in communication. Most basically, this is nonsymmetrical kinesthetic communication that increases over time in the womb. We are all born listeners; with extrication from that center, and quite gradually, oral communication develops. As the self begins to narrate its own story it situates itself as both speaker, intending the world and all that is within it, and listener, belonging to the world as the particular sort of object who is addressed and thus affected by another speaker. As listener, the voice of the other (the speaker) becomes part of the self-in-formation. This doubling anchors the self-in-formation to what is not yet accessible as the speaker's intentional object, but yet is (exists) in the saying, as that saying is heard. Typically, this doubling begins prelinguistically as the beginning speaker makes noises that others take to be evidence of its distinctive voice. It increases dramatically as those noises cohere around narratives in which the emergent self can say "I"; can posit itself as being active in a multiplicity of narratives and as affirming its ownership of those narratives—and thereby, its response-ability in relation to them.

This "global phenomenon of anchoring" by which directedness is unified is the second salient feature in Ricoeur's reflective analysis of the mediated formation of self.[48] The self's ability to say "I" of itself, and yet to recognize itself when spoken to as "you," relies upon what he calls "the anchoring of the I in use" so that "I do not leave my place and I do not eliminate the distinction between here and there."[49] Despite this immobility, the "agents and patients of an action are caught up in relationships of exchange which, like language, join together the reversibility of roles and the nonsubstitutibility of persons."[50] As I/agent, my living body remains "absolutely here, and so heterogeneous with respect to any set of geometric coordinates," which is to say that this I/agent is "nowhere in terms of objective spatiality."[51] Simultaneously, as me/patient, my living body undergoes, by passively synthesizing, the actions of others. The result of this doubled mode of being is "a twofold adherence of one's own body to the domain of things and to that of the self."[52] The self lives both as unifying I, agent who intends the things of the world and is always directed toward them, while having no place within them; and a fragmented me, patient who undergoes the actions of others and thus is dispersed among many places.

The anchoring of self in its living body reminds us that a third way in which the mediated formation of self is accomplished is by virtue of the ongoing composition of a living body from the physical constituents of other bodies. This giving-and-taking is hidden from reflection insofar as we direct our attention to the activities of individual selves and so attend, with Heidegger, to being "thrown" into a form of being that ends in death. A different analysis results from attending also to birth. Prior to birth, the self-in-formation receives its substance from another. It is paired with another by being a physical part of that other, and by being the literal continuation of the pairing of two other selves. After delivery—which is to say, after being given life, rather than "thrown" into an environment—that body remains paired with those other-thans whose human voices and physical substance reside within it. Along with literal rebirths, as the body regenerates throughout its life span, there are metaphorical rebirths: multiple instances of beginning again as the self engages in the generative intentionality which sustains its dialectical (mutually constituting) relation with the selves of others. The living body can only continue to be as the continually regenerated domicile of others: or, in Ricoeur's words, the sustenance of self is a continuing narrative of "oneself as another."[53]

NOTES

1. David Hume, *A Treatise of Human Nature*, ed. L.A. Selby-Bigge (Oxford: Oxford University Press, 1888; initial publication 1739), 252.
2. Ibid., 251.
3. OA, 20, 2–4.
4. OA, 20.
5. OA, 20.
6. OA, 19, 299, 318.
7. OA, 339, 341. This characterizing of noesis and noema as the conceptual structure of directedness relies upon an understanding of the noema as an intentional, rather than intensional, entity. For a discussion of that difference, see my "The Noema as Intentional Entity," *The Review of Metaphysics* 37 (1984): 757–784.
8. OA, 24.
9. Erazim Kohak, *Idea and Experience: Edmund Husserl's Project of Phenomenology in Ideas I* (Chicago and London: University of Chicago Press, 1978), 176.

10. Ibid., 175.

11. This particular formulation of a persistent theme is from a 1981 interview by Richard Kearney that is published in his *Dialogues with Contemporary Continental Thinkers* (Manchester: Manchester University Press, 1984), 32.

12. This is not to say that this view was ever totally eliminated from Christian tradition. Pual's letter to the Romans expresses an enduring theme when he bemoans "that the law is spiritual; but I am of the flesh. . . . I do not understand my own actions. For I do not do what I want, but I do the very thing I hate . . . nothing good dwells within me, that is, in my flesh . . . " (7:14–20). Descartes's epistemology retains this Pauline orientation. "The body," Susan Bordo reminds us, "is the chief impediment to human objectivity for Descartes" *(Flight to Objectivity: Essays on Cartesianism and Culture* (Albany: State University of New York Press, 1987), 26). However, "given the right method, one could transcend the body" (ibid., 94).

13. René Descartes, *Discourse on Method and The Meditations,* trans. F. E. Sutcliffe (New York: Penguin Books, 1968), 54, 106. The former expression is from the Fourth Discourse; the latter, from the Second Meditation.

14. OA, 267, 295–296.

15. These criticisms rely on the analysis of Carl L. Becker in *The Heavenly City of the Eighteenth Century Philosophers* (New Haven: Yale University Press, 1932) and on Susan Bordo's analysis of Cartesian ways of thinking in *Flight to Objectivity.*

Becker argues that "Man," for the thinking characteristic of modernity, "is but a foundling in the cosmos, abandoned by the forces that created him. Unparented, unassisted and undirected . . . he must fend for himself . . . " (15). Enlightenment philosophy did not so much discard a basis in faith, he continues, as it "demolished the Heavenly City of St. Augustine only to rebuild it with more up-to-date materials" (31; cf. 49).

Bordo notes that Medieval philosophy—the subject of this rebuilding process—"did not disparage the body's role in knowledge, nor was it especially impressed with distance and detachment as paths to understanding" (9). However, she argues, Descartes's *Meditations* instituted a "seventeenth-century 'masculinization of thought' . . . an acute historical flight from the feminine, from the memory of union with the maternal world, and a rejection of all values associated with it" (ibid.). This flight, I would argue, initiated the rebuilding discussed by Becker. The goal was a rebuilt conception of the subject founded in "a deliberate and methodical reversal . . . a beginning anew with reason as one's only parent . . . the body of infancy is transcended . . . " (98). In the last part of this essay, I propose that this birth narrative is refuted by phenomenological analysis.

16. A history of variation of and expansion upon the very notion of "science" and thus of the epistemology and ontology proper to the human/

social sciences enters into this difference between Husserl and Ricoeur. For a discussion of old and new logics of social science in relation to issues of unity and complexity, see James Bohman, *New Philosophy of Social Science* (Cambridge: The MIT Press, 1991).

17. Eugen Fink, *Sixth Cartesian Meditation: The Idea of a Transcendental Theory of Method*, with textual notations by Edmund Husserl, trans. and intro. Ronald Bruzina (Bloomington: Indiana University Press, 1995), xiviii. Hereafter cited as *Sixth CM*. Bruzina places an asterisk after the sentence ending "way to go" in this quotation from Fink, in order to mark the place of Husserl's marginal note.

18. *Sixth CM*, xiii–xlix.

19. *Sixth CM*, 1.

20. *Sixth CM*, xlvi.

21. *Sixth CM*, ix, xiiii.

22. *Sixth CM*, xiiii.

23. OA, 324, 334, 325. These phrases will be quoted in context below. I have altered the English translation (on p. 325) to reflect Ricoeur's reference to *une operation prereflexive, antepredicative* (Sa, 386). I use "living body," rather than the English translation's rendition of Ricoeur's *chair* as "flesh" in regard to Husserl's "Leib" (in contrast to "Korper"). My hope in doing so is to frustrate easy alignments of "flesh" with "body" as dichotomized from "mind," and also to accord with the prevalent practice in extant English translations of Husserl. Were it not for the dangers of neologizing, I would use "livebody" to correlate with "lifeworld." Rendering Korper as "corpse" does carry useful connotations; cf. Fink's remark, "Texts are the corpses of the living spirit" (*Sixth CM*, xxx).

24. Edmund Husserl, *The Crisis of European Sciences and Transcendental Phenomenology*, trans. David Carr (Evanston: Northwestern University Press, 1970), 154–155. Hereafter cited as *Crisis*. Bruzina notes that these passages "do not occur fortuitously in that section [43] of the *Crisis* or only as a last-minute realization on Husserl's part." (*Sixth CM*, xl).

25. *Sixth CM*, xxxi.

26. *Sixth CM*, xliii–xliv. Husserl's remark is quoted from Dorion Cairns entry for May 4, 1932, in his *Conversations with Husserl and Fink*, ed. and intro. Richard M. Zaner (The Hague: Martinus Nijhoff, 1976), 71.

27. OA, 310, 313, 311.

28. OA, 59.

29. OA, 60–61.

30. OA, 16–17. Cf. 297, 314. By "scientistic" I mean a faith in knowledge as grounded in observation of what is present (directly or through instrumentation), as relied upon by physical science research in Euro-American culture for the past three centuries or so. Causal relations between separable things are valorzied in this epistemology; thus product ("what") is

attended to over process ("how"), and relation ("why") is construed as causal or logical, rather than as plausible claims for multiple genesis and contingent possible goals. This epistemological structure, as Ricoeur says, accomplishes a "diversion from 'how' we act and 'who' acts" (OA, 60–61; quoted above).

31. Ronald Bruzina gives a moving account of these years in his Translator's Introduction to *the Sixth CM* (see especially xxiii–xxxii). Also, see Karl Schuhmann, *Husserl-Chronik: Denk und Lebensweg Edmund Husserls*, Husserliana I (Den Haag: Martinus Nijhoff, 1977), 337ff. Eugin Fink took up Ludwig Landgrebe's position as Husserl's research assistant in August 1928 and spoke at Husserl's funeral on April 29, 1938.

32. OA, 324–325, 326, 297.
33. OA, 1–3.
34. OA, 19.
35. OA, 19.
36. OA, 16.
37. OA, 1, 4; English version altered to reflect Ricoeur's reference (on p. 1) to "le primat de la mediation reflexive" (Sa, 1).
38. Sixth CM, xxxvii; quoted in context at the start of Part Two.
39. OA, 324–325.
40. OA, 51.
41. OA, 330.
42. For the equivalence of selfhood and ipseity, see OA, 331; for "constancy" as the form of coherence of selfhood, see OA, 267, 295, 319; for "perseverance" as the correlative form of coherence of things, see OA, 267.
43. OA, 349.
44. David Hume, *A Treatise of Human Nature*.
45. OA, 51.
46. Sixth CM, xliii.
47. Anthony J. Steinbock, *Home and Beyond: Generative Phenomenology After Husserl* (Evanston: Northwestern University Press, 1995), 172. Steinbock notes that "World constitutive . . . matters like birth and death" are excluded from the genetic analysis that predominates in Husserl's later work: "everything that lies prior to human childhood or after adulthood remains unquestioned" (189). Ricoeur's emphasis on the extent to which human being is an "undergoing" of others, and my analysis here, suggests that the dependency that characterizes the emerging self is a persisting dimension of human subjectivity. One way to interpret Husserl's neglect of this theme is suggested by Bordo's argument that Cartesian modes of thinking foster a "masculinization of thought" . . . an acute historical flight from the feminine, from the memory of union with the maternal world, and a rejection of all values associated with it" (*Flight to Objectivity*, 9).
48. OA, 319.
49. OA, 193.

50. *OA*, 193.
51. *OA*, 325.
52. *OA*, 319.
53. This essay owes much to conversations with colleagues at the University of Denver. I would like to thank Mary Jane Collier, Darrin Hicks, and Roy Wood for their insights in regard to the communicative constitution of self. Particular thanks are due to Alton Barbour for making those conversations possible. I would also like to acknowledge an extended debt to Raymie McKerrow for our efforts to articulate the body's priority over the subject.

THREE

Rethinking Subjectivity
Narrative Identity and the Self

David Rasmussen

In the following, I want to consider whether or not it is possible to retrieve the concept, or better, the phenomenon of subjectivity under the category of the narrative identity of the self. In so doing, I will be considering the question regarding the reemergence of subjectivity in a world of philosophical discourse that had conceived of itself as having overcome the perils of subjectivity, either in the form of the hermeneutic critique of early phenomenology or in the form of the analytical critique of skepticism. Conceived against the backdrop of the perceived achievements of a theory of interlocution, this will force us to reconsider the problem of the intersubjective achievement of valid knowledge one more time.[1]

In reflecting on the phenomenon of the reemergence of subjectivity, I want to consider a number of arguments presented in Paul Ricoeur's recent book *Oneself as Another*. In so doing, my task will be not simply to reduplicate Ricoeur's argument. Rather, my concern will be to attempt to consider the implications of the concept of narrative identity for the question of the reemergence of subjectivity as it relates to a theory of interlocution. To anticipate the argument, I am particularly interested in the implications of Ricoeur's critique of the theory of interlocution from the point of view of self-identity. If Ricoeur's critique is correct, it would follow that the attempted overcoming of the problem of subjectivity through a theory of interlocution is achieved only by undermining an adequate concept of self-identity. In order adequately to reconstruct the problem as it develops in Continental philosophy, it will be necessary to go back to Husserl.

For a certain form of European philosophy the dilemma associated with subjectivity reached its darkest moment in Edmund Husserl's "Fifth Meditation,"[2] where it was acknowledged that the phenomenological ego could not constitute the other in the same manner in which it could constitute itself. Husserl, through the use of apperception, appresentation, and pairing, attempted to find ways through which the other could be constituted by analogy to the self. In the end, his analysis appeared to pose an epistemological problem. Critics would point out that one could never know the other in the same way as one could know the self and, as such, the enigma of solipsism seemed to haunt Husserl's philosophy.

However, in retrospect, Husserl may have had a point. Perhaps there is a sense in which the other can never be known by the self in the same sense that the self can know itself. There is a certain duality at the heart of the problematic of self and other. According to Husserl, I can know the other only by analogy to myself. This is where apperception, analogical appresentation, and pairing applied in Husserl's reflections eventually become clues to the way the phenomenological ego can develop a "constitutional theory of the experience of someone else." For Husserl, at the most basic level one intuits the other as the other's "body" by a kind of "analogizing apperception" to one's own body. At a somewhat higher level one can make a differentiation between "ego" and "alter ego" as given in "an original pairing." Thus, according to Husserl, we have an account of the manner in which the other enters into my field of perception. But the other never enters my field of perception with the same originality as does the ego, and in this sense Husserl characterizes the transcendental synthesis to which ego and alter ego belong as a "passive synthesis" of "association" and not of "identification." The distinction is important from an epistemological point of view because from the standpoint of subjectivity from which Husserl begins his analysis one can never reach an identification with the other. That is because the alter ego can never be present to the ego in the same way in which the ego is present to itself. Hence, the problem of the other, the other as "mind" or as "body," could never be resolved in an originary way. It is this dilemma that Husserl gave to the philosophy of language. The philosophy of language would resolve the dilemma of self and other, but only by undercutting the radical dichotomy that exists between them. Hence, the problem becomes one of constructing a notion of intersubjectivity that preserves the uniqueness of self-identity while at the same time bridging the gap between self and other.

FROM IDENTITY TO SELF

At the heart of Ricoeur's reflections on the identity of the self is the thesis that identity can be conceived in the sense of either "the Latin *ipse* or *idem*." The latter term tends to emphasize sameness while the former term, and this is the interesting point, "implies no assertion concerning some unchanging core of the personality."³ *Ipse* then can be used to articulate the experience of the self in time, the category under which subjectivity returns.

Ricoeur's initial strategy is to think through the process of identification by considering the basic analytic transitions from semantics to pragmatics, keeping in mind the relationship of the problem of identity to that of self-identity. Inasmuch as semantics and pragmatics both claim to overcome the philosophy of subjectivity, there is an underlying polemical thrust to Ricoeur's argument. Ideally, the argument, which could be conceived as a critique of the analytic theories of reference and reflexivity, would read as follows: 1) while semantics can conceive of identity only on the basis of a conception of *idem* or sameness, 2) pragmatics (speech-act theory) attempts to get beyond the question of identity to self-identity through a theory of interlocution. 3) However, theories of interlocution are limited by being able to consider identity only on the basis of the concept of sameness or *idem*. 4) Finally, the basic thrust of the movement from semantics to pragmatics is toward particularity, which should be toward a conception of self-identity based on *ipséité*. This, of course, is a matter of contention. Can the logic of the move from semantics to pragmatics include a transition from the concept of self based on identity to one that can acknowledge otherness and temporal particularity? If the movement from semantics to pragmatics cannot account for this latter development, then one is left to ponder the achievement of the reconceptualization of the self at the level of a theory of interlocution. While Ricoeur wants to reconceptualize the basic thrust of the analytic arguments as arguments that drive toward *ipséité*, it is not at all clear that the authors of those arguments either can or wish to do so. While the basic thrust of the analytic arguments may be toward a more particular conception, their fundamental limitation is that they are unable to conceive of the self as an entity that changes over time. Without loading the argument, I will simply assume for the moment that this is an inadequacy.

Taking Strawson's *Individuals*[4] as representative of the semantic form of argumentation, Ricoeur argues that the self is "neutralized by being included within the same spatiotemporal schema as all the other particulars. The concept of identity is thus expressed as 'sameness (*mêmeté*) and not as selfhood (*ipséité*)."⁵ Hence, "in a problematic of identifying reference, the sameness of one's body conceals its selfhood."⁶ To be sure, Ricoeur acknowledges the uniqueness of Strawson's strategy:

> The advantage of this new strategic decision is certain: to say that bodies are the first basic particulars is to eliminate, as possible candidates, mental events; that is, representations or

> thoughts, whose shortcoming is that they are private rather than public entities. Their lot, as specific predicates of persons, is simply postponed. They first had to be dislodged from the dominant position of ultimate reference, which they occupy in a subjectivist idealism.[7]

Given the great advantage of this approach, the consequence is that it tends to eliminate the problem of the so-called "lived body," that is, the body that is experienced as belonging to a particular self. Hence, the actuality of selfhood is really concealed in a kind of likeness of one particular body with all other bodies, that is, as a predicate ascribed to an entity. And this is the overall point when it comes to the forms of ascription within the "primitive" concept of the person. While being able to characterize selfhood by reference to sameness, this view overlooks the particularity associated with the self as an entity living through and within time.

The theory of interlocution (pragmatics) moves beyond the problematic of identifying reference by considering the "speakers" who refer in specific ways. In this sense the "illocutionary act" is joined to the act of "predication" by concentration on the reflexive implications of the notion of utterance.

Ricoeur believes this concentration on the utterance of the speakers *could* lead to the notion of selfhood because the reference is to the event of utterance. In short, utterance equals interlocution. But what of this utterance? It would appear that the very emphasis on the one who utters would allow for the expression of the self as a unique someone who makes this particular statement as a testament to her identity. But that is precisely where speech-act theory becomes elusive. The very reflexivity that characterizes speech-act theory does not sustain the promise of highlighting the particularity of selfhood. Instead, it manifests itself as a form of sameness. "Ultimately, one would have to say that reflexivity is not intrinsically bound up with a self in the strong sense of self-consciousness."[8] As Ricoeur claims, the intersubjective character of speech-acts is derived by the fact that the utterance "is mirrored" in the act of another. The result is a "reflexivity without selfhood." However, Ricoeur thinks that speech-act theory can drive beyond itself in the sense that by "anchoring" interlocution in the "speaking subjects" the particular experience of the speakers would have to be taken into account.

In any case, if one chooses to step beyond Ricoeur, at this point a more general argument can begin to take shape. The move to speech-act theory has been taken to mean a step beyond the philosophy of the subject. Hence, the movement to the philosophy of language conceived in this sense was thought to overcome the dilemma of subjectivity. However, that step was achieved at a certain price. Only by reducing the phenomenon of subjectivity to sameness, and thereby sacrificing the temporality of the individual self, could speech-act theory achieve a rational explanation of interlocutionary activity. If one were to accept Ricoeur's argument, it would appear that the interlocutionary act taken as event would drive speech-act theory beyond itself. But even if it does not, it would still be impossible in purely illocutionary terms for one to account for the self as embodied and temporal. In other words, speech-act theory retains the Cartesian bias of the disembodied self. One might even go so far as to suggest that such an approach retains the traces of a philosophy of identity.

Here one could make a further point about the manner in which Continental philosophy has appropriated the philosophy of language, particularly in the form of speech-act theory. Immediate recourse to a theory of interlocution as the linguistic counterpart for a theory of intersubjectivity as, for example, in Jürgen Habermas's attempt to overcome the so-called dilemmas of the philosophy of consciousness by recourse to speech-act theory achieves its goal, but only at a certain price; namely, through a false reduction of self to other under the rubric of the identity of discourse. The problem is that the very philosophy of identity that such an attempt is tailored to overcome is suspect, inasmuch as it relies on another system of identities, namely, identical expression.[9]

Certainly, it is not possible simply to go back to Husserl. The wager is this: if we go forward remaining within the context of a philosophy of language, it is possible to reconceptualize self-identity as narrative identity. In brief, this is the potential for a theory of narrative.

THE SELF AND PERSONAL IDENTITY

Thus far we have established that the problematic of subjectivity reenters the philosophical scene because the analytic philosophies of language could only conceptualize an identity in terms of sameness. In order to take the next step in the argument it will be necessary to show, first, what it means to conceptualize an identity that can be characterized temporally and, second, how one can achieve such characterization linguistically. Following Ricoeur, the first issue centers around personal identity while the second concerns narrative identity.

The conceptualization of sameness privileges similitude. The most radical form of similitude is, of course, numerical. We say of two different things that they represent one and the same thing; for example, x equals p, cognition equals recognition. The criterion of similitude begins to weaken when applied to a "current perception" in relationship to a "memory." Ricoeur suggests that, in order to posit identity, one needs a category such as "uninterrupted continuity" that would postulate a relationship between present and past. Hence, the concept of similitude should be widened to include various discontinuities or changes in identity. Ricoeur suggests that at the base of this widening of the concept of similitude is the "principle of *permanence in time*."[10] One can anticipate the argument in terms of the already posited dialectic between sameness and selfhood, between *idem* and *ipse*. It is not the case that one gives up on sameness. But, through the introduction of the category of temporality, the question becomes one of attempting to get beyond the reduction to sameness, which eliminates the different forms that self-identity takes over time. One will then have to find a way in which the self endures, in the sense that earlier forms of identity can be associated with later forms of identity without reduction to sameness. Ricoeur's solution is to designate identity through character.

In its most elemental form character is defined as a "set of lasting dispositions by which a person is recognized."[11] Of course, the Aristotelian origin of this designation is apparent. The self is known by its character. In its most originary sense, character announces itself and can be so designated through habit. As Ricoeur puts it, "habit gives a history to character."[12] Habits can manifest themselves as in process of being formed, and they can be already acquired. In terms of the dialectic between *idem* and *ipse*, they give the appearance of sameness to a changing self. In fact, habit tends to abolish the appearance of innovation by giving the appearance of sameness. In Ricoeur's terms, it is here that *ipse* manifests itself as *idem*.

NARRATIVE IDENTITY:
THE DIALECTIC OF SELFHOOD AND SAMENESS

A narrative can link the past with the future by giving a sense of continuity to an ever-changing story of the self. Because narrative has this potentiality it is uniquely qualified to express the ongoing dialectic of selfhood and sameness while at the same time it can allow one to rethink the meaning of subjectivity. The way in which narrative is initially expressed is through fictional narratives. Fictional narratives disclose "character" through "emplotment." In Ricoeur's words, there is a kind of "discordant concordance," which is conveyed through narrative, that in philosophical terms may be conceived as a "synthesis of the heterogeneous."[13] The plot accounts for "diverse mediations" between "disparate components of the action—intentions, causes, and chance occurrences—and the sequence of the story," as well as mediations "between pure succession and the unity of the temporal form."[14] In other words, narratives link events together by giving account of the intentions of the actors so that the character appears to have a certain chronology. Narratives make sense out of self-identity in the context of time.

Narratives account for action, but they do so in complex ways. In the dialectic between plot and character narrative resolves the potential contradiction between the two by "granting to the character an initiative . . . and . . . by assigning to the narrative as such the power of determining the beginning, the middle, and the end of an action."[15]

This is, of course, the dilemma of tragedy. The protagonist appears to be the author of her own activity while spectator and chorus alike know that the narrative itself will eventually overwhelm the character in such a manner that she must succumb to the inevitable unfolding of events.

Ricoeur speculates that this dialectic between action and character produces a dialectic internal to the character. On the one hand the character draws her "singularity" from the "unity of life" which is, in turn, considered as "a temporal totality which is itself singular and distinguished from all others." This is the concordance side of the dialectic between concordance and discordance. On the other hand, "[f]ollowing the line of discordance, this temporal totality is threatened by the disruptive effect of the unforeseeable events that punctuate it."[16] This forces the "identity of character" to be summed up in the "history of a life." Thus chance is transmuted into fate."[17] Freedom succumbs to necessity.

One of Ricoeur's most brilliant insights is to reconceive this dialectic of concordance and discordance on a higher level as the dialectic between sameness and selfhood thematized as a set of "imaginative variations" entertained by the narrative. This is the very point of narrative. Narrative does not seek to conceal this dialectic but rather it seeks out the contradictions.

> In this sense, literature proves to consist in a vast laboratory for thought experiments in which the resources of variation encompassed by narrative identity are put to the test of narration.[18]

One can in fact generate a standard for the interpretation of fiction from this point of view. On the one hand, there is the kind of nineteenth-century literature that seeks to favor sameness of character, to which can be contrasted a kind of twentieth-century literature that subjects selfhood to almost infinite variation. The latter would reflect a loss of identity while the former would concentrate on identity. Selfhood is defined as sameness as, for example, the character of Raskolnikov, in Dostoevsky's *Crime and Punishment*, to be contrasted with the protagonist in Musil's *Man Without Qualities*. In the latter, speculates Ricoeur, selfhood is exposed by "taking away the support of sameness."[19]

Equally, this reflection on the imaginative variations between selfhood and sameness can be used as a clue to the distinction between literary and technological (science fiction) forms of narrative. Here, Ricoeur turns to his hermeneutic background to make the distinction. Literary fictions "remain imaginative variations on an invariant, our corporeal condition experienced as the existential mediation between the self and the world."[20] In literature we encounter beings like ourselves who are anchored to the world through their corporeal condition. One might even go so far as to state that, in literature, action is mediated through suffering. With science fiction the case is different. There the focus is upon technology. The brain is taken to be the equivalent of the person. The problematic for science fiction is the mediation of identity through sameness inasmuch as the resolution of identity is performed at the conceptual level. In contrast, the problematic of literary fiction can be said to be selfhood or "selfhood in its dialectical relation to sameness."[21]

NARRATION: BETWEEN PRESCRIPTION AND DESCRIPTION

Seen against the backdrop of analytic philosophies of identity, the concept of narrative identity opens up the realm of the particular self, whose identity would have been subsumed under the category of sameness. As such, narrative can reopen the question of the self as a subjective and particular self, but on the basis of a form of linguistic expression. As narrative can thematize action, so it can be the bridge to ethical life. Or to put it specifically, it can bridge the gap between the "ascription of action to an agent who has the capacity to act" and the "imputation to an agent who has the obligation to act."[22] Narrative has the unique capacity to conceive of that obligation mimetically. In this sense narrative provides an imaginative variation on practice. Hence, Aristotle could claim that "tragedy" can be conceived mimetically in relationship to, not persons per se, but to "action and life." Here, through narrative, we have the relationship between *mimesis*, *bios*, and *praxis*.

However, fiction cannot be applied to life praxis without complications. To be sure, the organization of one's own life history and a fictional account of a life are different. However, no one without the help of fiction can recount either their origin or death. Fiction complements life history by creating a framework where one's own life can be accounted for. It is in this sense that narrative identity has a relationship to ethical life. Hence, Ricoeur denies that the narration has a purely aesthetic dimension. Indeed, reflecting Kant's *Critique of Judgement*, one takes pleasure in following the destiny of a character through the narration, even to the extent that one can suspend the teleology of action itself. But this is just what narration contributes for ethics: namely, by analogy to the thought experiment, new ways to evaluate character and action.

> The thought experiments we conduct in the great laboratory of the imaginary are also explorations in the realm of good and evil. Transvaluing, even devaluing, is still evaluating. Moral judgment has not been abolished, it is rather subjected to the imaginative variations proper to fiction.[23]

Earlier, Ricoeur introduced the dialectic of selfhood and sameness under the categories of character and self-constancy. Self-constancy referred to "keeping one's word" while character referred to the different moments in which selfhood expressed itself. Narrative not only poses the possible imaginative variations on the problematic of selfhood and sameness; it also, when applied to real life, invites difficulties. When one moves from fiction to real life the potential for loss of identity, as in the case of Musil's *Man Without Qualities*, is refigured as the self in reality "confronted with the hypothesis of its own nothingness."[24] On the ethical plane, the problem becomes one of conceiving how the self, which is confronted with the potentiality of its own nothingness, can assert itself as a moral or ethical agent.

TIME AND NARRATIVE

I want to return now to a point made at the outset of this discussion. We began with the thesis that the failure of both a semantic theory of representation and a pragmatic theory of interlocution was that they were unable to render identity in any way other than through sameness. As such they were unable to render identity as selfhood that may be characterized by differentiation over time. Narrative identity has been able to overcome the dilemma that is at the heart of a theory of interlocution. Hence, the most important thing about narrative identity is its ability to make apparent the temporal dimension of selfhood, which must be obliterated if the theory of interlocution is said to be a triumph over the philosophy of the subject. In this sense it would be necessary to reconceive a theory of interlocution in the context of time. As Ricoeur suggests, "[E]very speech-act (or every act of discourse) commits the speaker and does so in the present."[25] In this sense, "assertions" are not mere empty identities. Rather, they are utterances in a temporal context, which carry with them the tacit implication of "sincerity."

> I cannot assert something without introducing a tacit clause of sincerity into my saying it, in virtue of which I effectively signify what I am saying, any more than I can do so without holding as true what I affirm.[26]

If we conceive of a promise or a commitment in time, it is clear that it will carry with it the implication that one will be bound to it. In order to account for that one would have to bring back some form of subjectivity in the sense of the reference to the intentionality of a subject. "By promising, I intentionally place myself under the obligation to do what I say I will do."[27] And if one obligates oneself in the present it is also clear that one will have some obligation toward the future. Indeed, to make a promise has the implication of keeping it. The force of the statement "I can" would then carry with it the implication of my initiative. If I say that I will do it, this implies, as Ricoeur suggests, not only that the statement becomes my act but that I will inscribe my act in the course of things. In this sense, the speech-act occurs at the juncture of internal and cosmological time. On the one hand, it forms my commitment to the living present, while at the same time, commitment to such an act coordinates the activity of an individual within the course of things. Such an act then has an ethical signification that commits one to a certain form of participation in a historical present.

NARRATIVE, SUBJECTIVITY, AND VALIDITY

In *Time and Narrative*, Ricoeur makes the claim that "narrative" is the "guardian of time, insofar as there can be no thought about time without narrated time."[28] Within this claim rests Ricoeur's fundamental reconstruction of the Husserlian thematic with regard to time, which in Husserl's context raised fundamental questions regarding the validity of intersubjective knowledge. In order to illustrate the problem, allow me to return to the "Fifth Meditation" from which this discussion began. When Husserl attempted to verify the experience of the other he did so within the framework of internal time-consciousness. What is shared between self and other is time, even though the other has to be experienced "somatically" in space. His claim is simply that "what is appresented by the 'body' over there, in my primordial 'surrounding world,' is not something psychic of mine, nor anything else in my sphere of ownness. I am *here* somatically."[29] In the terms of this spatial metaphor, I can build up my experience of the other through my sphere of ownness to include the otherness of the other but only through appresentation, that is, the indirect presentation of the other.

> My own ego however, the ego given in constant self-perception, is actual now with the content belonging to his Here. Therefore an ego is *appresented, as other* than mine.[30]

It is the bodily character of the other that raises real questions regarding validity, in the sense that valid knowledge can only be achieved at the appresentational level. How can one have valid knowledge of the other as a body? In this sense it is the other as flesh that forces one to raise the question of the validity of intersubjective knowledge. If, of course, one could reduce selfhood to sameness the problem would disappear.

When Husserl turns to temporality, which he actually presupposes in the above analysis of the spatial and perceptual character of bodily apprehension, he follows a similar pattern. Initially, of course, it is my experience of myself that is experienced temporally. Following Husserl, one constructs a phenomenological account of the experience of temporality as it effects knowledge by showing how, through experiences of past and future in an ever-expanding now, temporality is at the foundation of valid knowledge of the self. In other words, the temporal dimension of the experience of someone else follows a pattern similar to the spatial dimension. Husserl refers to a *"common time form"* that occurs as a consequence of the *"coexistence of my 'polar' Ego and the other Ego,* of my whole concrete ego and his, my intentional life and his, my 'realities' and his."[31] For Husserl that leads to the following proposition: "[E]very primordial temporality automatically acquires the significance of being merely an original mode of appearance of Objective temporality to a particular subject."[32] This leads him to make the claim, from the inside as it were, that internal time is related to objective time.

> In this connection we see that the temporal community of the constitutively interrelated monads is indissoluble, because it is tied up essentially with the constitution of *a world and a world time*.[33]

But "world time" is not the same as the time of the phenomenological ego, with the result that knowledge of the other as it is mediated through the temporality of the phenomenological subject is discontinuous with knowledge of the self. Again, one returns to the question of how valid knowledge can be conceived on the level of intersubjectivity.

Ricoeur has shown how narrative identity resolves the discontinuity between calendar or cosmic time and internal time through its ability to integrate an account of the self within the context of a larger temporal framework. And the unique advantage of such an approach is that one can preserve the distinctive character of the experience of the self within the framework of the constancy of time. Clearly, with reference to the theory of interlocution, this reconfigures the role of the subject and subjectivity within a framework that attempts to establish validity. One might conclude that this contribution will force us to rethink the problem of the intersubjective achievement of valid knowledge one more time.

NOTES

1. Refer to the numerous attempts to reconstruct a theory of intersubjectivity, from Hegel's concept of intersubjectivity as articulated through his critique of Kant's concept of autonomy, to Hurrserl's attempt to account for intersubjectivity in the context of his account of phenomenology, as well as the more recent attempts to account for intersubjectivity within the confines of language. To anticipate the argument of this argument, Ricoeur's reexamination of the notion of the self opens up the question of subjectivity again after recent attempts to overcome the notion of subjectivity through a philosophy of language. In particular, I am interested in Ricoeur's attempt to force the "theory of interlocution" associated with speech-act theory beyond the narrow confines of the "identity" problematic that characterizes it.

2. Edmund Husserl, *Cartesian Meditations*, trans. Dorion Cairns (The Hague: Martinus Nijhoff, 1960).

3. OA, 2.

4. Peter Strawson, *Individuals* (London: Methuen, 1957).

5. Ricoeur's critique is stated in the following way: "In Strawson's strategy, however, the recourse to self-designation is intercepted, so to speak, from the very start because of the central thesis that determines the criterion for identifying anything as a basic particular. This criterion is the fact that individuals belong to a single spatiotemporal schema, which, it is stated from the start, contains *us*, in which we *ourselves* take place. The self is indeed mentioned in the passing remark, but it is immediately neutralized by being included within the same spatiotemporal schema as all the other particulars" (OA, 32).

6. Ibid., 33.

7. Ibid., 33–34.

8. Ibid., 47.

9. The theory of communicative action, relying as it does on speech-act theory, is unable to contextualize self-identity. A discourse theory with its overly atemporal reduction of self-identity to identical expression requires a narrative theory as its complement.
10. OA, 117.
11. Ibid., 121.
12. Ibid.
13. Ibid., 141.
14. Ibid.
15. Ibid., 147.
16. Ibid.
17. Ibid.
18. Ibid., 148.
19. Ibid., 149.
20. Ibid., 150.
21. Ibid.
22. Ibid., 152.
23. Ibid., 164.
24. Ibid., 166.
25. TN 3, 232.
26. Ibid.
27. Ibid., 233.
28. Ibid., 241.
29. Husserl, *Cartesian Meditations*, 118–119; original emphasis.
30. Ibid., 119; original emphasis.
31. Ibid., 128; original emphasis.
32. Ibid.
33. Ibid.; original emphasis.

FOUR

Can There Be a Science of Action?

John van den Hengel

Essential to the Greek heritage of Western culture has been its determination to be delivered from the vagaries of mere opinion through the search for certain knowledge. Greek philosophy, and Western philosophy in its wake, was at great pains to distinguish clearly between what could be known with certainty (*epistémé*) and what could be accepted as a more or less vague opinion (*doxa*). This distinction between *epistémé* and *doxa*, first articulated by Plato, may have rested on the popular distinction between what can be known by sight and what can be known from hearing.[1] What I know from having seen personally is considered more secure as a knowledge than what I obtain from hearsay. Sight involves personal presence and experience whereas hearsay relies on the witness of others, on the authenticity or veracity of others. As a consequence, knowledge from hearing is secondhand knowledge. I am not as personally present or engaged in what presents itself to my hearing as I am to what presents itself or is present in my seeing. The aftermath of the distinction between *epistémé* and *doxa*, between certain knowledge and opinion, is to be found in the progressive refinement of the visual paradigm toward the eye of reason, and in our time in Dilthey's split between the empirical and human sciences and of C. P. Snow's distinction between the two cultures. The dominance of the "visual" paradigm in Western philosophy is shown in the preference of the epistemic over the doxic.

In this essay I want to explore the epistemic-doxic status of the knowledge of human action. I do so guided by the recent work of Paul Ricoeur, particularly in his masterly *Oneself as Another*. In *Oneself as Another* as well as in two other major texts, *Time and Narrative* and *From Text to Action*, Ricoeur has elaborated a hermeneutical approach to a theory of action with a specific emphasis on its epistemological status. His position is unique inasmuch as it safeguards both an ontology of human action and an epistemology. For Ricoeur, understanding and explanation are not unbreachable opposites. There can be no understanding without explanation and no explanation without understanding. Both are required for a proper application of action to the various spheres of life where action is at stake. At issue in this essay is the type of explanation that in Ricoeur's view is available to the understanding of human action.

Before delving into Ricoeur's analysis of the epistemological status of the theory of action, it is worthwhile to paint the larger picture within which Ricoeur develops this theory of action. His venture into practical philosophy must be seen in the light of his perception of the current crisis of Western civilization. For Ricoeur, a pivotal event marks our era, which calls for a new thrust in philosophy. He identifies this event at the level of human consciousness as the shattering of the Cartesian *cogito*. Nietzsche and the deconstructionists of this century perpetrated this "humiliation of the human subject."[2] The overevaluation and exaltation of the human subject as primary certainty and ground that played such an important role in the idealist rendition of the human subject in a dominant strand of interpretation of Descartes (Kant, Fichte, and Husserl) lost its force through the critique of Nietzsche. For Nietzsche, philosophy's claim to give certitude and to ground science seemed only a rhetorical strategy, one that ended up in the illusion of a solid foundation. Ricoeur's practical philosophy is an attempt to forge a new space for the human self beyond these epochal movements of the undue exaltation of the subject by the Cartesian tradition on the one hand and the declared rhetorical emptiness of the human subject by the deconstructionists on the other hand. But with the demise of foundationalism, the purely rhetorical position is not an acceptable alternative. If foundationalism promised too much certainty, deconstructionism holds out too little. For Ricoeur, the debate is not solely an academic exercise. At stake is the new possibility of the self beyond the dichotomy of the foundational and the illusory self. The primary intent of Ricoeur's practical philosophy, therefore, is to establish a new perspective on the identity of the self. His practical philosophy is at its core a hermeneutics of the self. In the context of this hermeneutics of the self we want to take up again the ancient and modern quarrel between *epistémé* and *doxa*.[3]

Ricoeur locates his development of the epistemological status of action theory within the framework of a refurbished interpretation of Aristotle's practical philosophy. He believes that such a revitalized Aristotelian practical philosophy could lead us beyond the current impasse. In practical terms, it means taking some of the aporetic positions or ambiguities in Aristotle's metaphysics, such as its blindness to the world to which we belong as we think and act, and seeking to resolve them by engaging Aristotle in a dialogue with a different perspective. Ricoeur had already tried to do something similar in one of his earlier works.[4] In *Oneself as Another,* he does it more systematically. As in the case of other authors, the dialogue partner of Aristotle is Heidegger. Ricoeur has come to accept that in *Sein und Zeit* Heidegger was in fact giving a reinterpretation of Aristotle's practical philosophy.[5] In *Oneself as Another* he not only accepts this new interpretation of Aristotle but also enters into discussion with the philosophers who promote this dialogue of Aristotle and Heidegger. *Oneself as Another* is Ricoeur's somewhat tentative projection of such a renewed practical philosophy.[6] But Ricoeur's sustained disagreement with Heidegger's unmediated ontology also has its repercussions on this practical philosophy. For Ricoeur, Heidegger's direct ontology, that is, an ontology without an epistemological mediation, is not acceptable. Ricoeur's hermeneutics of the self is less afraid than is Heidegger of the possible alienating influence of explanatory procedures in ontology. This essay is meant to examine how far Ricoeur is prepared to go in this epistemological mediation.

The theory of action that I examine in this essay is part of the analytic or explanatory feature of such a practical philosophy. A hermeneutics of the self, according to Ricoeur, cannot rely on intuition but must have recourse to analysis. Hermeneutics is a philosophy of detours, seemingly endless detours, unraveling the question "who," that is, "Who is this self?". An analysis of action and agency is the subtext of these detours. The theory of human action, underpinning practical philosophy as part of its analytical detours, is constituted out of fragments from the analysis of action in the philosophy of language, the philosophy of action, narrative theory, and ethical, moral, and political determinations of action.[7] Each of these divergent discourses of human actions must be allowed a place in the kind of understanding of the human self promoted by practical philosophy. For Ricoeur, they form part of the explanatory mediation of understanding in accordance with his tenet of "no explanation without understanding, and no understanding without explanation."[8] These different discourses form part of the unending analytical detour that is required for an ever-closer understanding of the human self. To understand Ricoeur's theory of action within a practical philosophy is to become aware of the analogical unity that he wishes to forge among the various discourses of human action in a manner not dissimilar to Aristotle's effort in his first philosophy. Such an ontological attempt goes clearly beyond the framework or limit that analytic philosophy normally imposes upon itself.⁹ A discussion of human action is not a neutral exploration but a passionate concern to understand and promote the humanly good life as an ethical, moral endeavor.¹⁰ Ricoeur's approach to a renewed practical philosophy avows that an ontology—however fragmented and tentative it appears at present—is able to pull together into an analogical unity the various considerations of action as a countermeasure to the demise of the foundationalist and rhetorical self.¹¹

In this essay I wish to examine the epistemic level that Ricoeur attaches to action theory as the analytical moment of his practical philosophy. Can there be, in his estimation, a science of action? If not, why not? If so, what level of certainty can be attached to such a theory after the collapse of the foundationalist theses? I shall take up these questions by taking up three points that are pivotal to his thesis.

First of all, in adopting the conceptual framework of action from analytic philosophy, Ricoeur insists more than does the analytic tradition on the "who" of action rather than on the "what" and "why" of action. This insistence is not to be attributed solely to his interest in the self. It emerges out of an unreflected potential of meaning in the action theory of representative analytical philosophers, particularly Donald Davidson. Ricoeur shows how they leave unreflected the central concept of the agent, the "who" of action in their analyses. The "who" of action has primacy in Ricoeur's theory, although it is the logic of action theory itself that has led him to redress the role of the agent, the self, with regard to meaningful action.

A second trait of this approach to action is the role of narrative. Ricoeur refuses to limit the discussion of action to simple actions and action propositions in the manner of analytic philosophy. He casts his eye on higher-order practical units such as are operative socially in crafts or games, the so-called practices,¹² and linguistically in the narratives of life stories.¹³ Narratives are the closest available reproduction of human action both structurally and existentially. Because of their capacity to interconnect action sentences, Ricoeur finds narratives—and through them, the narrative unity of life—the nearest imitation or recreation of the liveliness of the practical field.

A third trait of this action theory is its reformulation of the ontological thrust of action theory. If the ontological thrust is evoked in the mainstream analytical tradition, it is based on an ontology of events. Ricoeur's refurbished theory of action by returning to Aristotle's ontology of actuality and potentiality *(energeia-dunamis)*, on the contrary, is based on an ontology of person or the self.

AN ANALYTIC OF HUMAN ACTION

The philosophy of language has generally functioned as the organon for the theory of action of analytic philosophy. It relies in its analyses on the linguistic descriptions of action, that is, on "utterances in which individuals state their actions."[14] Since actions are essentially not observable, particularly those that are called meaningful actions, analytic philosophy turns to language and its capacity to explain action by its distinctive traits. In order to delimit our discussion of action, we will refer mainly to those actions that C. Moya calls meaningful. Meaningful actions are actions that do not require bodily movements.[15] But they have certain constitutive rules or performance norms.[16] By way of this performance, they become accessible. Language can describe the rules and norms of such action. This choice is made in order to avoid the confusion that continues to exist between actions and observable events. Analytic philosophy has insisted throughout that actions are not events or happenings. Actions, unlike events, it has argued, do not happen; actions are what *make things happen*. Meaningful actions, because of this orientation, are not observable and therefore less likely to be confused with an event.

In sorting out the concept of action, the analytic tradition has further recognized that action operates in a network of concepts, the one calling forth the other and all of them interacting with one another. This network constitutes the line of demarcation distinguishing actions from happenings or events. The language game of action includes such concepts as intention, goals, motive, agent, doing, and initiative, whereas events happen and are observable psychic or physiological movements. These concepts of action language are such that whenever one concept is used, the others are implied as well. For example, intention calls forth motive, and together motive and intention call forth the concept of agent. In *Time and Narrative*, Ricoeur summarized this network with the questions: Who? What? Why? How? With whom? Or against whom? Under what circumstances? With what outcome?[17] Although he pushes hard for the intersignification of all these questions, it is fair to say that the discussion centers on the three questions: "Who?" "What?" and "Why?" That is, on the concept of action, its goals and motivations, and the agent. Thus, by his insistence on the priority of "who" in the analysis of action, Ricoeur differs from the conventional approach to action.

It is Ricoeur's contention that current action theory favors the "what-why" correlation at the expense of the agent. Action theory considers actions from the perspective of "something that occurs." He seeks to correct this imbalance by exposing a logical inconsistency and bias in the current theory. The bias lies in the inability of action theory to escape the pressure to consider actions as events.[18] The analytic philosophers of action have trained their eyes to look for action among the events in the world. In order to determine what counts as an action, analytic philosophy looks for an explanation for the action taken as what happens. This emphasis on the "what" of action has led almost automatically to consideration of the "why" of action. Among events, actions are intentional activities.[19] Meaningful actions, such as promising, greeting someone, or making an offer, are different from involuntary bodily movements or happenings because they are such intentional doings. But the very language of "intentional" betrays the express exclusion of the agent who makes it all happen.

Analytic philosophy identifies three ways in which intentionality is expressed. The first type of intentionality can be stated as "I do or have done something intentionally." In the adverbial form of intentionality, the action is mostly a past action. The same can be said of the second linguistic expression of intention: "I act with a certain intention." In its desire to avoid intuitive, internal realities, analytic philosophy shows a clear bias for actions that are observable and as such appear as events. Hence, there is a preference in analytic circles for the first two expressions of intentionality but also a prejudice for actions in the form of events.[20] But there is also a third expression of intentionality: "I intend to . . . " Here the action to be undertaken is obviously not yet a *fait accompli*. It is not an event because it has not happened yet. According to analytic philosophers, expressions of future actions such as promissives and commissives are not verified yet by the action and are thus accessible only "to the agent who expresses it" and as a declaration.[21] A primary example of such a meaningful action is a commitment to a future course of action. For Ricoeur, it is just these projective actions that set the authentic paradigm for the understanding of action. In other words, according to Ricoeur, action is better understood in terms of what I commit myself to do than in terms of what I have done. If anything, he is consistent in his refusal to acknowledge actions as events.

Although we cannot go into details here, this has at least three interesting repercussions. First of all, promissives and commissives with their inescapably temporal orientation toward the future are least like observable events. The "what" of promissive actions is not an observable event. They are available only as declarations of an intention. In an "intend-to" statement such as, "I am going to row the boat across the lake," it is possible to analyze the expression of the intention,[22] to delve into memory procedures or scripts for "rowing a boat across the lake," or to search out narratives or navigational procedures and practices of rowing. But these analyses display only possibilities of "how-to" or give statistical probabilities about the fulfillment of my intention to row the boat across the lake. They shift the focus away from the action of rowing to the probability of the agent undertaking such an action. The rowing is still future; my intent to row is in the present. According to Ricoeur, analytic philosophy seems constantly tempted to let these actions be dealt with in the same manner as past actions. Actions intended to be done, however, are not events. They are not a "something" that I can describe.[23] If we seek an explanation of such projected actions, we must look for it in the motivation, the expression of intention, and the ability of the agent. This explanation is generally known as teleological "causality." In other words, an analysis of promissives ought to give wider attention to the pro-attitude or belief of the agent, something rarely done in analytic philosophy in its analysis of action.[24] This shift of emphasis toward the agent does not mean that action is some sort of internal (contemplative) event, modeled after external observation, which can then be called volition, desire, or wanting. This leads directly to the second observation.

Analytic philosophy tends to place its emphasis upon descriptions of actions. This emphasis on description manifests a concern for a particular type of knowledge in current action theory. It wants to know actions in terms of the adequacy of their description, that is, in terms of the truth of this description.[25] But intentional actions are fundamentally known without observation: "I do not say that I knew that I was doing this or that because I had observed it. It is in doing that one knows that one is doing something, what one is doing, and why one is doing it."[26] Because these intentional actions are not some internal event but reveal themselves in the doing, they call not for a descriptive knowledge but a practical knowledge: a knowing-how rather than a knowing-that.[27] Practical knowledge therefore poses the problem of truth not in terms of the adequacy of the description but in terms of veracity, that is, in terms of honesty or attitude. As we shall see later, Ricoeur calls this attitude toward practical truth *attestation*. This is the realm of "being-true" or "being-false," the realm of authenticity or of "lies, deceit, misunderstanding, and illusions."[28]

Finally, as a third observation, a more epistemological approach to action also reveals the necessity of recognizing the primacy of the agent. Davidson explains actions through motive and intention. To describe an intentional action, he says, is to explain it by way of the reasons for the action. Actions are that which make things happen. But the relation between the action and the motive tends to be described in analytic philosophy by the term *reason for* in order to avoid causal language. Davidson is less reluctant to perceive motives or intentions as "causes," citing common usage as evidence. He maintains that explanation by reasons is a subset of causal explanation. However, Davidson shows the tenacity of the Humean model of causality where cause and effect remain extraneous to each other. It leads him, according to Ricoeur, to the somewhat contradictory position of making intention not only extraneous to the action but also to considering intention as an internal event. Like Davidson, Ricoeur rejects the dichotomy between "reason for" and "cause," but, drawing on phenomenology, he bypasses the Humean model. The word *cause* can be used justifiably to describe what prompts one to do something. Cause in these cases usually refers to an affect or passivity such as hunger, a disposition, or an external force. If applied to actions, cause (motivation) is not extraneous as in the Humean causality but internal and necessary for the very constitution of action. In order to explain actions, Ricoeur draws instead on what he calls "singular causal explanation." Intentional actions are some type of efficient causality: they make things happen. The explanatory form of such intentional action is best described as "teleological explanation," where actions are explained by the very conditions that produce them.[29] But what are these conditions? By identifying these conditions as "motives," one is not implying some type of hidden internal "entity" or "event." We must avoid the temptation to objectify motives as something substantive. Motives do not belong to the realm of "some thing."

What the common approach of analytic philosophy almost imperceptibly leaves out in its approach, according to Ricoeur, is something that ordinary language makes explicit. What remains implicit in teleological explanation is its reference to the agent whose motive it is.[30] Teleological explanation describes (it states the goal) and it explains (that in view of which something is done). The "who" of action is implied but not clearly articulated. This is Ricoeur's basic critique of Davidson.[31] While Davidson refers to motives as the pro-attitude of the agent, he writes about motives without clearly thematizing the agent. The source of this bias lies in the subtle substitution of events for actions in a manner that makes actions appear like substances or fixed objects. But a teleological explanation desubstantializes action toward an articulation of the agent's inclinations and beliefs. Ricoeur expresses astonishment about the ease with which Davidson ignores a primary phenomenological attribute of intention, which is the "aiming of a consciousness in the direction of something I am to do."[32] In its fear of the intuitive and its attraction to the observable, conceptual analysis of action shies away from any consideration of the self-transcendence of a consciousness. Nevertheless, Ricoeur recognizes a durable validity in Davidson's search for an explanation of action by way of motives despite his obliviousness to the agent. His descriptive approach to action by delimiting or determining actions through their motives or causes is a welcome mediation for the understanding of action from the perspective of the agent. What counts as an action is explained by why the action was undertaken. "The use of 'why?' in the explanation of action thus became the arbiter of the description of what counts as an action."[33] However, the ascription to an agent is deferred by the way of the "what-why" question.[34] Ricoeur, on the other hand, insists for that reason that the agent's projection of the self into a future action—or what he calls ascription of action to an agent—must pass through this explanatory mediation. He thus seeks an analytical or explanatory moment in his theory of action. The priority of the agent is not such that it can bypass the analysis of the "what" of actions by way of their "why."

Up to this point there are at least two limitations to be placed upon the response to the question with which we began: Can there be a science of action? 1) If Ricoeur's distinction between intentional actions and intended actions is valid, the question of an empirical approach to action must be validated first of all for intended future actions such as promissives or commissives. These act as a paradigm of action. However, intended future actions do not qualify as events in the manner that past actions can. 2) Is an epistemic approach possible for such projected actions? An epistemic approach would consider projective actions as possible actions. At this point, one can go in two directions. By means of procedural theory and script theory in memory one can seek to determine the statistical probability of the action taking place. The emphasis remains on the action, but only in terms of the likelihood of its occurrence. The aim of this approach is to transform action once more into an event. Ricoeur does not choose this route, but he does not deny its validity. His desire to approach action in a way other than as an event leads him to look instead at actions first from the perspective of the agent. This leads for him to the much more interesting question of the capacity of the agent to initiate changes into the world. What is it that allows the human self to undertake initiatives of the kind projected by promissives and commissives?[35] Hence, for Ricoeur there occurs a shift away from the "what?" of action to the "who?" of action. This also implies a shift away from an epistemology of actions as events toward an epistemology of the agent. For Ricoeur, the autonomous discipline of action theory, however, cannot rely solely on the analytic tradition to answer this question. It must acknowledge as well the phenomenological and hermeneutical traditions, particularly because the major issue of action theory resides less in determining the distinction between actions and events but more in "determining what specifies the self, implied in the power-to-do, at the junction of acting and the agent."[36]

EXPANDING THE FRAMEWORK OF ACTION

Up to this point we have limited the concept of action to its functioning in sentences and the logical connections that exist between action, intention, motive, and agent. But these action sentences present only the logic of a conceptual network of action. Action in its manifold manifestation of human life requires a broader mirror in which to view itself. Ricoeur therefore insists that a revision of action theory toward a more adequate recognition of the agent requires a revision of action itself. Already Aristotle understood action as a synthesis of incidents and facts. He saw the scope of action to lie in the broader configuration of action produced by the tragedy. Tragedy, he held, was an imitation of human action and life. It composed or brought together the incidents of action into an imitation of action. In *Time and Narrative*, Ricoeur developed this theme at length, showing how narrative's discordant concordance is a productive imitation of action.[37] This expansion of the notion of action into a narrative configuration will have further repercussions upon a scientific approach to action. Only a scientific theory that can incorporate such a narrative would qualify.

Ricoeur indicates three different units of praxis that an expanded theory of action ought to encompass. They are arranged hierarchically.

The first unit of praxis he has called "practices." These refer to the network of subordinate actions governed by constitutive rules that are operative in professions, arts, and games. Ricoeur calls these relations "nesting relations" because they are not linear, rather they pertain to the complex of subordinate actions that make up, for instance, the profession of a lawyer or the game of chess. These actions gain meaning by the notion of constitutive rules that states that a given action or move has meaning and effect only in the context of the profession or game. Such rules govern the meaning of the particular gestures, stating, for example, that shifting a pawn in chess constitutes a move or that a promise is accepting the obligation to keep one's word. Such an extension of action theory places action into a social environment. These practices are meaningful and comprehensible only in a pragmatic social context, which means in interaction with others even when they are solitary practices. At the same time, the placing of action into these larger complexes such as professions and games manifests that acting and interacting can also become an acting upon or undergoing action. It suggests that action is closely allied with passion or suffering.[38]

The second unit of practice is a higher unit of action. Ricoeur calls them "life plans," by which he means the "vast practical units that make up professional life, family life, leisure time."[39] Here, he focuses on the life plans in which we move between certain ideals and practices in which we seek to realize these as our life project.

The third unit of practice touches what Alasdair MacIntyre has called "the narrative unity of life." However difficult it might be to conceive such a narrative unity because of the difference but also similarities between a literary composition and real life, it suggests that narrative (as an "unstable mixture of tabulation and actual experience")[40] plays the role of gathering together into a whole the real beginnings that constitute our initiatives with an anticipation of an ending of the course of our action. For Ricoeur, this narrative unity of life is the broadest context for a theory of action.

It is in this sense that, for Ricoeur, action becomes available for analysis and explanatory procedures, not only in the form of action sentences but also in terms of practices with their rules for understanding, as well as in terms of the more illusive life plans, but particularly in terms of the intelligibility of narrative configurations. In light of the above expansion of the field of action, Ricoeur has suggested that action is like a lingual text. This makes action analyzable in a manner that a literary text or narrative is analyzable. Action has what he calls "readability characters," that is, action becomes like an event that leaves traces such as in documents, monuments, course of events, history, institutions, great works of culture, constitutive rules of behavior, tradition, etc.[41] But as we saw above this is only one aspect of the realm of meaningful human action. It does not take into account the projective character of human life, which Ricoeur insists is a search first of all for a narrative unity of life and secondly for an ethical project. He sees it as the aim of a life. This would mean that, at the projective level, action as encompassing human life has an ethical coloration and should be investigated by ethics, politics, and the resources of practical wisdom. To the extent, however, that narratives and the literary tradition operate as "an immense laboratory for thought experiments" and "imaginative variations" of human life, Ricoeur also seeks to use these literary resources as a link to life.[42] Explanations of action sequences at this level are modeled, according to Ricoeur, on lingual texts.[43] Like grammar in language, actions are rule governed. Social action is motivated through symbols and values that express public features of desirability, and is codified in the cultural network of symbolic mediations that create patterns of interactive meanings. These codes confer a readability character upon these action sequences that allows them to become communicable and to be committed to writing. At this point, action becomes "transposed into a cultural text."[44] By the same token, actions enter into the public domain and become accessible to description (e.g., ethnology) and even more so to practical reason, understood in an adapted Aristotelian sense as deliberative desire. Practical reason fulfills the role here as an arbiter between conflicting claims of desirability. Ricoeur suggests that this level of rationality is governed by practical reasoning.

But is there a possibility to have this practical reasoning incorporate empirical rationality? To answer this question, one must sound two warnings. Ricoeur identifies the attempt to model practical reasoning after the scientific model as the Kantian fallacy. "Few ideas today," he says, "are as healthy and as liberating as the idea that there is a practical reason but not a science of practice."[45] Practical reason operates in the order of changing things where universal norms must come to terms with human desire and freedom. It is situated between logic and alogic and deals with the plausible and probable. Only a scientific model that takes account of the probable and the plausible can be considered as respectful of the field of practical reasoning. The second warning concerns the temptation to divorce action from particular persons, identifiable through personal pronouns, to abstractions such as the State as a hypostatized entity. Action remains personal and any scientific approach to action will have to safeguard singularity.[46]

FROM AN ONTOLOGY OF EVENTS TO AN ONTOLOGY OF THE PERSON

In his essay "Event and Cause," Davidson advances the thesis that events—and they include actions since actions have been classed as a subset of events—are primitive entities. Accordingly, events are true realities because of the propositions referring to them. For that reason, actions are like substances, with this difference that the logical form of action sentences sits somewhere between "substance" (fixed entity) and "even" (transitory entity).[47] At the ontological level this identifies actions as events and leads to an ontology of actions as events, that is, of actions as "something," as being on the side of substance. This has consequences for the unarticulated agent of action in analytic philosophy. In Ricoeur's terms:

> In fact, persons in Strawson's sense are more on the side of substance, to the extent that it is to them that action-events happen. In the logical analysis of the sentence "Pierre struck a blow," what matters is that the verb "to strike" is said of both Pierre and the blow. The blow is in the position of a particular event. Pierre is in the position of substance, not so much as a person distinct from material things . . . but as bearer of the event.[48]

CAN THERE BE A SCIENCE OF ACTION? 83

For Ricoeur, this fading away of the person, the self, in the mass of events is unacceptable. He does not deny that the logical form of action sentences shows that actions are events and, since these actions are amenable to several descriptions, they must be entities. They are individuated. Some type of qualitative identity can be said to exist between two actions. All the evidence points, therefore, to actions having substantial reality. This suggests that an ontology of events as a primitive entity has validity. But does this also cover those actions that we identified above as promissives or commissives? Here, the weight shifts from action as events to action as agent driven. The ontological question here too must shift to the agent. Is the agent something substantial inasmuch as she or he is the possessor of her or his action? Having established the primacy of the agent, must not the appropriate ontology move out of the radius of an ontology of event and into the orbit of an ontology of the person or self?

Before we can present such an ontology, Ricoeur's carefully constructed concept of the self must be considered. In the discussion of analytical philosophy it has become clear that actions can indeed be considered from two angles: as past and therefore observable actions, which makes actions become like entities, comparable to events,[49] and as future, not-yet existing, anticipated actions, which are not like entities. If this twofold perspective of event-action is transferred to the agent, a similar dialectic emerges. For who or what is this self mediated by human action? The self, Ricoeur insists, is not synonymous with the "I." The self that is mediated by action becomes most visible in the reflexive indefinite form of the predicate (e.g., to conduct *oneself*). It is indefinite before it becomes the self in the personal pronouns (myself). It is therefore not the equivalent of the solipsistic self or the ego. For Ricoeur, the self is a mediated self. It is constituted first of all in an unending process whereby the self encounters explanations of the self in the human and social sciences and all the disciplines and narratives that analyze and present the variations of the human self. This dialectic of explanation and understanding is complemented by a dialectic, on the one hand, of the self as *idem* (human identity as being the same) and the self as *ipse* (human identity as not-yet, as ipseity or the "kept word"), and, on the other hand, of the self and the other. For the moment, I would like to concentrate on the dialectic of sameness and ipseity because it allows Ricoeur to demonstrate the same bifurcation of the self as occurs in action.

The identity of the self in this view is constituted between "sameness" (*idem*) and "ipseity" (*ipse*). Ricoeur demonstrates this dialectic through narratives. Besides being an imitation of action—understood in the Aristotelian sense as productive of reality—narratives also configure temporality.[50] In the development of the characters, narratives account for existence as temporal. Now self-identity is a temporal process. The temporal process inscribed in narratives shows this self-identity to be moreover a dialectical process. In the narrative, there is an interaction of a self that, on the one hand, maintains an identity of constancy (a self that remains the same, hence, "sameness"), with a self that, on the other hand, projects itself into the future and commits itself to change and transformation (a self that is not yet but that becomes, which Ricoeur calls "ipseity").[51] The human self is constituted in this dialectic of sameness and ipseity. The self develops in a process, on the one hand, of actions that have "sedimented" themselves in what may be called human character. Here, the self displays a consistency, a constancy. As such, the self appears to possess a substantive identity, which endures as something that can be identified again and again as being the same. On the other hand, the human person is notonly a settled self. He or she undertakes initiatives, makes something happen which inserts itself as novelty. He or she projects into the future through promises and commitments. At this level, which Ricoeur calls ipseity, the self consists in remaining truthful to a given word. The self is determined by anticipated actions. In these projected actions, the identity is not substantive but in the process of becoming. In narratives, this twofold identity is configured by the plot. In the change of fortune (*peripeteia*), the self as *idem* encounters a new opportunity or crisis. In the capacity of the character to respond with a new initiative committing him or her to new possibilities, the self is shown as being more than inflexible constancy. It becomes other without losing personal identity, that is, it becomes itself without in some manner remaining the *same*. The self accordingly is a dialectic of "sameness" and "ipseity." In an ontology of the person, this dialectic pits "sameness"—which, because it can be identified again and again, appears as something substantive, as an entity—with "ipseity," which is projective and based on the "kept word."

But narrative action takes the personal identity of the agent beyond the internal dialectic of the self. Narrative action insists that human identity or the self is constituted even more strongly by the presence of the other in the narrative. Action is interaction, and at the same time undergoing action. Action and passion, that is, actions undergone or suffered, are inseparable, for every action is simultaneously a power "over." Human agency affects the other, so that the power to act is "grafted upon the initial dissymmetry between that which one does and that which is done to the other."[52] Or as Ricoeur says, "Every action has its agents and its patients."[53] To the abovementioned ontology of the self with its twofold orientation, therefore, we must add the dimension of the other with its passive component for both self and other. Ricoeur outlines this passivity in a threefold experience: the experience of one's own body, which mediates between the self and the world; the experience of the intersubjective other for whom I experience an ethical responsibility; and the experience of conscience as a relation of indebtedness to oneself. To what type of ontology does this perception of the self lead and what repercussion does this have upon the possibility of a scientific approach to action?

We will address first the ontological question and in conclusion the epistemological possibilities.

Above, it was stated that an ontology was necessary in order to allow practical philosophy to bring together into an analogous unity the various discourses on human action. But what sort of ontology undergirds the fragments of discourse that Ricoeur has assembled to address human identity? If the ontology of the self is constituted out of these various discourses on action, it cannot turn to traditional metaphysics, which is too solidly rooted in Being as substance or presence. It requires a concept of Being that is, at least in part, nonsubstantialist. After all, only the self as sameness appears substantial. Where does he find such an ontology? Surprisingly, in a revitalized Aristotelian practical philosophy. In Aristotle's metaphysics, Ricoeur has uncovered unresolved aporias that might be exploited for a nonsubstantialist concept of Being. He lights upon this in Aristotle's treatment of action and potency as modes of Being.[54] In Aristotle, these concepts are left ambiguous, for action is defined through potency. What is missing, Ricoeur argues, is the obvious temporality of action and passion. And that was precisely that great contribution of Heidegger's *Sein und Zeit*. If this book is indeed a rereading of Aristotle as some have suggested,[55] this book as Heidegger's rereading of Aristotle succeeds in tying temporality to an ontology. Hence, Heidegger's *Selbst* has become an existential, *Dasein,* a temporal openness to the world. In the self's projection into the future by way of initiatives the self becomes a "specific coordination with the movements of the world."[56] That is the reason why this ontology finds its roots not in substantial being but in being as act/potency. For Aristotle, act/potency is described in terms of *dunamis/ energeia*. Aristotle's *dunamis/energeia* is being at once actual and in potentiality.[57] Heidegger has called Aristotle's being as *dunamis/energeia* facticity, indicating thereby the givenness of reality *(es gibt).* For Ricoeur this is an inadequate articulation of Being as *energeia*. He translates it instead by Spinoza's *conatus,* which he understands as the desire and effort to be or "the effort through which each thing applies itself to persevere in existence."[58] Spinoza's *conatus* expresses this being as act and potency more clearly than does facticity because for Spinoza this effort to persevere in existence is of the very essence of a thing. The self is this energy, this desire and lack connoted by the very term *conatus*.

Being as act/potency allows Ricoeur also to root the third—the most fundamental—dialectic of the self: the self in relation to the other. The other is constitutive for the self. The self cannot be thought without the other. In its becoming, the self must encompass otherness, the dissimilar. That means Being includes passivity: all the experiences in which the self is forbidden to occupy the place of foundation.[59] This is why the self can attest to itself only in a broken fashion because it must recognize difference and otherness. The self must incorporate this other whether as one's own flesh, or as the intersubjective other, or as the "call" of one's own conscience. The self can no longer exist as an imperial self.

AN EPISTEMOLOGY OF THE AGENT OF ACTION

It was indicated above that Ricoeur insisted that understanding, an appropriation of the self, was not possible outside of explanatory ventures. The self is only available in mediations. That is why the appropriation of the self demands the effort of working through the analytical explanations of the self. The self is not intuitively obtained through introspection but only via the long detour of the traces of the self. We have already seen how fruitful such a mediation of explanation is for the understanding of the agent of action.

The self that emerges out of this analysis is not a radical origin or a foundation. It becomes in the interplay of action and passion. It is more fragile than the Cartesian subject who needed to be absolutely certain in its thrust toward the world and reality in the face of a deceptive evil genius. The only manner in which Descartes could save the certainty of knowledge was to interject God as the absolute guarantee of the possibility and certainty of knowledge. God could not consistently deceive human knowledge! Descartes's Achilles' heel lay in his need for a guarantee or verification of knowledge. All knowledge had to overcome the principle of doubt. For Ricoeur, this absolute certainty and final verification of knowledge is not possible. Once again, he turns to Aristotle's *Metaphysics* to overcome this bias toward guaranteed certainty.[60] For Aristotle, "to be true" and "to be false" were among the original meanings of being. "To be true" and "to be false" are modes of being. This brings us back again to the debate between *epistémé* and *doxa*. In Ricoeur's terms, the Aristotelian modes of being "to be true" and "to be false" become "attestation" and "suspicion."[61] For Aristotle, to put it another way, there exists a knowledge of things in between the necessary and immutable (*epistémé*) and arbitrary opinion (*doxa*). Practical reason lies in this median zone of a sobered reason that is open to discussion and criticism.[62]

What epistemological status does Ricoeur attach to this sobered reason? He insists that the speaker of a language and the agent of action both make a commitment to the real that takes them beyond themselves. In a constative proposition a speaker affirms, "This is so." Similarly, in a promissive proposition an agent commits, "This I will do." This is the "ontological vehemence" of the speaker or the agent.[63] The speaker and the agent make an affirmation not only about reality and about the world of action but also about a mode of existence of the self. This mode of existence of the self Ricoeur names "attestation."[64]

Attestation as an ontological vehemence of the agent is not only a commitment of the self but also an epistemic thrust.[65] Against the relativist claims of the deconstructionist and despite the lack of an absolute guarantee of truth, there is a confidence in the self—an unverifiable confidence—in what the self says and in what the self believes it can do. The self, in other words, exists as a belief, as a credence, as an assurance of truthfulness. Ricoeur calls it a *mode aléthique,* a truthful mode, which expresses not so much "I believe that..." but "I believe in..."[66] This must not be reduced to a psychological argument. But it is not located only on the scale of knowledge or at the level of epistemic truth. And yet it is deeply epistemological. At one level attestation resembles witnessing, inasmuch as in witnessing the equilibrium is easily disturbed by doubt and suspicion cast upon it by more progressive theories, other actions and stories, other ethical or moral predicates. In attestation the self expresses the assurance that, in spite of suspicion, meaning and the self are possible. Truth here is not necessarily verifiable truth. Attestation is the self in its commitment to the world. Attestation, to use Heidegger's language, is the self as Care.[67] The self exists as an attestation of the truthfulness of being. In attestation one expresses the confidence that everyone exists as a self. At another level, this attestation, like witness, calls for a criteriology. The ontology of the self has explanation as its first dialectical opposite. As Ricoeur insists, attestation must be mediated by analysis just as the "who?" must pass by the "what?" and the "why?" Attestation relies therefore upon analytic philosophy as well as pragmatic philosophy and narrative theory, as well as other explanatory disciplines of action, to provide it with a "realist twist." For Ricoeur, these explanatory opposites have been mainly linguistic. Nevertheless, the restriction to language aside, these analyses provide an epistemological core at the heart of attestation.[68]

CONCLUSION

Where does this leave us with the question of a science of action? For Ricoeur, the dialectic between *epistémé* and *doxa* will never be completed. What he seeks therefore is a space between "mere" opinion and science. That is the space of Aristotle's *doxazein*, that is, the space of the dialectic. Ricoeur has long maintained that the dialectic between explanation and understanding is ontological, that is, that it pertains to the constitution of reality. In *Oneself as Another* he maintains that this dialectic pertains to the ontological constitution of the self. It is this interminable dialectic, this broken dialectic, with its endless detours fed by an indefatigable ontological vehemence, that has become for Ricoeur the less than secure haven of the self.[69]

NOTES

1. Rémi Brague. *Aristote et la question du monde: essai sur le contexte cosmologique et anthropologique de l'ontologie* (Paris: Presses Universitaires de France, 1988), 10.
2. OA, 16.
3. Ibid., 11–16.
4. See PA.
5. In the 1920s it was announced in Husserl's *Jahrbuch* that Heidegger would write a book on Aristotle based on his courses at Freiburg and Marburg. But the publication of the *Nachlass* during the 1980s shows no such commentary. Instead of the explicit commentary, what did appear was the book *Sein und Zeit* (1927). Authors such as Rémi Brague, *Aristote et la question du monde* (Paris: Presses Universitaires de France, 1988); Franco Volpi, *Heidegger e Aristotele* (Padua: Daphni, 1984); Jacques Taminiaux. *Lectures de l'ontologie fondamentale. Essaid sur Heidegger* (Grenoble: Jérôme Millon, 1989); and Manfred Riedel, *Für eine zweite Philosophie: Vorträge und Abhandlungen* (Frankfurt: Suhrkamp, 1990) speculate that *Sein und Zeit* is a substitute for this book on Aristotle. *Sein und Zeit* is seen by these authors as Heidegger's creative rereading of certain ambiguities left unthought and unexpressed in Aristotle's metaphysics.
6. The tentativeness of Ricoeur's position is scripted into the book by his decision to call the divisions "studies" rather than chapters. Also the final chapter manifests this scruple. The quest for an ontology of action is introduced with a question mark: "What Ontology in View?"
7. OA, 16–19.
8. "What is a Text? Explanation and Understanding," in HHS, 145–161.

9. The main area of application of analytical philosophy has been narrative in relation to historiography. See, for example, William H. Dray, "On the Nature and Role of Narrative in History" and "Narrative and Historical Realism," in *On History and Philosophers in History* (Leiden: E. J. Brill, 1989); Arthur Danto, *Analytic Philosophy of History* (Cambridge: Cambridge University Press, 1965); and W. B. Gallie, *Philosophy and the Historical Understanding* (New York: Harper and Row, 1964). *TN*, vol. 1, gives a lengthy, mainly appreciative, analysis of these efforts (ibid., 121–161).

10. This practical concern has been present in Ricoeur's philosophy from the beginning. His doctoral dissertation, *FN*, already sought to create a bridge between a theoretical and practical philosophy. It is in his latest work, particularly in OA, that the ethical, practical thrust of all his work becomes most apparent.

11. The limits Ricoeur set for himself regarding the epistemic approach to action by restricting himself to actions mainly in linguistic propositions and texts need not be exclusive of other approaches to action. Elsewhere, together with Paul O'Grady and Paul Rigby, we have argued for the validity of more empirical approaches of human action in the human and social sciences as the dialectic explanatory counterpart of the appropriation of action. It is our conviction that the dialectic interplay of explanation and understanding in the realm of human action needs to be broadened. See "Prelinguistic Action: A Narrative and Psychological Approach" (under review).

12. See OA, 176.

13. See "Life: A Story in Search of Narrator," in *Facts and Values*, ed. M. Danser and J. N. Krary (Dordrecht: Nijhoff, 1986), 121–132.

14. OA, 57. We will ask below whether such a linguistic approach to action is too narrow a base to investigate the complexity of action.

15. C. Moya. *The Philosophy of Action: An Introduction* (Cambridge: Polity Press, 1990), 40.

16. Ricoeur defines meaningful action as "that action which an agent can account for—*logon didonai*—to someone else or to himself in such a way that the one who receives this account accepts it as intelligible." Meaningful means that the account "meets the conditions of acceptability established within a community of language and of values." See his article "Practical Reason," in *TA*, 189.

17. *TN*, vol. 1, 55. This practice is continued in OA. In an earlier text on action, *sa*, 21–63, Ricoeur deals at length with the concept of action, intention, motive, and agent.

18. Ricoeur shows how despite an initial opposition to considering actions as events, analytic philosophy ended up by taking event as its real term of reference. What happens and what makes things happen distinguishes events (happenings) from actions. What makes things happen is neither observable nor true or false. Only of the "done" action can one make a

constative utterance. But this emphasis of analytic philosophy on the accomplished action brings action within the sphere of events. See OA, 59–61.

19. Hence the influence of such authors as G. E. M. Anscombe, A. C. Danto, D. Davidson, A. Kenny, J. L. Petit, P. F. Strawson, L. Wittgenstein, and G. H. von Wright. Ricoeur gives no attention to the volitional theory or to the theory of mind that are sometimes evoked to overcome the eternal regress-problem in action theory in its attempt to distinguish between actions and happenings.

20. That is Ricoeur's basic insight in light of Donald Davidson's approach to action. Ricoeur recognizes that Davidson's essay "Actions, Reasons, and Causes" is an attempt at realigning the philosophy of action, but it leads to a favoring of the descriptive approach to action. See Davidson, *Essays on Actions and Events* (Oxford: Clarendon Press, 1980), 3–19.

21. OA, 68. It is worth remarking here that the fact that these actions are not observable does not make them incommunicable. We can discuss what we are going to do and why we are doing it. Our language can explore this with a richness of expression and with a grammar that makes the future action communicable. Future actions are not private: they are as public as the language in which we declare them. See "Practical Reason," in TA, 189–190.

22. OA, 68.

23. Ibid., 59.

24. Ricoeur recognizes the pressure in analytic philosophy toward description and to knowledge that can be true or false. Analytic philosophy has an abhorrence for the positing of internal events to which the criterion true-false does not apply. For more detail see below. OA, 70.

25. Ricoeur notices this particularly in Anscombe's position in *Intention* (London: Basil Blackwell, 1979).

26. OA, 70.

27. This does not mean that practical knowledge is excluded from the analysis of cognitive psychology.

28. OA, 72.

29. Ibid., 78.

30. Ricoeur relies on Charles Taylor's definition of teleological causation: it "is an explanation in which the global configuration of events is itself a factor in its own production." The intention or motive, in other words, are part of the know-how needed for the action. Charles Taylor, *The Explanation of Behavior* (London: Routledge & Kegan Paul, 1964). See "Practical Reason," 191.

31. Ricoeur refers here to Davidson's position articulated in *Essays on Actions and Events*, particularly in the first essay, 3–19.

32. OA, 67.

33. Ibid., 61.

34. Ibid., 96–99.

35. See the interesting reflections on initiative in the essay entitled "Initiative," in *TA*, 208–222.
36. *OA*, 113.
37. See particularly *TN*, vol. I, 52–87.
38. *OA*, 153–157.
39. Ibid., 157.
40. Ibid., 162.
41. Paul Ricoeur, "The Model of the Text: Meaningful Action Considered as a Text," in *TA*, 150.
42. *OA*, 158–162.
43. "The Model of the Text: Meaningful Action Considered as a Text," 144–167.
44. Ricoeur frequently refers to the cultural anthropology of Clifford Geertz, *The Interpretation of Cultures* (New York: Basic Books, 1973), to explain how actions too become part of a system of interacting symbols. If actions are governed by rules they become accessible to description and to interpretation (the "as" structure of interpretation: an action signifies this or that). See "Practical Reason," 194–195.
45. Ibid., 199.
46. Ibid., 201.
47. *OA*, 83.
48. Ibid.
49. This is how Ricoeur approached action in the above-mentioned article "The Model of the Text: Meaningful Action Considered as a Text." These actions leave traces or marks that allow them to become part of a history.
50. This is Ricoeur's main thesis in his three-volume *TN*. Narratives configure temporality not only of actions but also of the characters, the agents inscribed in the text.
51. *OA*, 116–123. See also "Ipséité, alterité, socialité," *Archivio di filosofia* 54 (1986): 17–34, and "L'identité narrative," *Esprit* (juillet-août 1988): 295–304.
52. *OA*, 256.
53. Ibid., 155.
54. Ibid., 302–317.
55. See beside the authors mentioned in Note 8, Thomas Sheehan, "Heidegger, Aristotle, and Phenomenology," *Philosophy Today* 19 (1975): 87–94.
56. *OA*, 309.
57. Ibid., 315.
58. Ibid., 316.
59. Ibid., 318.
60. Aristotle, *Metaphysics*, 6.2.1026a32–b2.

61. OA, 299.
62. "Practical Reason," 206.
63. See for example, "Ontologie," *Encyclopaedia universalis*, vol. XII (Paris: Encyclopaedia Universalis France, 1972), 94–102.
64. OA, 22.
65. Paul Ricoeur, "L'attestation: Entre phénoménologie et ontologie," in *Les métamorphoses de la raison herméneutique*, ed. Jean Greisch and Richard Kearney (Paris: Cerf, 1991), 382.
66. OA, 299.
67. Ibid., 300.
68. Ibid., 16, 299–302.
69. I gratefully acknowledge the contribution that a grant from the Social Sciences and Humanities Research Council of Canada (410-91-0422) made to the research of this article. I thank my co-researchers Paul O'Grady and Paul Rigby and research assistant Murray Littlejohn for their helpful comments.

FIVE

Literary and Science Fictions
Philosophers and Technomyths

Don Ihde

> I enter the Teletransporter. I have been to Mars before, but only by the old method, a space-ship journey taking several weeks. This machine will send me at the speed of light. I merely have to press a green button. Like others, I am nervous. Will it work? I remind myself what I have been told to expect. When I press the button, I shall lose consciousness, and then wake up at what seems a moment later. In fact I shall have been unconscious for about an hour. The Scanner here on Earth will destroy my brain and body, while recording the exact states of all my cells. It will then transmit this information by radio. Traveling at the speed of light, the message will take three minutes to reach the Replicator on Mars. This will then create, out of new matter, a brain and body exactly like mine. It will be in this body that I shall wake up.
>
> —Derek Parfit, *Reasons and Persons*

Those who have carefully read Paul Ricoeur's *Oneself as Another* may recognize this as the more complete text of a sci-fi imaginative variation developed by Derek Parfit in *Reasons and Persons* (Oxford, 1986). And those who read analytic philosophy will recognize this as a clever, but typical fantasy using sci-fi literary examples rampant in this phenomenological genre. Brain transplants, body teletransportations, mind/body switches, all play roles functioning not unlike phenomenological imaginative variations within this philosophical culture. Parfit is identified by Ricoeur as one of his most formidable philosophical others in his attempt to meld into a "discipline [requiring] . . . a new alliance between the analytic tradition and the phenomenological and hermeneutic tradition . . ." Following his long and deep seated habits of dialectically interrogating philosophical others—structuralism, psychoanalysis, critical theory, and here most focusedly, Anglo-American analytic philosophy—he produces what may be the capstone book of his career. For even though his dialectical and hermeneutic moves remain discernible in Oneself as Another, they are more subtly made, less visible in the foreground, and placed in the most complex and synthetic display of his philosophy to date. Ricoeur does continue to surprise me: he does not falter, he sharpens his tools, and he never fails to deliver new insights and challenges—and for those of us who have reached graybeard stage, we can note with envy and hope that Ricoeur has produced and published more books since he retired than in his career up to that time!

Is Ricoeur too friendly and easy on his critics and others, as Charles Reagan alleges in his new biography of Ricoeur?[2] And is this particularly the case with his detour into analytic philosophy concerned with a theory of the self? Surely the sparse, virtually monodimensioned sense of analytic self-identity, identity in a desertscape, stands in sharp contrast to the richer, narrative, and polymorphic sense of the self that emerges in the rainforestscape of Ricoeur's theory. And one could, point by point, make these comparisons—but that is not what struck me in reading Oneself as Another. Rather, I shall turn to a crucial set of parallelisms which emerge in the fulcral fifth and sixth studies in the very middle of Oneself as Another. For it is precisely in the Ricoeurean attempt to forge an alliance between analytic and phenomenological-hermeneutic traditions that these interesting parallelisms appear.

TWO PHILOSOPHICAL CULTURES

Ricoeur's take upon analytic philosophy—which includes discussion of Strawson, Ryle, Davidson in addition to Parfit—is one that sees a symptom of two cultures in the differing uses of fictive, imaginative variations. Ricoeur begins by simultaneously identifying the different preferred literary, fictive examples as variations and by differentiating between "literary" fiction and "science fiction."

It will be one of the functions of the subsequent comparison between science fiction and literary fiction to place back on the drawing board the question of the presumed contingency of the most fundamental traits of the human condition.[3] So the first parallelism is the type and use of imaginative variations, in these cases exemplified in the two cultures by two different genres—literary and science fiction—each favored by one of the two traditions. This far I simply accept and agree with Ricoeur's insight into two parallel uses of fictive variations.

LITERARY AND SCIENCE FICTIONS 95

But, then, in a second move, Ricoeur surprises me and enters a territory he has seldom talked about or worked upon. He identifies science fiction variations with "technology" (perhaps better capitalized as Technology):

> What [Parfit's] puzzling cases render radically contingent is this corporeal and terrestrial condition which the hermeneutics of existence, underlying the notion of acting and suffering, takes to be insurmountable. What performs this inversion of meaning by which the existential invariant becomes a variable in a new imaginary montage? This is done by technology [my emphasis]; better, beyond available technology, this is the realm of conceivable technology—in short, the technological dream.[4]

It was, in fact, this identification that gelled my response and, now departing from Ricoeur's stance, I will claim a second and much deeper background parallelism and argue that the two philosophical cultures are motivated—exemplified in Ricoeur and Parfit—by two contrasting technomyths. Ricoeur clearly recognizes Parfit's technomyth, but, I shall argue, he does not recognize his own. For deeper and broader than the preference for literary, fictive devices is the appeal to contrastive utopian and dystopian technomyths.

Deepest of all, however, is a third set of parallelisms, for embedded in the technomyths are two, radically different body ontologies. Here, Ricoeur reemerges with clearer insights and, by returning to the phenomenological sense of body distinguished from flesh, shows how—in a new and more subtle way—analytic body theory might be called a "new" or neo-Cartesianism.

I shall examine each of these philosophical cultural differences in turn, and then conclude with a suggestive reconstruction of the technomyths, which constitute a hidden agenda between the traditions.

ANALYTIC SCI-FI VERSUS NARRATIVE FICTION

I return to Parfit's teletransportation: Parfit self-consciously worries, at least a little, that technologized fictions may extend too far. He notes that there is some hesitation and doubt within the Anglo-American traditions about the relevance and usefulness of such variations. Parfit points out that:

> Some believe that we can learn little. This would have been Wittgenstein's view. And Quine writes, "The method of science fiction has its uses in philosophy, but . . . I wonder whether the limits of the method are properly heeded . . . [such uses] suggest

that words have some logical force beyond what our past needs have invested them with."⁵

Yet, for the most part, among those I shall call the "new Cartesians," sci-fi variations are the means of choice, now resonating with strong trends in popular culture with its cybercinema and "wired" embodiments.

If science fiction is the preferred mode of imaginative variations (to make logical points, to be sure), it is merely the foreground indicator of a much deeper background set of philosophical assumptions. I shall here focus upon two levels of these backgrounds, the implicit technomyth that seems to be functioning, along with a powerful reductionist notion of embodiment. Both of these background assumptions reinforce each other. But first, a look at what Ricoeur calls the difference between "literary" and "technological" fictions:

> Literary fictions differ fundamentally from technological fictions in that they remain imaginative variations on an invariant, our corporeal condition experienced as the existential mediation between the self and the world. Characters in plays and novels are humans like us who think, speak, act and suffer as we do. Insofar as the body as one's own is a dimension of oneself, the imaginative variations around the corporeal condition are variations on the self and selfhood.⁶

In short, implied in what Ricoeur is calling the literary fiction is an embedded, implied theory of body as mine (me). Technological fictions—sci-fi analytic fictions—disrupt this ultimately phenomenological feature and attempt to make embodiment itself contingent:

> Are we capable of conceiving of (I do not say realizing) variations such that the corporeal and terrestrial condition itself becomes a mere variable, a contingent variable, if the teletransported individual does not transport with himself some residual traits of this condition, without which he could no longer be said to act or to suffer, even if it were only the question of knowing if and how he is going to survive?⁷

Clearly, the crucial difference, then, between what Ricoeur calls the literary fiction and the technological fiction is the implied sense of embodiment which the two variants display. Literary fictions, which Ricoeur prefers and illustrates in *Oneself as Another* in his discussion of *Antigone*, *In Remembrance of Things Past*, etc., naively accept and contain what I shall later discuss as the embodied self within a world and experientially centered variation. Technological fictions displace embodiment and do variations upon fictive non-experienced (or non-experiencable) possibilities. (As a minor caveat, I do want to note that Ricoeur does to literary fictions precisely what Heidegger does to poetry: Were poetry only that which can "reveal Being," then a lot of what passes as poetry simply doesn't count, including most of what could be considered to be ironic, humorous, or satyric. Similarly, in Ricoeur the reduction is to the great novels, plays, and other literary vehicles that are primarily narrative in form, with distinct characters, voices, and identities. I wonder where Kafka's *Metamorphosis* or other nonhuman imaginations would fit, which are clearly not distinctly sci-fi or "technological" nor do they retain human corporeality.) So, here we have the first parallelism, two distinctly different styles of fictive imaginations, but variants that point to much deeper and broader cultural philosophical styles.

CONTRASTING TECHNOMYTHS

I shall now move to the first background feature that distinguishes the two philosophical cultures. At this level this feature is one of an implied "technomyth," or deep seated and not always specified attitudes toward technologies. At the most extreme the technomyths take utopian or dystopian trajectories.

Analytic philosophers are rarely technological dystopians. In part, this should not be surprising given the historical associations of analytic philosophy with what was explicitly a central and highly valued appreciation of science. Not only was much of analytic philosophy to be an emulation of the "scientific," but it also brought with it a culture of the quasi-religious dimension of scientific utopianism. Science, if not now surely in the future, would make almost anything possible. In the contemporary situation, however, what was once "science" has become technoscience, science embodied through technologies. Repeating Ricoeur's critique of Parfit: "What [Parfit's sci-fi] . . . puzzling cases render radically contingent [the corporeal and terrestrial] . . . is done by technology; better, beyond available technology, this is the realm of conceivable technology—in short, the technological dream.[8] What Ricoeur is calling "the technological dream" is part of what I am calling a technomyth. In its analytic version it is utopian, fictive, and holds implicitly that the conceivable is ultimately technologically feasible. And, in the contemporary situation the technological dream often turns biotechnological. Thus, the imaginations of transplants, teleportation, mind/body changes, have a technobiological shape and "causation." Nor can I too often point out that the slide from conceivability to future actuality not only barely conceals the utopian beliefs that go back all the way to Roger Bacon, Bruno, da Vinci, to reach a peak in the Enlightenment, but that these also are today rampant in popular culture.

The problem of critique here, however, does not lie with the task of distinguishing between the quasi-religiosity of utopianism and what can become actual, but with a much deeper "contradiction" within which the "technological" remains concealed in science fiction forms. This contradiction is deeply embedded in what I have heretofore termed embodiment relations in which humans relate to and through technologies quasi-bodily.

It takes particularly poignant shape in the cases of prosthetic devices and at the edges of the technologies that fictionalized are termed *bionic*. But the contradiction lies in a more general desire relating to all embodiment possibilities:

> There is ... a deeper desire which can arise from the experience of embodiment relations. It is the doubled desire that, on one side, is a wish for total *transparency*, total embodiment, for the technology to truly "become me." Were this possible, it would be equivalent to there being no technology, for total transparency would be my body and senses; I desire the face-to-face that i would experience without the technology. But that is only one side of the desire. The other side is the desire to have the power, the transformation that the technology makes available. Only by using the technology is my bodily power enhanced and magnified by speed, through distance, or by any of these other ways in which technologies change my capacities. These capacities are always *different* from my naked capacities. The desire is, at best, contradictory. I want the transformation that the technology allows, but I want it in such a way that I am basically unaware of its presence. I want it in such a way that it becomes me. Such a desire secretly rejects what technologies are and overlooks the transformational effects which are necessarily tied to human-technology relations. This illusory desire belongs equally to pro- and antitechnology interpretations of technology.[9]

This applies, I believe, to Parfit's teleportation fantasies, and Ricoeur is right in calling it a "technological dream"—it is a fantasy exercised by the contradictory desire that both wants and does not want technology and thus hides the technological.

If Parfit's agenda embeds its fantasies in technological utopianism, does Ricoeur's agenda do the same with respect to a technological dystopianism that for so many Euro-American philosophers also entails continued Romanticism? At no point in *Oneself as Another* does Ricoeur explicitly either take a distinctly anti-technological stance, nor does he even clearly link his fictive devises with "technology." Indeed, the technological is almost invisible for his side of the cultural gap.

A version of Continental Romanticism, however, does appear. It lies in what I shall call a "slide" from the phenomenologically established ontological relation between an embodied self and the environing world. Regarding literary fiction and its sense of embodied self:

> In virtue of the mediating function of the body as one's own in the structure of being in the world, the feature of selfhood belonging to corporality is extended to that of the world as it is inhabited corporeally.[10]

Then, in a distinctly Heidegger-like move, Ricoeur identifies the phenomenological world with "Earth," which then gets toned down to the notion of terrestrial condition:

> This feature defines the terrestrial condition as such and gives to the Earth the existential signification attributed to it in various ways by Nietzsche, Husserl, and Heidegger. The Earth here is something different, and something more, than a planet: it is the mythical name of our corporeal anchoring in the world.[11]

I shall not here follow, but simply assert, that in Heidegger the notion of Earth becomes a key variable in his critique of Technology, the calculative way of seeing the world that contains and belongs to Modern Science, which is a tool of Technology-as-Metaphysics. In the "world-as-view," Earth can be degraded into a mere planet, but as a result of technological seeing. Does Ricoeur fall into this dystopian stance? I cannot make a strong case that he does, although his frequent use of "terrestrial condition" identified with a mythical Earth seems to suggest an affinity. The one clue that an implicit antitechnological trajectory may be part of a technomyth is his worry about a Parfitlike projection in which the sci-fantasy could become actual. Ricoeur interestingly argues that (phenomenological or) literary corporality carries something like a moral implication:

> For if an imaginary system which respects the corporeal and terrestrial condition as an invariant has more in common with the moral principle of imputation,—would not any attempt to censure that other imaginary, the one which renders this very invariant contingent, be in its turn immoral from another point of view for the reason that it would prohibit dreaming?[12]

Caught now in not wanting to censure dreaming—technological fantasies—but at the same time wanting a morality that protects corporality and the terrestrial condition, Ricoeur cautiously worries:

> It will perhaps one day be necessary to forbid actually doing what today science fiction is limited to dreaming about.... Let us simply express the wish that the manipulative surgeons in these dreams never have the means—or more especially, the right—to perform what is perfectly permissible to imagine.[13]

Ricoeur is not about to wish himself teletransported to Mars! But this caution falls short of the call to remain en-Earthed or stay in the forest cottage of his German counterpart. Ricoeur's caution, however, insofar as it entertains both a fear of technological possibility without recognizing the contradictory nature of the dream, remains in precisely the same dilemma as Parfit regarding the technological. I argue that technological utopianism and the technological dystopianism equally hide the technological:

> The [contradictory] desire is the source of both utopian and dystopian dreams. The actual, or material, technology always carries with it only a partial or quasi-transparency, which is the price for the extension of magnification that technologies give. In extending bodily capacities, the technology also transforms them. In that sense, all technologies in use are non-neutral. They change the basic situation, however subtly, however minimally; but this is the other side of the desire. The desire is simultaneously a desire for a change in situation—to inhabit the earth, or even to go beyond the earth—while sometimes inconsistently wishing that this movement could be without the mediation of the technology.[14]

DIFFERENT BODIES

We now arrive at the most crucial of the parallelisms that lie in the *body-ontologies* which are radically different between analysis and phenomenology. Ricoeur, in the tenth, ontological study, returns to the phenomenological sense of embodiment and the distinctions of Husserl and Merleau-Ponty between "body" and "flesh":

> To say that the flesh is absolutely here, and so heterogeneous with respect to any set of geometric coordinates, is equivalent to saying that it is nowhere in terms of objective spatiality.... And

> the "over there" where I could be if I transported myself there ... has the same status of heterogeneity as the here of which it is the correlate.... [This is within an] *environing world*, taken as the correlate of the body-flesh ... the world as practicable completes fortuitously what has just been said about the internal, as it were, spatiality of the flesh.[15]

He also returns to the pre-extra linguistic meanings of the fleshworld correlation:

> It is upon this prelinguistic relation between my flesh localized by the self and a world accessible or inaccessible to the "I can" that a semantics of action is finally to be constructed which will not lose its way in the endless exchange of language games.[16]

Flesh, phenomenological body, is mineness, experiencable. So, when Ricoeur turns to Parfit's body-ontology, it must appear reductionist. And, while I would claim that the neo-Cartesianism of Parfit also reintroduces a "god's eye view" into his technological fictions, Ricoeur's critique is one that emphasized what is new in this revived Cartesianism:

> What the reductionist thesis reduces is not only, nor even primarily, the mineness of experience but, more fundamentally, that of my own body ... Thereafter, the true difference between the nonreductionist thesis and the reductionist thesis in no way coincides with the so-called dualism between spiritual substance and corporeal substance, but between my own possession and *impersonal description* [my emphasis].... The most radical confrontation must place face-to-face two perspectives upon the body—the body as mine, and the body as one body among others.[17]

Then, in one of the most thoroughly phenomenological descriptive arguments in the book, Ricoeur goes on to show how "This neutralization, in all the thought experiments ..., will facilitate focusing on the brain the entire discourse of the body."[18] Here is part of his phenomenological description:

> The *brain* ... differs from many other parts of the body, and from the body as a whole in terms of an integral experience, inasmuch as it is stripped of any phenomenological status and thus of the trait of belonging to me, of being my possession. I have the experience of my relation to my members as organs of movement (my hands), of perception (my eyes), of emotion (the heart), of expression (my voice). I have no such experience of my brain. In

truth, the expression "my brain" has no meaning, at least not directly: absolutely speaking, there is a brain in my skull, but I do not feel it. It is only through the global detour by way of my body . . . that I can say: "my brain." . . . Its proximity in my head gives it the strange character of *nonexperienced inferiority* [my emphasis].[19]

The body-as-brain, the reduced impersonal and nonexperienced body in Parfit, is adjoined to another favorite notion, the "cerebral trace" as the substitute for memory, another case of reducing the personal to the impersonal, which slides the discussion over into the language games of "causal dependence" and other forms of physicalism still favored by analytic philosophers. Ricoeur concludes that: "Parfit's fictions . . . concern entities of a manipulable nature from which the question of selfhood has been eliminated as a matter of principle."[20]

Perhaps, at this most extreme juncture, I should not call the divergent body-ontologies a "parallelism" because there is much greater contrast here than in any of the previous comparisons. A body-ontology in which "mineness . . . constitutes the core of the nonreductionist thesis"[21] and constrained by the phenomenological notion of body as flesh, simply contrasts with the reductionist thesis that locates identity in brains, cerebral traces, and other impersonal, inexperiencable entities. Thus, the parallelisms, instead of gradually converging, diverge.

RICOEUR'S ANALYTIC DETOUR

A detour presumably takes one on a side road, but eventually must return to the highway—does the detour via analytic philosophy do this? Probably not. If not, why not? I think that the reason ultimately lies in the two radically different body-ontologies, which motivate analytic philosophy on one side, and hermeneutic phenomenology on the other. *Oneself as Another*, perhaps unintentionally, reveals this fissure. As I draw to a close, I want to observe that the two styles employ—in the services of their ontologies—two very different constraint systems. I shall contend, with some irony concerning the self-interpretations by these traditions, that analytic philosophy (here Ricoeur) operates with a tight constraint system.

At the level of fictive variations, it is easy to point out the looseness in Parfitian teletransportation fantasies. He begins with an easily imaginable transportation example: the "old method," a space ship, is not only logically, conceptually, but technoscientifically possible—"by today's lights," to employ a Quinean phrase. Such imaginations are implicitly constrained by the context of the best known technoscientific parameters of the present. To be sure, he has reduced the time of a current probe from eighteen months to several weeks, a factor of six. The leap to the new method, the "Replicator," radically loosens the constraints to the merely logically, conceptually possible with only minimal caveats to retain a "scientific aura." The Replicator still seems constrained to the speed-of-light speed limit of known science, and seems to imply a biotechnology related to the beginnings of genetic, atomic, and molecular manipulations. The looseness of this constraint may be seen when the giganumbers implied in the fantasized technologies are noted: Currently it is possible to send a million bits per minute (for example, a single frame of an image from Mars contains ten-million bits and takes ten minutes to transmit). Were it possible to reduce the human body, with its ten thousand trillion cells, multiplied by the ten thousand protein units in each cell, yielding a billion trillion bits, and send these in today's technologies, it would take 750 days plus to get a body's information to the Replicator. Clearly, this is no advance since it is slower than the space probe. But is we increase it by a factor of six, it still will take at least 150 days and still be slower than the probe.

The very absurdity "by today's lights" of this situation only serves to further sharpen the notion that the thought experiment is a wild and barely constrained fantasy. Admittedly, Parfit does not take the even easier route of *Star Trek*, which loosens the constraints far beyond the physics, let alone the technologies, of today. Parfit's Replicator does not have the capacity to go from "impulse" to "warp" speed and thus break the speedlimit of the known universe. But the constraint system is largely open to mere logical and conceptual possibility. This leaves it far more loose than any scientific constraint system which must take account of the known laws and patterns of physics, chemistry, biology, and technology.

Ricoeur's constraint system is much tighter, although it cannot be said to be a technoscientific set of constraints. It is rather a set of existential constraints governed by experiencable bodies in correlation with an experiencable surrounding world. His favored literary fictions also presuppose embodiment, temporality, and bodily spatiality. These are constraints that cannot "violate a constraint of another order, concerning human rootedness on this earth,"[22] and which must contain the full sense of "mineness, which ... constitutes the core of the nonreductionist thesis."[23] But, if Parfit's constraints are too loose, perhaps Ricoeur's are too tight. Humans have, after all, actually escaped—temporarily and in a phenomenological cocoon to be sure—the earth; and the perspectives that show earth as (also) planet are not totally alienating since they show the finitude of our dwelling place and also begin to make it appear as a kind of integral whole. I even think that the ontological correlation of embodied self within a world might be able to include "worlds" if they are complex enough to have the ecosystems that are necessary to sustain us (we are, after all, not solitary beings, but beings-in-a-system). So, in my own way, I accept Parfit's rendering of myself and my world as contingent, although by a different route. But I suggest the dreaming that makes this possible needs to be constrained by a deeper recognition of the phenomenological, taken existentially.

TELETRANSPORTATION REDUX

I press the green button and fall unconscious. The worrisome dreams I had before this moment, about all the glitches early replicators had, when like computers they used to "crash" in the middle of a transportation, do not occur. I am, of course, unaware that the residual effects of a solar flare have passed by during my own weeks of transportation. I wake up and announce: [Read in falsetto] "I'm here; everything seems to be fine; I'm me. But there does seem to be something a little different...."

NOTES

1. OA, 113.
2. Charles E. Reagan, *Paul Ricoeur: His Life and His Work* (Chicago: University of Chicago Press, 1996), 136.
3. OA, 150.
4. Ibid., 150.
5. Derek Parfit, *Reasons and Persons* (Oxford: Oxford University Press, 1986), 200.
6. OA, 150.
7. Ibid., 151.
8. Ibid., 150.
9. Don Ihde, *Technology and the Lifeworld* (Bloomington: Indiana University Press, 1990), 75.
10. OA, 150.
11. Ibid., 150.
12. Ibid., 151.
13. Ibid.

14. Don Ihde, op. cit., 75.
15. OA, 325.
16. Ibid., 325.
17. Ibid., 132.
18. Ibid., 132.
19. Ibid., 132–133.
20. Ibid.
21. Ibid., 137.
22. Ibid., 135.
23. Ibid., 137.

PART TWO

RICOEUR IN RELATION TO OTHERS

SIX

Ricoeur and Levinas
Solicitude in Reciprocity and Solitude in Existence

Patrick L. Bourgeois

Paul Ricoeur's recent ethico-moral project, culminating in three of the last four chapters of *Oneself as Another*, consists in polarizing the ethical philosophies of Aristotle and Kant, and integrating a critically adjusted version of each into a unique and encompassing ethical framework. Within this entire enterprise he likewise develops many opposing polarities which he similarly proceeds to interarticulate and appropriate into a coherent position. One such opposition is that between the exteriority at the heart of the ethical philosophy of Emmanuel Levinas and the interiority of Husserl's transcendental philosophy. And within this context he employs elements of Heidegger's existential analysis of Dasein to flesh out the way of a satisfactory interarticulation, from which he appropriates his own position.

It is within this context that the accusation has been made that Ricoeur is too severe in his critique of Levinas. Although we must concede to this accusation in a qualified way, such an admission must not prevent us from appreciating the fullness and the richness of Ricoeur's contemporary ethico-moral philosophy, especially in the light of the recent contrasting works on deconstruction and ethics.[1] I intend in this chapter to enter this present conversation on deconstruction and ethics by proposing a complex thesis: first, that Ricoeur's critique of Levinas is indeed a bit too severe, but when understood in his own context, the place of this critique in his overall project of an ethico-moral foundation and principle comes to light. It will be seen that Levinas's own position already contains in principle a fundamental dimension that Ricoeur wants to supply, even though it is in need of further development. This then becomes the context for adjusting Ricoeur's interpretation in deference to Levinas, but without altering Ricoeur's own position. Thus, after investigating Ricoeur's critique of Levinas and briefly defending Levinas's own position, I will attempt to work toward interarticulating the positions of Ricoeur and Levinas, incorporating both the solitude of interiority and the solicitude that Ricoeur incorporates from Heidegger. This leads into the second part of my thesis, arising from the treatment of the first: that Ricoeur, precisely by incorporating an essential element from Levinas, provides a viable ethics as an alternative to postmodern deconstruction.

At the outset, however, it must be admitted that Ricoeur's and Levinas's projects are entirely different and somewhat opposed. For, from Levinas's point of view, it could be claimed that Ricoeur's whole enterprise fits into the context of totality, thus constituting precisely what Levinas intends to interrupt with infinity. Even in this apparent opposition, however, it must be admitted that Ricoeur's project, always considered to be ethical, has certain explicit affinities with that of Levinas. For Ricoeur has constantly adhered to the need in ethics precisely for Levinas's "face to face," even contending that ethics has its beginning in the second person's recognition of the other's will and freedom. And, on the other side, Ricoeur says that he has not ever assumed Levinas's ontology of totality, showing how Levinas restricts identity to the point that it "results that the self, not distinguished from the I, is not taken in the sense of the self-designation of a subject of discourse, action, narrative, or ethical commitment" (OA, 335). I believe it is here, with the notion of totality, that the difficulty between them is found. And Levinas's notion of totality in the context of the identity of the self needs to be extended, just as Ricoeur's interpretation of Levinas regarding the place within interiority for an encounter with the other will be adjusted. It is to Ricoeur's critique that we must now turn.

Ricoeur contends that Levinas, with his powerful message of responsibility elicited within the face to face epiphany of the other, describes the other as so separate, isolated, and solitary that no real encounter is possible without a supplementary dimension to give a basis for a response of responsibility, one that makes it possible. In spite of an intense respect for Levinas, Ricoeur has found the account of the face to face incapable of establishing the relation required for such a response. He, rather, sees Levinas's entire philosophy as resting "on the initiative of the other," but this initiative establishes no relation. According to Ricoeur's terse formulation, "E. Levinas's entire philosophy rests on the initiative of the other in the intersubjective relation. In reality this initiative establishes no relation at all, to the extent that the other represents absolute exteriority with respect to an ego defined by the condition of separation. The other, in this sense, absolves himself of any relation. This irrelation defines exteriority as such" (OA, 188–189). It is this lack of relation that defines exteriority. It seems that even in the contention by Levinas that escaping the solitude of existence, in the face to face encounter, involves a glimpse of the infinite, its trace in the face. There is no possibility for such a response, because there is no possibility of a relation that would allow it or elicit it.

Ricoeur's reading of Levinas involves a move from *Totality and Infinity*[2] to *Otherwise than Being*,[3] showing the development of this point in Levinas to the point of exaggeration. This reading interprets the role of the self before the encounter with the other face to face as "a stubbornly closed, locked up, separate ego" (OA, 337);[4] the other is an "absolute exteriority which can present itself to the separate ego by the epiphany of the face."[5] This hyperbole of the separation is carried further in the notion of the "the substitution" in *Otherwise than Being*. Ricoeur contends that here Levinas's hyperbole reaches the point of paroxysm when "Levinas speaks about responsibility which 'under accusation by everyone' goes to the point of substitution of the I for the Other. Here the other is no longer, as in *Totality and Infinity*, the master of justice, he is 'the offender, who, as offender, no less requires the gesture of pardon and expiation'" (OA, 338).[6] In this later account a subject becomes a hostage.[7] In spite of Peter Kemp's criticism of Ricoeur's reading of Levinas from *Otherwise than Being* to *Totality and Infinity*, it seems that Ricoeur's reading of Levinas in terms of the later work is justified, in that Levinas's thought should be assumed to develop and become more mature so that the later thought is contained in the earlier, at least in some form.[8] According to Richard Cohen's view of the progression of Levinas's view of alterity, Ricoeur is not wrong in interpreting back to *Totality and Infinity* from *Otherwise than Being*. What is wrong, however, is that Ricoeur overlooked something in *Totality and Infinity* presupposed by the epiphany of the face: that is the role of other people in interiority, with its economy, enjoyment, and hospitality. The face to face, even in *Totality and Infinity*, presupposes this life with others. The precise point for Levinas is that the face to face goes beyond this—and so does the epiphany in *Otherwise than Being*. And, for the face to face encounter, the two, the same and the other, must be separate and exterior to one another or there is no infinite beyond the totality.

In an attempt to do justice to Levinas's position, independent of Ricoeur's critique, two basic points need to be explicitly laid out: first, transcendence in Levinas's sense requires that the two terms (persons) be external to each other, or there is no real transcendence in the face to face; and second, that interiority or totality in Levinas's sense already contains a capacity for relation with the other, as mentioned above. There is an exteriority already there that makes the exteriority of transcendence possible, without jeopardizing the transcendence of the latter. In addition, the two-sided dimension of desire further illuminates these two issues.

Even if a place stressed for the possibility of an encounter, the two terms dealt with in *Totality and Infinity* must be external to one another *in the strong sense*. Otherwise, there is only all-encompassing totality at the expense of exteriority. To obliterate this is to destroy the possibility of any relation between the totality and the face of the other. Levinas has correctly indicated, than, that we cannot characterize the other as a reality that can be "integrated" or 'sublated' into any consciousness, spirit, or other form of interiority."[9] Yet, Levinas admits the transitive relation in which we live, but indicates that: "I *am* not the Other, I am all alone. It is thus the being in me, the fact that I exist, my *existing*, that constitutes the absolutely intransitive element, something without intentionality or relationship. One can exchange everything between beings except existing."[10] In developing his view of solitude of existing, Levinas is pitting himself against Heidegger, for whom Dasein is transcendence and being-in-the-world with others, but, from Levinas's point of view, all within totality. Further, when Phillipe Neno asked Levinas regarding the ethical relation making us escape this solitude, Levinas shot back immediately regarding the infinite that, "I am not afraid of the word God, which appears quite often in my essays. To my mind the infinite comes to the signifyingness of the face. The face *signifies* the Infinite." This infinite is insatiable, it is the "exigency of holiness."[11] Thus, it can be seen that Levinas, with his complex statements of solitude and infinity, is clear in emphasizing that solitude is a mark of the fact of being, and being, rather than solitude, is what one must escape.[12] He further affirms that *Time and the Other* represents an attempt to escape from this isolation of existing, as the preceding book, *Existence and Existents*, signifies an attempt to escape from the "there is."[13] And it is precisely this "escape" character of Levinas that must not be lost. For Levinas, the fact of being is private, and existence alone cannot be communicated, cannot be shared as such. "Solitude thus appears here as the isolation which marks the very event of being."[14] And we come back to the affirmation of the transitive dimension. We can indeed be with others through sight, touching, sympathy, etc. Yet, although these are all transitive, we cannot be the other. The pivotal question for the present discussion is whether saying that solitude is a mark of existence, and that it is being that we must escape can give a proper possibility for a response of responsibility to the other, in alterity. Is the other so other that a relationship is impossible? Must something further be supplied to Levinas's view to make the face to face possible?

Ricoeur, of course, does not exclude the fact that the two terms, the same and the other, or interiority (totality) and exteriority (infinity), must be external to each other, even though at times he seems to be oblivious to this point. For he cannot employ Levinas's face to face with the other in his own polarization of Levinas and Husserl unless he maintains the exteriority of the terms as the main point of Levinas's *Totality and Infinity* before he integrates these oppositions within his own developed position. It is in this general movement that Ricoeur is certainly not oblivious to the required exteriority of the other. His critique challenges the other main point, claiming that interiority or the totality has no base for being called by the epiphany of the face of the other. The positive contribution of Ricoeur is that he expands Levinas in a needed direction to round out and render explicit the place in the subject for such a response as solicitude and self-esteem, as will be seen. These, however, from Levinas's point of view remain within the context of totality of the subject. And likewise, Ricoeur's fundamental point in *Oneself as Another* presents a complex identity not found as such in Levinas, a point to which Ricoeur explicitly adverts in his comments on Levinas. Let us now turn to the second point of Levinas's view mentioned above.[15]

Ricoeur's omission mentioned above is precisely what Kemp is indicating in accusing Ricoeur of having missed an equilibrium among the levels of analysis that allows *Totality and Infinity* to make sense out of a separation. This equilibrium allows for the separation between ethical existence and pre-ethical life to be without contradiction. In *Totality and Infinity*, according to Kemp, there are three levels of description of existence, none of which excludes the others: "that of enjoyment and habitation (called 'Interiority and Economy'); that of the face (called 'Exteriority and the Face'); and that of love and fecundity (called 'Beyond the Face')." Kemp goes on to show on the first level how the other is included in the enjoyment of life, but not strictly as face. The other is seen to be "present in intimacy and sweetness, in familiarity and feminity."[16] He goes on to say the same about the analysis by Levinas of the economy of labor in the home, which can become a home of hospitality. But the hand may be "a manipulator, and one may close one's house instead of opening it to the poor and the stranger."[17] In these cases, the same closes in on itself, "so that interiority and the economy of the home cannot constitute an ethics. Indeed, it is only the face entering from the exteriority which assigns us to responsibility."[18]

Even in the preface of *Totality and Infinity* Levinas has already set the stage for this insight in the context of eschatology, where a continuity between totality and that which is outside the totality can be clearly seen. Levinas says explicitly that "this 'beyond' the totality and objective experience" is "reflected *within the totality and history, within experience.* The eschatological, as the 'beyond' of history, arouses them (beings), and calls them forth to their full responsibility."[19] Yet, in the very context of establishing the connection, Levinas is quick to indicate that the seeds of a break are already within this totality. For, as he says: "The first 'vision' of eschatology... reveals the very possibility of eschatology, that is, the breach of the totality, the possibility of a *signification without a context.*"[20]

Levinas, in preserving this distinctness or separation between totality and infinity, has overstressed the identity of the same or interiority at the expense of what Ricoeur has always supported as the alterity within an identity of a self. Levinas consequently passes over the twofold sense of identity in Ricoeur's account of the identity of the same and the identity of the self: *idem* identity and *ipse* identity. Although his recent *Oneself as Another* is his most explicit and best development of this break within the reflecting existent, Ricoeur has been articulating in one way or anther this view since the beginning of his writings, coming to emphasize this aspect of reflective philosophy in the Yale Terry Lectures followed by the book on Freud. Here in *Oneself as Another*, he has developed explicitly the alterity within oneself, which, in our present context, allows a mediation between oneself and the other. It is true that Levinas would certainly consider this whole project of reflective philosophy of Ricoeur to be a matter of totality and identity of self, but he would here indeed sell Ricoeur short, for Ricoeur is quite correct in stating that Levinas has no such dual sense of self-identity, but a rather simple same. This, even for Ricoeur, does not preclude the need for the exteriority of the other mentioned above in order to have a transcendence in the call of the other in the face to face epiphany. And that is perhaps the point Ricoeur most admires in Levinas, the transcendence of the face to face which entails an encounter between two independent and solitary existents. In this sense, Ricoeur does not want to exclude the solitude of each individual, a solitude that cannot be overcome. Yet that is not the end of the issue. For he considers the solicitude of which Levinas's position does not take account to be equiprimordial. Yet, in defense of Levinas, in spite of what has been said, perhaps one could stretch the point and consider both of Ricoeur's senses of identity to be collapsed in Levinas's same, which must be somehow identical with itself independently of an encounter with the other. This point is possibly borne out by Peperzak's observation that this "self-identity of Me is... the concrete activity of self-identification through which I establish myself as inhabitant and owner of my world..."[21] The point to be emphasized here is that the very project of *Totality and Infinity* attempts to establish the separation and difference between totality as same and the infinity as other, thus refusing to encompass them both within the same horizon of totality.[22] It is precisely this point that Ricoeur tends to overinterpret when looking to the interiority's inability to respond, missing something of that dimension in Levinas's own *Totality and Infinity*.

Ricoeur and Levinas both similarly take a positive attitude toward desire, which requires a transformation of the treatment of Kant. First, in liberating the will from its identity with the Kantian pure practical reason, overcoming Kantian epistemological priority, they both give a more positive place for desire. Desire is thus redeemed from its role of pollution and defilement and rather takes on a positive role in the activity of the will and in action in general. It is in this context that the double-sidedness of desire must be considered in the face to face transcendence.

It is the double-sidedness of desire that indicates the transcendence in the epiphany of the face and the possibility within interiority for the epiphany of exteriority. On the first side of desire, the satisfaction of needs stands within the economy of totality. Levinas employs the experience of enjoyment as a fulfilled need on the affective level to highlight the isolation of the enjoying subject. Someone else cannot feel my pleasures and pains, which confirms the enjoying subject in its identity with itself. Such being at home with oneself separates from all other as a unique and original substance not absorbed by the continuity of the universe. The opposition between the interior and the exterior must not be interpreted in terms of the traditional opposition between the ego and its world or between subject and object.

> Through its needs and its enjoyment, but also through representation and objectifying knowledge, the solitary ego is related to the "exteriority" of elements, equipment, things, and objects, but *this* "exteriority" cannot resist the ego's encompassing capacity of appropriation and integration. The exteriority revealed by the face is that by which the alterity of the Other escapes from the dimension where interiority and exteriority, subject and object, mind and matter, traditionally are opposed and put into contradiction or mediated dialectically as moments of a differential whole.[23]

The face of the other is an expression that cannot be reduced to my world nor to the task of self-realization; "it is the interdiction of killing this vulnerable defenseless, and naked other in front of me."[24]

On the other side of desire is the concrete way of transcendence to the other, but this is not a desire that satisfies a need, for that remains within the context of totality and focuses on relations with others that do not yet involve transcendence in the fullest sense. This whole phenomenon is recast in relation to desire that is not the satisfaction of a need.[25] Rather than grasped in fulfilled satisfaction, this aspect of desire cannot be integrated, and thus is transcendent and exterior. Hence, the other, not represented or comprehended, does not become something that is mine. Thus, for Levinas, this desire does not have the structure of intentionality. "It is, thus, neither the natural tendency that was thematized in Aristotle's ethics as a teleological striving for self-realization nor a nostaligic 'eksisting' toward a contentment that—although delayed—could fulfill the longing subject and bring it to its rest."[26] In a sense, the will and desire reach out toward an object or person as it is, while cognition brings something into the subject, into interiority. The desired thus remains transcendent and, as such, exterior. This is an essential point of Levinas.

The crucial aspect of this side of desire is the fact that it shows an essential impossibility of fusion or union. The desired has one thing in common with death, that both are absolutely other, so that neither death nor the other can take place within the unfolding of my possibilities. This is because desire and the desired are insatiate and insatiable, so that the distance separating them cannot be abolished. It is precisely this double-sidedness of desire as separation and relation that, preserving the exteriority of the two terms and thus allowing for transcendence in the epiphany of the face, opens the space for an analysis of human existence as two-dimensional reality. Here, we follow Peperzak, who agrees in substance with the point made above from Kemp. First, "as separated individuals, we are independent and egocentric, centers and masters of an economy that is also an egonomy." Second, "as transcending toward the Other, we live in a different dimension, the structure of which is made transcendence, alterity, and the impossibility of totalization and identification." The difficulty of Levinas's enterprise, especially in this context of Ricoeur's interpretation, "lies in the task of showing—in the form of a thematic, and thereby necessarily gathering, discourse—that gathering, coherence, and unity do not constitute the ultimate horizon of such a discourse, and that otherness, separation, and transcendence are irreducible to any unity."[27]

From what has already been considered above about the exteriority within interiority, Ricoeur's main point of critique of Levinas, that there is no place within interiority for a response to the face of the other, must be mitigated in the light of what has been seen in Levinas's own view. Ricoeur's critique overemphasizes the exteriority at the expense of this very possibility of relation to the transcendent other as within interiority. Again, it must be emphasized that *Totality and Infinity* was written to emphasize the exteriority of the face of the other precisely as a break with interiority. This however does not necessarily preclude some place within totality for the experience of the face of the other. In a sense, the other is already included in the enjoyment of life, in economy, and in hospitality, but not strictly as face, which remains transcendent. But here we have a place to anchor such an epiphany of the face. And it is only the face entering from the exteriority that "assigns us to responsibility."[28] For Levinas, the face breaks with the usual cultural meaning and hence calls into question the horizon of the world. As Bernasconi observes: "[N]o face can be approached with empty hands and closed home,' is Levinas's way of saying that the relation with the absolutely Other who paralyzes possession presupposes economic existence and the Other who welcomes me in the home. Thus in the movement parallel to that found in the account of representation and enjoyment, Levinas reverses the movement by which it seemed that the face of the Other was being made an ultimate ground. Hence the intimacy of the home is the 'first concretization.' "[29]

The only adequate response to the revelation of the absolute in the face is respect, generosity, and donation. It is because the other's face is naked, that it commands and obligates. The other's emergence is the "refutation of my egoism and therewith the fundamental dispossession that is needed for the possibility of universalization and objectification by putting the world of things in common.... The face-to-face of a living discourse is the concrete way in which the fundamental relation is practiced. It is neither mediated nor otherwise preceded by an original 'we' or 'being-with': on the contrary, all forms of association or community are founded in the relation of the Same and the Other."[30] Thus, the tension between the views of Levinas and Ricoeur comes to the fore, for it is to this very Heideggerian context castigated by Levinas that Ricoeur wants to turn for his expansion upon Levinas's doctrine. Thus, Ricoeur has to adjust Levinas here, since he advocates Heidegger's solicitude and also self-esteem and need of others as the place of the possibility for a response, which is supposedly cut off by the lack of relation due to separation, isolation, and solitude of the same. We must turn back now to Ricoeur's critique in the light of this further development of Levinas's thought in order to see what legitimacy his remarks have, and then to see how Ricoeur, enlightened by Levinas, proffers a more viable ethics than that of postmoderns, who are influenced by Levinas, yet want to divest his ethics of any real ethical relation.[31]

Ricoeur's critique of Levinas regarding the separation and exteriority of the other and the initiative from the other as incapable of establishing the relation allowing a response of responsibility takes place within the context of bringing two entirely different directions of movement together: the movement from the other (exteriority) to me (interiority); and the movement of inwardness toward the other. Ricoeur admits having to adjust each of these views. But what cannot be overlooked is that for Levinas the relation is between two that are external to one another, and not reducible to the totality of the same. The stress on the separation, isolation, solitude, exteriority keeps the distance between the two as other than a mere opposition within the context of totality. Further, it must be kept in mind that Ricoeur is not entirely oblivious to this, since his negative comment on Levinas's view of "totality" shows that he sees the alterity between the infinite and totality not to require such an interpretation of totality as so closed up.

Ricoeur, in interpreting the face as the "master of justice," since, as Levinas says, it forbids murder and commands justice, and is thus the source of the injunction, immediately contrasts its dissymmetry with the reciprocity of friendship. Although not mentioned here, his own view puts justice consequent upon friendship in the formation of communities, following Aristotle. Perhaps Levinas would respond that the face to face does not require friendship, and his alterity as a call elicits the response of responsibility. But, it must be admitted that these are two different contexts of discourse: one of transcendence; the other of the framework of ethics. And within the first context of discourse, Ricoeur questions whether the injunction, to be heard and received, must not call first for a response that compensates for the dissymmetry of the face-to-face encounter without which the exchange would be broken off. In other words, the other's initiative, to be reciprocated, must somehow free the capacity for giving (OA, 189). He suggests that goodness could spring forth in a being who does not detest himself to the point of being unable to hear the injunction from the other. And the goodness, for Ricoeur, is connected to the aim at the good life, which is often tied to doing for others out of regard for them.

In the context of Ricoeur's own conviction of the priority of the ethical over the moral, Levinas's language of summons and injunction seems already too moral in a way similar to Kant in relation to Aristotle: that is, the ethical is the foundation of the moral, and the injunction, duty, and the law should not arise on the ethical horizon too soon. Ricoeur delves below moral duty to find a latent "ethical sense" (OA, 190) which can be invoked in cases of "undecidable matter of conscience" (OA, 190). It must be remembered that Ricoeur, in the seventh and eighth studies of *Oneself as Another*, polarizes Aristotelian ethics of virtue and Kantian morality of obligation, showing all the while the more fundamental dimension of the ethical aiming at or seeking of the good life. It is clear, then, why solicitude of the ethical is presupposed for the injunction: the critique of Kant in the eighth study could well be applied to Levinas, that the injunction is invoked too soon, even with the substitution of the face and the infinite for the Kantian pure rational moral law. Thus, in this present context, it is clear why Ricoeur shows that Levinas needs the ability to respond and the ability for some kind of reciprocity based on solicitude, which itself is caught up in seeking the good life or human good.

But one has to admit that, in defense of Levinas, even Ricoeur has recognized the basic dimension of the face to face for ethics. And earlier in *Oneself as Another*, before confronting the position of Levinas, Ricoeur has already laid bare the notion of self-esteem latent within and intrinsic to the ethical aiming at the good life, from which he now extracts, or within which he interprets, a basic solicitude having the status of a "benevolent spontaneity" (190). Such benevolent spontaneity is the basis of a receiving at the same level as being called to responsibility in acting in accordance with justice, which is presupposed by any response of responsibility. This reciprocity, or receiving and reaching, is not the same as the equality of friendship, but it does compensate for the dissymmetry. Although the whole of the Aristotelian framework eventually comes to light in reflection as the prerequired framework for morality, it does not necessarily get the first focus within a philosophical reflection. And even for Ricoeur, as has been seen, it is freedom in the second person or the face of other in the personal relation that begins ethics and takes on the connotation of transcending the values of our culture and times. Further, it is violence and evil that demand that the limit of the Aristotelian framework is recognized.[32]

Ricoeur contends that it is the search for equality across inequality which establishes the place of solicitude in ethics. Solicitude bespeaks a lack belonging to self-esteem, as the reflexive moment of the wish for the good life, constituted with a lack evolving with a need, a need for friends, and giving rise to the awareness of the self among others. Thus, it is seen that solicitude is not external to self-esteem, but is constituted as a moment of self-esteem in its lack and need.

Ricoeur sees another inequality emerging from the figure of the other as master of justice in suffering, which takes the form not merely of pain, but of reduction or destruction of the power for acting or being able to act. Again, the other seems to be reduced to receiving, and the self who responds is again the one who gives. Ricoeur, however, sees a subtle form of giving emerging from the very weakness of the one suffering. "A self reminded of the vulnerability of the condition of mortality can receive from the friend's weakness more than he or she can give in return by drawing from his or her own reserves of strength" (OA, 191). Here, magnanimity enters. On this phenomenological level, feelings must be considered as affects that enter into motivation. This in Aristotle's context of "disposition." And it is feelings (here as affects) in solitude that are revealed in the self by the other's suffering and by the moral injunction (OA, 191). For Ricoeur, "[T]his intimate union between the ethical aim of solicitude and the affective flesh of feelings seems to me to justify the choice of the term 'solicitude'" (OA, 192). Thus, it is seen that, between the extreme poles, in the call to responsibility the initiative comes from the other, and in sympathy for the sufferer, the initiative comes from the living self, where a quasi friendship appears as a midpoint in which the sufferer and sympathizer share the same wish to live together (OA, 192).[33]

In the tenth study, in accord with his own dialectical procedure, Ricoeur polarizes the most extreme positions, finds a crack by means of which to open them, and brings out something implicit that allows a rapprochement, or better put, an interarticulation that, as he works it out fully, becomes his unique position. His own position is constituted from elements of opposing positions that he critiques, adapts, and then creatively appropriates in a new and better integration. And it is noteworthy that the "analogical transfer" considered in the context of Husserl, not Heidegger, is somewhat independent of the movement from the other toward me, even though it intersects with it. Neither Husserl's nor Heidegger's accounts get to the necessary point of addressing the other's movement toward me, and that is precisely why they need the movement of Levinas analysis. I believe in fact that in Ricoeur's appropriation of this opposition, Levinas requires and supplies to a limited extent this ability of myself to receive and to approach the other; and that the accounts of both Husserl and Heidegger lack and require the other before their analysis closes themselves of from such an encounter. "It is here that the analogical transfer from myself to the other intersects with the inverse movement of the other toward me. It intersects with the latter but does not abolish it, even if it does not presuppose it" (OA, 335).

Ricoeur says: "At the origin of this movement [of the other toward me] lies a break. And this break occurs at the point of articulation of phenomenology and of the ontology of the 'great kinds,' the Same and the Other" (OA, 335). It misses the twofold sense of identity as *idem* identity and *ipse* identity. This is precisely the place where Kemp's remarks are relevant. The question for us is the status of this break, since Levinas does allow for it in principle as seen in the reading of those sections of *Time and Infinity* mentioned above. Ricoeur considers Levinas's account to so radically oppose the other and the same as to exclude his own twofold sense of identity, that of *ipse* and *idem*, so central to his position and to this *Oneself as Another*. This exclusion is the result of Levinas's ontology of totality that houses his view of the identity of the same. And this ontology of totality "results that the self, not distinguished from the I, is not taken in the sense of the self-designation of a subject of discourse, action, narrative, or ethical commitment" (OA, 335). It is the case that, even after the attempt made above to mitigate the point Kemp makes concerning the pre-ethical levels that are not exclusive of the ethical and its exteriority, they indeed still can be seen not to adequately supply this twofold sense of identity in which the self, considered as another, has a bridge across the gap between the self and the other. We have found, however, that there is a place at the point of the exteriority within interiority to graft Ricoeur's double view of the self, inclusive of the ipseity of the self as well as *idem* identity, mentioned above.

Ricoeur considers both the break effect of Levinas and the reduction to ownness in Husserl to stem from the use of hyperbole as the "systematic practice of excess" (OA, 337). In Ricoeur's mind this hyperbole is precisely the closing up of the inwardness of immanence of transcendental phenomenology. And Ricoeur sees Levinas's hyperbole to reach both the same and the other, so that first the closed, locked up separate ego, before the other is spoken of hyperbolically as absolute exteriority. Ricoeur goes on to interpret the even greater hyperbole of *Otherwise than Being* in the development about "substitution of the I for the Other" (OA, 338–341). The conclusion to this section on Levinas returns to the confrontation between Husserl and Levinas. He again emphasizes that there is no contradiction in the dialectical complementarity between the two movements: that of the other toward the same, and that of the same toward the other. These two movements do not annihilate one another "to the extent that one unfolds in the gnoseological dimension of sense, the other in the ethical dimension of injunction. The assignment of responsibility, in the second dimension, refers to the power of self designation, transferred, in accordance with the first dimension, to every third person assumed to be capable of saying 'I'. Was not this intersecting dialectic of oneself and the other than self anticipated in the analysis of the promise? If another were not counting on me, would I be capable of keeping my word, of maintaining myself?" (OA, 340–341). This is at the heart of Ricoeur's ethico-moral position.

In taking Ricoeur to task for a too severe criticism of Levinas, Kemp admits that Ricoeur's critique is not too severe if one agrees with Ricoeur that "grounding ethics requires one to ascribe to solicitude a more fundamental status than obedience to duty."[34] This is a critical point, for it focuses precisely on Ricoeur's basic aim: to provide a quasi Aristotelian ethical framework and an adjusted Kantian deontological principle. The total backdrop and context for this critique of Levinas is Ricoeur's own efforts to critique and open up Kantian ethics of duty or obligation to its proper grounding in an ethics or an ethos, coming from the opposed direction. And in this Ricoeur's critique makes sense. But both Ricoeur and Levinas disagree with Kant to the extent that they each remove the priority from the absolute a priori moral law given to pure practical reason; and each opens the way to the fundamental role of desire, liberated from the Kantian interpretation, as seen above. While Ricoeur wants to ground the obligation to law in the ethics of teleology, and in this context we could fix solicitude, Levinas wants to bring obligation alive in the concrete situation of the face to face, thus breaking out of totality, including even breaking out of the framework that Ricoeur is so careful to provide. Ricoeur's criticism of Kant can well be levied against Levinas in that he could be considered to bring up the injunction too soon, but he now has to supply for Levinas what he supplies for Kant, a foundation and a framework for ethics, which is precisely what he has intended all along. Although in reflecting on the moral situation one might first begin with the transcendence of the "face to face," this beginning does not supply an adequate foundation for ethical life, which has transpired at a basic level long before this reflection catches it in the act, so to speak. And this is precisely where Ricoeur incorporates a quasi Aristotelian teleological dimension into the ethicomoral situation. And while Ricoeur might want to add this to Levinas, and rightly so, it can be found that in the context of totality, Levinas has already to some extent included the situation that makes the "face to face" possible within totality.

Retaining Levinas's responsibility within Ricoeur's ethicomoral integration allows Ricoeur's place of receptivity to be integrated with an element of Levinas's view of totality, the latent exteriority. But this must preclude any subordination of Levinas's exteriority of the face and infinity to the totality, which he so consistently and rigorously avoids, and which would falsify or remove precisely the uniqueness of his view of alterity. In accepting the role of solicitude in human existence, Ricoeur has developed a place within interiority that really allows a response to the face of the other. And in doing so, he has accounted for a central, indeed, the central point of Levinas, that a breakthrough—a break out—out of the "totality" of traditional philosophy is necessary for there to be a face to face encounter. This is precisely what Ricoeur has done in interarticulating the two movements of Husserl and Levinas. And incorporating this alterity of the other is not entirely alien to Ricoeur's previous work, for he has encountered similar elements within his recent philosophy. For instance, in his development of time in *Time and Narrative*, he has focused upon and accounted for the alterity of cosmic time.

So too here, the exteriority of the other is outside the domain of the Heideggerian or Husserlian world, and of Levinas's totality. This is precisely the element of Levinas that must not be jeopardized in our present expansion of Levinas's view in order to clarify how a relation is possible within interiority. And, I dare say, Ricoeur seems to want to embrace this face to face in indicating it as the place where ethics really begins. And it is precisely in accepting the alterity of the other that he has taken a positive element in agreement with Levinas, a point that even deconstruction likes. But this affinity with deconstruction cannot be exaggerated, for, in this context of even a mitigated deconstruction, Levinas's account of the ethical relation is lost to the deconstructive process, so that what remains is only the obligation of deconstructing. And nothing of Ricoeur's undertaking as a project of ethicomoral philosophy, except this same alterity, which he shares with Levinas, can survive this deconstructive process.[35]

Ricoeur's use and adjustments of Levinas in a dialectic with Heidegger-Husserl provides an ethics of responsibility and obligation as an alternative to postmodern deconstructive writings on/against ethics. In this, he has a basic rapport with the position of Levinas, which can be seen from what has been said. Due to his critique of and expansion of the Kantian philosophy, Ricoeur is able to interarticulate the ethical as encompassing the aim of an accomplished life with the moral as encompassing the actualization of the ethical aim in norms that are characterized at once by "claims to universality and by an effect of constraint" (OA, 170). Following from his critique of Kant's practical reason and freedom, and from the expansion of Kantian themes, Ricoeur is able to turn in a positive way to a priority of the teleological, putting into place the evaluative element of Aristotelian ethics to subtend the moral imperative of Kant, Levinas, and deconstruction. As to the positive element of deconstruction, Ricoeur's recent dwelling on alterity of cosmic time and his addressing the alterity of the other of Levinas in the tension that he sees between Husserlian inwardness and Levinas's exteriority reveals the alterity the face to face manifests beyond interiority. He has clearly appropriated a certain positive element from Levinas in terms of the alterity of the other, the epiphany of the face, and its assignment of responsibility. Ricoeur and Levinas, against the so-called deconstructive ethics that deconstructs the ethical relation, both invoke the face to face of the personal other at the heart of ethical response.[36] Ricoeur's rich and full treatment of ethico-moral philosophy, entailing the points above, and because of his positive relation to Levinas, emerges as one of the most viable ethics today in contrast to deconstructive ethics, which is hardly an ethics.

NOTES

1. It is my contention, not to be developed here, that Ricoeur's ethics, instructed by Aristotle, Kant, and the entire tradition of philosophy, even postmodern deconstruction, proffers a very viable contemporary ethics. This would contrast his work with that of postmodern deconstruction especially that of Derrida. Some recent secondary literature to which this relates by contrast are the following: John D. Caputo's, *Against Ethics* (Bloomington: Indiana University Press, 1993); Drucilla Cornell's *The Philosophy of Limit* (New York and London: Routledge, 1992); and Simon Critchley's *Deconstructive Ethics: Derrida and Levinas* (Oxford and Cambridge: Blackwell, 1992). These works all respond to the dialogue between Levinas and Derrida. Cf. especially Jacques Derrida's "Violence and Metaphysics: An Essay on the Thought of Emmanuel Levinas," in *Writing and Difference* (Chicago: University of Chicago Press, 1978). It is this essay by Derrida that in some measure put Levinas's work on ethics in the heart of postmodern discussions.

2. Emmanuel Levinas, *Totality and Infinity: An Essay on Exteriority*, translated by Alphonso Lingis (Pittsburgh: Duquesnes University Press, 1969), hereafter referred to as *TI*.

3. Emmanuel Levinas, *Otherwise than Being or Beyond Essence*, translated by Alphonso Lingis (The Hague: Martinus Nijhoff, 1974), hereafter referred to as *OB*.

4. See Peter Kemp, "Ricoeur between Heidegger and Levinas: Original Affirmation between Ontological Attestation and Ethical Injunction," in *Philosophy and Social Criticism* 21 (1995) 56. See OA, 337.

5. Kemp, "Ricoeur between Heidegger and Levinas," 54.

6. See also Kemp, "Ricoeur between Heidegger and Levinas," 55.

7. Levinas, OB, 112. Kemp, 55.

8. It is clear from reading the introduction of Cohen to *Time and the Other*, trans. Richard Cohen (Pittsburgh: Duquesne University Press, 1987), hereafter referred to as *TO*, that the later thought is contained in the earlier. Following Cohen's view of the progression of alterity, Ricoeur is not wrong in interpreting back to *TI* and *OB*. Kemp, on the other hand, makes a point of indicating that one should read Levinas in such a way as to give more importance to *TI* than to *OB*.

9. Adriaan Peperzak, *To the Other: An Introduction to the Philosophy of Emmanuel Levinas* (West Lafayette: Purdue University Press, 1993), 120.

10. Levinas, *TO*, 42. Quoted, too, in *Ethics and Infinity*, trans. Richard Cohen (Pittsburgh: Duquesnes University Press, 1985), 59, hereafter referred to as *EI*.

11. Levinas, *EI*, 105.

12. Ibid., 59.

13. Ibid., 57.

14. Ibid., 57–58.
15. It is not possible here to do an in-depth study, but only to indicate certain focal points. An in-depth study would require a rather lengthy work.
16. Kemp, "Ricoeur between Heidegger and Levinas," 56.
17. Ibid., 55.
18. Ibid., 57.
19. Levinas, *TI*, 23.
20. Ibid.
21. Peperzak, *To the Other*, 136.
22. Ibid., 138.
23. Ibid., 161.
24. Ibid., 164.
25. Ibid., 133.
26. Ibid., 134.
27. Ibid., 135.
28. Kemp, "Ricoeur between Heidegger and Levinas," 56.
29. Robert Bernasconi "Rereading Totality and Infinity," in *The Question of the Other: Essays in Contemporary Continental Philosophy*, ed. Arleen Dallery and Charles E. Scott (Albany: State University of New York Press, 1989), 33–34. Quoting Levinas (*TI*, 172 and *TI*, 153).
30. Ibid., 145.
31. Robert Bernasconi, "Deconstruction and the Possibility of Ethics," in *Deconstruction and Philosophy: The Texts of Jacques Derrida*, ed. John Sallis (Chicago: University of Chicago Press, 1987), especially 135. Bernasconi admits that deconstruction (at least Derrida in "Violence and Metaphysics") does seem to preserve the ethical relation, but only in the sense of the thought of the ethical relation, not yet a practice, in its insistence that the logos of it is the impossible–unthinkable–unsayable. This, for Bernasconi, is deconstruction's rigorously holding to the limits of thinking. In this context, the ethical enactment lies especially in the refusal of deconstruction to take on the standpoint of critique, thus not passing judgment in its own voice on its own behalf. So understood, deconstruction as such cannot accept anything of the ethical, even the ethical relation as Levinas had it, and must deconstruct it in terms of the non-logocentrism, the ellipsis, of its own view. The only ethical relation allowed here is the impersonal deconstructive process itself.
32. Paul Ricoeur "The Problem of the Foundation of Moral Philosophy," *Philosophy Today* 28 (1978): 178 and 182–184.
33. Levinas does not give such a positive or prominent place to sympathy in his critique of Husserl. Richard Cohen points out that "it is at the level of the 'decency' of 'everyday life' then, that Levinas finds a place for the sympathy and pairing that he has rejected as ultimate constitutive of the inter-subjective relationship." In Cohen's footnote 62, p. 83 of *TO*. Alterity

is precisely what Levinas wants to emphasize, while Ricoeur is trying to round it out and make it more viable in taking Husserl's direction into account.

34. Kemp, "Ricoeur between Heidegger and Levinas," 55.

35. See note 28 above.

36. Although some deconstructionists such as Critchley and Cornell advance a deconstructive ethics, and hold onto the term, the ethics they allow amount to no more than the responsibility in the process of deconstruction.

SEVEN

Moral Selfhood
A Levinasian Response to Ricoeur on Levinas

Richard A. Cohen

INTRODUCTION

Given its title and subject-matter, it is no surprise that Paul Ricoeur's most recent work, *Oneself as Another (Soi-meme comme un autre)*, based on his 1986 Gifford Lectures, concludes with three discussions of the work of Emmanuel Levinas. No one more than Levinas has made the relation of self to other, as ethics, more central to philosophy. And now in *Oneself as Another* Ricoeur, too, wants to highlight the ethical character of selfhood and its intimate relation to the alterity of other persons. That the confrontation with Levinas strikes close to Ricoeur's efforts is underscored by the fact that Levinas appears at the two culminating moments of *Oneself as Another*: at the beginning (chapter 7) and at the end (chapter 10) of its fourth and concluding part on the moral and ontological character of the self. Furthermore, since its last chapter, chapter 10, was developed two years after the rest of the work, for the Cerisy Decade of 1988, it represents not only two more years of reflection on all the themes presented in 1986, but especially, as the text bears out, two more years of reflection on the criticisms of Levinas initiated in chapter 7. The object of this chapter is to show how and why Ricoeur criticizes Levinas, and how and why these criticisms miss their mark.

Oneself as Another is a dense, layered, complicated, and nuanced text. Ricoeur's overall critical intention is one shared by Levinas and by most contemporary thinkers, namely, to challenge the modern philosophical conception of selfhood determined as posited ego. In challenging selfhood qua posited ego, Ricoeur and Levinas share a further aim, but one that this time separates them from many of their philosophical contemporaries. Aiming to obviate the Cartesian "thesis of the indecomposable simplicity of the cogito" (19), they aim also to avoid the antipodal thesis, the "Nietzschean deconstruction" or "vertigo," as Ricoeur expresses it, "of the disintegration of the self" (19). To elaborate an alternative conception of selfhood than that of a posited ego, *Oneself as Another* is split into four related parts, based on four levels of meaning essential to selfhood: discursive (chapters 1 and 2); practical (chapters 3 and 4); narrative (chapters 5 and 6); and prescriptive (chapters 7 through 10). Each dimension of the self is approached from two points of view: the analytical and the hermeneutical. No wonder, then, that Ricoeur invokes and criticizes Levinas in part four, when he treats the prescriptive dimension of selfhood.

CHAPTER 7: "THE SELF AND THE ETHICAL AIM"

Ricoeur's first discussion of Levinas, whose thought centers on selfhood, alterity, and the ethical, occurs when Ricoeur first considers the moral dimensions of selfhood, beginning in chapter 7, entitled "The Self and the Ethical Aim." Chapter 7 is split into three subsections, based respectively on the three components of Ricoeur's "definition" of "ethical intention." "Ethical intention" is the cornerstone of moral selfhood, and hence the pinnacle of the entire conception of selfhood in *Oneself as Another*. "Let us define 'ethical intention,'" Ricoeur writes, "as *aiming at the 'good life' with and for others, in just institutions*" (172). These three clauses: (1) "aiming at the *good life*"; (2) "with and for others"; (3) "in just institutions," provide the topics of the three subsections of chapter 7. The number, relation, and movement between them is basically "Hegelian": starting with the self as moral character, one then moves to the alterity of moral sociality, to finally return to the reconciliation of moral self and other as justice. The discussion of Levinas in chapter 7 quite naturally occurs in its second subsection, on moral sociality.

The first of the three components of "ethical intention," "aiming at the good life," which I will call "moral character" for short, has the status of *primus inter pares*. Its primacy appears first in the fact that the other two components of moral life, moral sociality and justice, are part of its definition. Its primacy appears second and more deeply in the fact that establishing the primacy of moral character over moral sociality is the specific aim of chapter 7, and the basic reason Ricoeur criticizes Levinas, who in sharp contrast gives primacy to sociality. The primacy of moral character in ethics is reflectively grasped as the primacy of what Ricoeur calls "self-esteem." Ricoeur's argument is that the second component of moral life, moral sociality, only makes sense as "the articulation of this aim"—self-esteem—"in norms" (170). "Self-respect," the reflective grasp of this second component, is thus a development of and as such remains dependent upon "self-esteem."

The differences separating Ricoeur and Levinas are sharp. First, Ricoeur's hierarchy of self and other is exactly the reverse of Levinas's, for whom moral sociality precedes moral character. Second, Ricoeur equates moral sociality with normativity. For Levinas, in contrast, moral sociality does not by itself, or does not at first manifest itself as normativity. Normativity, for Levinas, is a conditioned development which appears later or consequent at the level of justice. The initial morality Levinas discerns emerging with sociality is "purer" or more stringent than normativity, if one can say this, commanding prior to and without commandments. To be sure, laws are a part of a developed morality, but they are not its initial moment. Levinas's antinomianism, though restricted, separates him from Ricoeur, and from Kant. The different way these two thinkers part company from Kant is instructive. Ricoeur gives precedence to moral character over moral sociality, and hence rejects Levinas, precisely because Ricoeur also insists, following Kant, but contra Levinas, on binding moral sociality to normativity. Ricoeur and Levinas agree, in other words, that norms are not the ground zero of morality; they part company over whether norms are or are not synonymous with moral sociality.

In the first subsection of chapter 7, on "aiming at the 'good life,'" Ricoeur examines Aristotle's account of virtue, friendship, and *phronesis*, in the *Nicomachean Ethics*. The analyses are complex and nuanced. What Ricoeur takes from them, however, to apply in the second subsection of chapter 7, "with and for Others," where Levinas appears, is less so. "From Aristotle," Ricoeur writes, "I should like to retain only the ethics of reciprocity, of sharing, of living together" (187), in a word, of mutuality. Mutuality serves a bridge from the first subsection on moral character to the second subsection on moral sociality because the mutuality of genuine friendship, as Ricoeur understands Aristotle, comes from two persons each aiming at the same good life, united by the same aim. The genuine friend, then, is in this respect actually "another self *[allos autos]*" (185). Thus conceived, mutuality is not an affirmation of the alterity of the other person, as it is in Buber, but rather a social or shared confirmation of the primacy of each person's correct aim or moral character.

In the second subsection of chapter 7, without altering its function as a bridge, Ricoeur shifts from Aristotle's notion of mutuality to his own more "inclusive concept of solicitude," as the basic meaning of the moral self in its ethical intention toward another. Constructively specifying the "equality" that informs Aristotelian friendship, Ricoeur conceives the sociality of solicitude on an economic model, based "principally," as he writes, "on the exchange between *giving* and *receiving*" (188). Even without the Kantian practical rule of noncontradiction, we can see why, following Aristotle's notion of equality or mutuality, Ricoeur equates social morality and normativity: norms regulate judgments regarding equality. Good solicitude, then, means equal exchange. Bad solicitude means unequal exchange. Proper solicitude, upon which the reflexive concept of self-respect is based, is thus "a fragile balance in which giving and receiving are equal, hypothetically." In contrast, if "in the initiative of exchange" (188) one or the other pole predominates, if the self's solicitous relation to the other is not mutual, reciprocal, or equal, to that extent moral sociality fails, and to that extent the self loses its self-respect.

It is precisely at this point, when speaking of bad solicitude as an imbalance between giving and receiving, that Ricoeur invokes Levinas. Levinas represents a radical imbalance: the extremity of all initiative coming from the other, the extremity whereby all is received and nothing is given. "Levinas's entire philosophy rests on the initiative of the other in the intersubjective relation" (188). Having situated Levinas thus, Ricoeur's argument is transparent: because Levinas has made extremity rather than mutuality the basis of ethics, his is surely a false and perhaps even an evil path. Even worse, Levinas's privileging of the other is so unbalanced, so extreme, as to be more than a moral impediment: it is a philosophical impossibility; it establishes no link at all.

So, first of all, Levinas mistakenly gives priority to moral sociality over moral character. Second, within the social domain, Levinas mistakenly exaggerates the initiative of the other, hence mistakenly gives priority to an unbalanced alterity over the balance of good solicitude. The impossibility of Levinas's position hinges on Ricoeur's unswerving allegiance to a Parmenidean-Hegelian conception of the nature and limits of relationality and transcendence. Levinas's fundamental error is to attempt, per impossible, to think what Hegel called "external relation," when in truth such an alleged relation is no relation at all, an "irrelation" (189), as Ricoeur calls it. Although Levinas seems to be in the good company of Kant and Plato on this point, for Ricoeur, as for Hegel, genuine philosophy must be limited to "internal" or "dialectical" relations, that is to say, relations whose terms do not in any irreducible sense exceed their relationality.

In the wrong on all three of the above requirements—begin with the self, link sociality and normativity, stay within internal relations—it follows that Levinas's essentially futile effort to upset the balance of solicitude results in a number of more specific but interrelated problems. Ricoeur isolates three, all having to do with excess: (1) The other person's exteriority is so excessive he/she is out of contact; (2) The separation of the self is so excessive, so passive, that it is inviolate, that is to say, again, out of relation; and finally (3) Reviving Derrida's 1964 criticism, violence and war, not morality, remain as Levinas's only avenues to breach the "irrelation" between self and other. The following citations from chapter 7 articulate these three lines of criticism:

> This [Levinas's unbalanced] initiate establishes no relation at all, to the extent that the other represents absolute exteriority with respect to an ego defined by the condition of separation. The other, in this sense, absolves himself of any relation. This irrelation defines exteriority as such. (188–189)
>
> The summons to responsibility has opposite it simply the passivity of an "I" who has been called upon . . . . Taken literally, a dissymmetry left uncompensated would break off the exchange of giving and receiving and would exclude any instruction by the face within the field of solicitude. (189)
>
> This is why the Other . . . has to storm the defenses of a separate "I." (190)

Such is Ricoeur's rejection of Levinas in chapter 7.

But far from deviating from or capitulating to the hegemony of the Parmenidean-Hegelian heritage of philosophy, Levinas's thought intends to directly challenge it. This challenge, as Ricoeur obviously recognizes, strikes at the heart of the meaning of selfhood. It is not at all likely, then, that Ricoeur's appeal to the logic of Parmenidean-Hegelian philosophy will carry much weight with a ontological deliberately and conscientiously set upon casting aside the gravity of this heritage. For Levinas the uniqueness of the ethical relation, and its importance for philosophy, is precisely that its terms, self and other, are both out of relation and in relation. Their "dephasing" or "diachrony" is the very force of ethics, not merely contrasting with but contesting the priorities of epistemology and ontology, determined as they are, and as Ricoeur would have all domains determined, by an attachment to internal and dialectical relations.

Levinas raises the priority of the encounter with the alterity of the other, ethical priority, to the status of the very humanity of the human. Humanity arises in moral responsibility. Moral responsibility, for its part, is inaugurated by overturning *conatus*, "perseverance in being," natural indifference to alterity. Radical alterity, far from leaving the self unmoved, as

Ricoeur suggests (relying on the circular or self-defensive requirements of epistemology), radically moves the self, "reconditions," "transubstantiates" its naturally selfish inclinations and autonomous syntheses into moral responsibility for the other. Levinas's responsive *"me voici,"* "Here I am,"[1] formula for the moral self, is not undercut by an allegedly deeper "Here I stand" (*"Icije me tiens"*; 339), Ricoeur's counterformula, but rather arises as morality arises: as a displacement, a hollowing out, a being-for-the-other, a "despite-oneself" *(malgré-soi)*, to invoke several of Levinas's formulae for the moral self.

In contrast, the moral self in society is for Ricoeur not a hollowing out, but rather the tragic (cf. 241–249) taking of a stand in the face of compossible moral alternatives. The tragic character of Ricoeur's moral self in society is not our primary concern, however. What is important is to note that for Ricoeur social alterity stimulates an *already* morally inclined solicitude, drawing out moral character by drawing upon what Ricoeur calls its *"benevolent spontaneity"* (190). This move is perplexing, however, and not only from a Levinasian point of view. We must ask a hard question: independent of sociality and the complexities of choice introduced therein, from whence is selfhood inclined to benevolence? With the notion of "benevolent spontaneity," do we not see Ricoeur succumbing, in company with such English moralists as Shaftesbury and Hutcheson before him, to an unwarranted moral optimism, to what Freud called "wishful thinking"? Ricoeur posits what he cannot prove. No wonder he will later, in chapter 10, rely on the moralistic language of "conscience," "attestation," and "conviction." No evidence supports his optimism, or, rather, equal evidence opposes it.

Only a transcendental argument (such as that which motivates Kant's *third* critique), which Ricoeur disclaims, could postulate the goodness of natural being as an explanation for morality. Levinas, in contrast, does not equivocate on this point: "No one is good voluntarily." Only the unassumable alterity of the other person has the moral force—though not the necessity—to convert, to shame the natural self into moral being. As for Ricoeur's related equation of social morality with a normative economic model, and the criticisms of Levinas that follow from this equation, it smacks of the procrustean bed—for Levinas, and for Ricoeur. Because he rejects external relation a priori and gives priority to character, Ricoeur argues: "On the basis of this benevolent spontaneity, receiving is on an equal footing with the summons to responsibility" (190). "This is why," he continues, "it is so important to us to give solicitude a more fundamental status than obedience to duty" (190). But why in the first place does Ricoeur limit the question of social morality to a choice between solicitude and norms? Levinas would argue, in contrast, that the moral status of both norms and solicitude depends on a prior opposition between natural indifference or perseverance (*conatus*) in being and moral responsiveness, between the for-itself and the for-others. *Conatus* plays a completely different role in Ricoeur's thought. Far from representing a morally reprehensible indifference to alterity, for Ricoeur *conatus* has only an epistemological function: the "priority of the *conatus* in relation to consciousness . . . imposes on adequate self-consciousness" the "very long detour" (317) of analysis and hermeneutics, that is, Ricoeur's program.

What is procrustean, then, for both Levinas and Ricoeur is the latter's supposition that giving priority to moral sociality means giving priority to moral norms, hence reducing alterity to moral law, and moral selfhood to obedience to duty. This fundamental misrepresentation is summed up in Ricoeur's reduction of the Levinasian other to a "master of justice" (189). We have seen Ricoeur's alternative economic model, but we must insist on our question regarding how the authority of the "good life" inclines solicitude. In contrast to the empty abstraction that allegedly results from Levinasian excess, Ricoeur's "benevolent spontaneity" is said to be concretely disciplined by means of "the self's recognition of the superiority of the authority enjoining it to act in accordance with justice" (190). That is to say, Ricoeur's concept of moral sociality requires that the self recognize the legitimate superiority, the authority, of what Gadamer in *Truth and Method,* to which Ricoeur refers (177 f. 8), calls "the legitimacy of prejudices" (TM, 246).[2] What Ricoeur refuses to accept is that without resorting to norms the authority of alterity in Levinas operates at an altogether different level than does Gadamerian authority. Gadamerian authority is epistemological. To cite from the page in *Truth and Method* to which Ricoeur refers, the other's "authority has nothing to do with obedience, but rather with knowledge"; the agent's recognition of the other's superiority is "an act of freedom and reason, which fundamentally acknowledges the authority of a superior because he has a wider view of things or is better informed, i.e., once again, because he has superior knowledge" (TM, 248). Levinas's objection (made years earlier to the entire ecstatic apparatus of Heideggerian fore-structure [*Vor-Struktur*]), is that the moral dimension of social encounter cannot be preserved against a critique of representational consciousness by deepening the meaning of knowing, incarnating knowing. Rather, the moral dimension of social encounter operates beneath and sustains all levels of understanding, precisely because—contra the Parmenidean-Hegelian heritage—it is an encounter with alterity as such.

For Levinas, as I have indicated, humanity and moral humanity arise together. Morality is neither a prior constituent nor a gloss added to an already constituted humanity. Rather, the other qua other and moral alterity emerge together: the only genuine other is the commanding-obliging other, the moral other. This level, Levinas would argue, must be presupposed by any analysis or hermeneutics of moral life. Without it one could not even begin to speak of such things as the goodness of the "good life," or the benevolence of spontaneity. Spontaneity, unless it is already socially conditioned, is neither benevolent nor malevolent but amoral—hence malevolent. The superiority of the other in an exchange of giving and receiving, even if based on the most careful epistemological assessment of the other's attributes, cannot be called moral, rather than simply economic, unless the moral dimension as such is already operative through a prior encounter with alterity as such.

It is because he misunderstands the level or significance of the alterity of the other in Levinas, that Ricoeur misunderstands, in addition, the passivity of the self that responds to alterity. The Levinasian self is not so separate as to be inviolate, simply passive, or, as Ricoeur would have it, the (im)possible object of violence and war. Rather, it is, as Levinas writes, "more passive than any receptivity," "more passive than any passivity." These superlative expressions do not refer to an inertia, since for Levinas the inertia of the self is its natural *conatus*. Rather they refer to the moral self's irreplacability, its nonsubstitutability, and to it inexhaustability. The moral self arises as pure subjection to the other, as a subjectivity irreplaceably subject, hence as "elected" by the other. While the *conatus* is *soi-même*, it-self, one-self, the moral self is *malgré-soi*, despite-itself, despite-oneself. In the face of the other, no one but myself, no one but me (*"moi"*), "I" am responsible. Not only is this fixing of the moral self, its irreplacability, extraordinary, but so too is its sufficiency. Just as the alterity of the other is irreducible and unassumable, so too the hollowing out of the moral self—its desire for goodness—is endless. What this means, concretely, is that the moral reserves of the self are in principle inextinguishable. Beyond giving or attempting to give food, shelter, clothing, employment, etc., that is, beyond giving *things*, and beyond the kind word, warm hand, or even silent company, that is to say, beyond any giving *of* the self, the responsibility of the self exceeds the very limits of finitude. The oneself of response goes all the way to giving the very self or the self, all the way to death, the ultimate self-sacrifice. One can be for-the-other all the way: one can die for another—such is the ultimate structure of morality, or the "unrelating relation" (*TI*, 295), as Levinas calls it, at the heart neither of knowledge nor being, but better, more demanding, of morality.[3]

CHAPTER 10: "WHAT ONTOLOGY IN VIEW?"

In chapter 10, more specifically in its second subsection, entitled "The Otherness of Other People," we find (335–341) the central and most extended critical discussion of Levinas in *Oneself as Another*. In addition to reasons already noted above, Levinas's prominence in this chapter is due to its level, approach, issue, and chief figure. The level is ontological. The approach is a "second-order discourse" (298), utilizing the "metacagories," as Ricoeur writes, of "the 'great kinds'; akin to the Platonic Same and Other" (298). The issue—by far the most complex and most inclusive, as it involves the very title of this work" (298)—"concerns the specific dialectical structure of the relation between selfhood and otherness" (298). The chief figure is Martin Heidegger, the *Dasein-analytic of Being and Time*, more specifically, the nature and role of conscience *(Gewissen)*.

Regarding the latter, an important way to grasp the difference separating Ricoeur and Levinas is in terms of their fundamentally different responses to Heidegger. First some similarities. Both thinkers acknowledge Heidegger's tremendous and inescapable contribution to philosophy, especially the brilliant phenomenological analyses of *Being and Time*. And neither thinker is a Heideggerian in any simple or straightforward sense, although Ricoeur is by far closer to Heidegger, as we shall see, than Levinas, who is not a Heideggerian at all. In criticizing Heidegger, too, Ricoeur and Levinas share a bond. Both find his thought morally deficient, especially his conception of the self. Rectifying this deficiency is the work of the third and concluding subsection of chapter 10 (341–355), entitled simply "Conscience," where Ricoeur will a second and final time engage Levinas critically. Despite their many agreements regarding Heidegger, it is precisely in their critical relation to his thought that Ricoeur and Levinas radically part company.

Though more intimate, Ricoeur's critical relation to Heidegger is on a par with his relations to other major figures in the history of philosophy. As one sees at each step of the way through *Oneself as Another*, Ricoeur takes up texts—of "Plato, Aristotle, Descartes, Spinoza, Leibniz, and so on" (298)— close to his position, in order to critically and creatively rework them to suit his own vision. We have witnessed this approach very briefly in relation to Aristotle's conception of virtue and friendship in the *Nicomachean Ethics*. Ricoeur gives credit to his "reinterpretations and reappropriations, thanks to a meaning potential left unexploited" (298). It is here precisely that we see Ricoeur's special methodological intimacy with Heidegger. His reconstructive approach to the history of philosophy, his revisionary manner of philosophizing, exploiting "meaning potential left unexploited," is precisely the approach taken by Heidegger, especially in his many works after *Being and Time*. So, while Ricoeur does indeed criticize Heidegger's results, specifically the moral deficiency of Dasein in *Being and Time*, he will do so in a Heideggerian manner. We shall have to see to what extent this deforms Ricoeur's alleged independence.

Levinas, in contrast, opposes both Heidegger's results *and* Heidegger's manner of thinking. Levinas does not tease out or put in "a meaning potential left unexploited" in Heidegger's *Dasein-analytic*, at the price of leaving its overall structure or issue intact, as does Ricoeur. Rather, he offers a radical alternative, and thereby criticizes Heidegger through and through. Displacing and recontextualizing all meanings to his own bent—which is another way of saying that Levinas's is a truly original thought—it follows that they are stripped of a Heideggerian sense. This difference is one between critique, an internal variation, and criticism, an external alternative. This difference explains why, despite Ricoeur's concluding moral reconstruction of Dasein's conscience, *Oneself as Another* ends where Heidegger's work ends, in ontology. In contrast, Levinas's work begins and ends elsewhere, in ethics.

Ricoeur's moral criticism of Heidegger aims no to overthrow Heidegger's conception of Dasein but to fix it, in a word, to moralize Dasein. Levinas's moral criticism of Heidegger, in contrast, intends not to fix Heidegger's conception of Dasein, but to oppose it—in the name of morality. Thus, Ricoeur, while standing within Heideggerian ontology, supplements and corrects it with morality, while Levinas, standing in an ethics outside Heideggerian ontology, uses morality to overthrow it. Obviously, then, Levinas's criticism of Heidegger is more radical than Ricoeur's critique. And yet, it is precisely for this greater radicality that Ricoeur takes Levinas to task, going so far as to deny the very possibility of Levinas's criticism.

Before turning to a detailed reckoning with Ricoeur's criticism of Levinas, a preliminary but disturbing perplexity must first be assuaged. Ricoeur begins his discussion of Levinas in chapter 10 stating that "we have reserved until this moment the encounter with the work of Emmanuel Levinas" (335). But obviously, as we have seen, this is not true. Ricoeur has already "encountered" the work of Emmanuel Levinas in chapter 7, and encountered it critically. An even greater perplexity with Ricoeur's statement emerges insofar as in chapter 10 Ricoeur reactivates several of the earlier criticisms found in chapter 7. What then has Ricoeur "reserved until this moment"? While only close examination of the criticisms proper can answer this question fully, two preliminary remarks help pave the way.

One answer, not especially deep, but worth noting, is that the repetition might simply result from the fact that chapter 10 was given as a free-standing lecture at Cericy-la-Salle in 1988, two years, that is to say, after chapter 7 had been given as part of the Gifford Lectures in Edinburgh. Inasmuch as criticism of Levinas is the culminating critical moment of the Gifford Lectures, and hence also of chapters 1 through 9 of *Oneself as Another*, there need be no surprise, really, that it is repeated and incorporated into the later ontological resurrection of the lectures. This reiteration would mark the importance of Levinas for Ricoeur.

A second, deeper reason has to do with the significance Ricoeur gives to his own work, the significance, that is to say, of doing ontology, and hence of chapter 10 and *Oneself as Another* as a whole. I have already noted this significance but want to underline that it is Ricoeur's. Shifting from the "first-order" discourse of chapters 1 through 9, to the "second-order" ontological discourse of chapter 10, does not simply mean that the latter is about the former. Ricoeur puts much more stock in his method of "reinterpretations and reappropriations." The difference is between the old and the new. Chapter 10, in other words, represents an "innovation" (299)—much like the Hegelian *Aufheben*, uplifting sublation—relative to the earlier first-order discourse, and indeed to all prior discourse, Levinas's included. The aim and result of *Oneself as Another*'s many "reinterpretations and reappropriations" of the history of philosophy is thus neither a dry "repetition" (299) nor an "aimless wandering" (299), but rather a creative development in the history of thought. Although I have characterized Ricoeur's relation to Heidegger as one of revision, rectification from within, Ricoeur sees his own reconstructions more grandly as fundamental innovations, indeed as fundamentally original thinking. Thus, Ricoeur's perplexing statement about reserving his encounter with Levinas for chapter 10 would mean, in this perspective, that here in this chapter Ricoeur sees himself opposing Levinas, opposing Levinas, that is, with Ricoeur's own proper or original thought.

For this reason, in addition to reviewing and challenging two explicit criticisms of Levinas found in subsection two, where (a) the charge of irrelation is renewed and (b) a new charge of hyperbole is introduced, what follows will review and challenge (c) the critical force of the positive alternative conception of selfhood as "being-enjoined," which Ricoeur develops in subsection three by creative supplementation of Heidegger's conception of conscience, and the explicit criticisms of Levinas found there, on the very last pages (354–355) of *Oneself as Another*.

Irrelation

Ricoeur's first and most fundamental criticism is familiar to us from chapter 7. It derives from what I have been calling the "Parmenidean-Hegelian" heritage of philosophy to which Ricoeur subscribes. The argument is that Levinas's account of the self and intersubjectivity is flawed, indeed impossible, because it makes the unforgivable error of trying to overstep the bounds of relationality per se. Levinas is guilty of the ultimate nonstarter in philosophy: treating a nonrelation as a relation. "No middle ground," Ricoeur writes, "no between, is secured to lessen the utter dissymmetry between the Same and the Other" (338). Here, as earlier, Ricoeur specifies this broad criticism in terms appropriate to his topic, namely, self and other. Because the Levinasian self is too separate, the other is taken to be too other, hence they cannot be put into relation. "Because the Same signifies totalization and separation, the exteriority of the Other can no longer be expressed in the language of relation" (336).

What the above citation makes clear is that for Ricoeur the basic flaw of Levinas's account is to have overly insularized, overly isolated, overly separated the self. The real truth, so Ricoeur argues, is that in order to receive the other, as the self surely does, the self must first have it own prior moral capacity of reception, its own prior moral self-subsistence. Such a prior capacity, as we have seen, is the key to Ricoeur's alternative conception of moral selfhood, and indeed of selfhood altogether. Although, in proleptic response, Levinas time and again refers to the self in terms of a passivity deeper than receptivity, there is an entire alternative avenue of response, having to do with eros, and more specifically with familiality.

This first answer, regarding the familial dimension of selfhood, an answer that stands in obvious and ready opposition to Ricoeur's depiction of Levinasian selfhood and the critical charges built on that depiction, is one that has been entirely ignored by Ricoeur, for whatever reasons. Ricoeur is thus tilting at a straw man. He nowhere touches upon Levinas's very fine analyses of the self's capacity of reception found in Part Four of *Totality and Infinity*. There the separated self—the self susceptible to moral relations—is determined as capable of moral encounter precisely because of its created rather than its caused or posited being. This distinction and Levinas's account of selfhood starting with created being, is of the utmost importance. Levinas's point is that the self's is first the product of familial relations, is conditioned by birth, filiality (paternity, maternity), and fraternity. The self is susceptible to radical alterity because it is a being that is *born*, born from and into a web of familial relations.[4] These analyses are not only original, then, but "solve" the basic charge regarding a lack of receptivity that Ricoeur lays against Levinas.

Levinas is quite explicit on this point, even to the extent of anticipating a criticism such as Ricoeur's, as the following citation from *Totality and Infinity* bears witness:

> The acuity of the problem lies in the necessity of maintaining the I in the transcendence with which it hitherto seemed incompatible. Is the subject only a subject of knowings and powers? Does it not present itself as a subject in another sense? The relation sought, which qua subject it supports, and which at the same time satisfies these contradictory exigencies, seemed to us to be inscribed in the erotic relation. (*TI*, 276)

Unfortunately, Ricoeur nowhere refers to these all important analyses of the erotic relation, of the self as born, the self as a child of parents, as a sibling, etc., which for Levinas are in no way to be understood as merely psychological or sociological attributes. Rather, Levinas presents them as part of "a new ontological principle" (*TI*, 276): "Sexuality is in us neither knowledge nor power, but the very plurality of our existing.... Fecundity is to be set up as an ontological category" (*TI*, 277). At this level they represent Levinas's answer to the problem Ricoeur repeatedly harps upon and takes to be insoluble, namely, establishing a selfhood capable to receiving transcendent alterity without at all diminishing the radical transcendence of that alterity. "[B]ecause the son owes his unicity," Levinas writes, "to the paternal election he can be brought up, be commanded, and can obey, and the strange conjunction of the family is possible" (*TI*, 270). Too many pages would be necessary to fully explicate this dimension of the Levinasian conception of selfhood; I have attended to this topic elsewhere (see Note four above). Having noted the existence and importance of the erotic and familial dimension of selfhood in Levinas, and that in this dimension lies the basic answer to Ricoeur's criticism, and without diminishing the importance of this answer (as a response to Ricoeur and as an original account of selfhood in its own right), we will move on and respond to Ricoeur's criticism without tapping these Levinasian resources that Ricoeur has ignored.

Ricoeur's criticism is even more specific: in addition to lacking the basic capacity of reception, Ricoeur argues that Levinas's separated self also lacks requisite capacities of discrimination and recognition. "[A]wakening a responsible response to the other's call," Ricoeur writes, cannot work "except by presupposing a capacity of reception, of discrimination, and of recognition" (339). We will look in turn at these three necessary characteristics of selfhood—reception, discrimination, and recognition—that Ricoeur finds lacking in Levinas. First, reception: "If interiority were indeed determined solely by the desire for retreat and closure," Ricoeur writes, renewing the argument of chapter 7 against the irrelation of a monadic self, "how could it ever hear a word addressed to it, which would seem so foreign to it that this word would be a nothing for an isolated existence?" Ricoeur is claiming, of course, that the Levinasian self has fallen into the solipsistic abyss from which the Cartesian ego only emerges with divine help. To remedy such an isolated insularity, Ricoeur writes: "One has to grant a capacity of reception to the self that is the result of a reflexive structure, better defined by its power of reconsidering preexisting objectifications than by an initial separation" (339). The latter, "separation," refers to Levinas's position, the former, "reconsidering preexisting objectifications," is Ricoeur's. By "reconsidering preexisting objectifications," Ricoeur means his own union of analysis and hermeneutics, which both uncovers and reflects a self always only partially known to itself. Such a self has not just "fallen" (*verfallen*), to use Heidegger's terminology, into the inauthentic superficiality of the concerns of the "they" (*das Mann*), but is also never fully able to recover itself even when authentically focused upon itself. As such it is ontologically "in debt," "guilty," *schuldig*. It is the latter term, Dasein's guilt (like "mutuality" in Aristotle), that holds Ricoeur's attention, and which will, later in *Oneself as Another*, be subject to reinterpretation. In any event, an unending spiraling self-illumination is the only avenue of self-understanding that obviates the aporias that inevitably arise, or so Ricoeur believes, from an account such as Levinas's, which is not at bottom ontological, not oriented by the question of being or essence, that is to say, not hermeneutical.

One answer to this charge, Ricoeur acknowledges (335), is to aver that Levinas's account of the self's encounter with the other works "at a level of radicality where the distinction I [Ricoeur] propose between two sorts of identity . . . cannot be taken into account" (335). Although Ricoeur clearly intends this comment as a criticism, as if Levinas had missed a crucial distinction, the truth of the matter is that Levinas's account does operate at a level more radical than Ricoeur's. This difference of level, which is also a difference in aim, makes all the difference in distinguishing between their accounts. Levinas's account aims to grasp a more radical aspect of the self-other encounter than does Ricoeur's, namely, encounter with alterity as such. Taken up in this problematic, Levinas is indeed in a more Cartesian mold, as it were, than is Ricoeur. But by being so he is able to break it up more radically than Ricoeur by shattering the basic commitment to epistemology upon which all Cartesianism is constructed. Thus, while Ricoeur rejects Cartesian epistemology for the foundation of his thought, Levinas rejects epistemology as the foundation of thought altogether. It does no good, then, for Ricoeur to criticize Levinas for missing out on the advantages of a hermeneutic-analytic epistemology over an obsolete Cartesian-representational epistemology—because Levinas rejects both.

For all that, Levinas does not give up philosophy. Rather, he reorients or disorients philosophy from its usual epistemological base to an even more exacting ethical height. This does not mean, lest we misinterpret the consequences of such a radical shift, that Levinas gives up epistemology in a Nietzschean frenzy. Rather, he reorients it to the essential disorientation effected by ethical exigencies. Levinas articulates the priority of prescription over description or denotation. After acknowledging in his own way and for his own purposes their differences in level, Ricoeur writes: "[I]n Levinas, the identity of the Same is bound up with an ontology of totality that my own investigation has never assumed or even come across" (335). And this is precisely right. It is precisely right because concerned as Levinas is to account for a more originary encounter with alterity, the emergence of alterity as such, it follows that the appropriate conceptual alternative must be totality. Because Ricoeur never accounts for the emergence of alterity as such, he never comes across, as he says, "an ontology of totality." Their difference, then, comes down to asking different questions and thus exposing different answers. The Levinasian rebuttal, then, is to point out that this difference cannot authorize Ricoeur, or anyone else at a conditioned level, in this instance a level of inquiry that takes radical alterity for granted, to criticize its own conditioning level, where alterity first takes shape.

Let us recall that in chapter 7, where Ricoeur defended the priority of the self-directed orientation of self-esteem over the other-directed orientation of self-respect, the self's autochthonous capacity to receive the other, its "solicitude," was characterized as "benevolent spontaneity." We questioned and, outside of certain logical and epistemological considerations, could not find Ricoeur's grounds for introducing the term *benevolence* to characterize the self's spontaneity independent of or prior to its response to the other. At the conclusion of chapter 10 Ricoeur addresses this question anew by means of a positive account of moral selfhood developed by means of "reinterpretations and reappropriations" of the Heideggerian notion of conscience (*Gewissen*). We will turn to this shortly. In subsection two of chapter 10 Ricoeur is once again relying on a logical and epistemological argument, compelling within the Parmenidean-Hegelian (and let us add Heideggerian) horizon of philosophy, to renew his charge that Levinas has failed to establish a relation between self and other. But what Levinas wants to account for, as has been indicated, is not the relation *between* self and other, but the encounter with alterity as transcendence, as the outside, the other. And he does so not by a "pretention" (355)—Ricoeur's word—greater than Fichte's, but by recognizing the inadequacy of the entire epistemological framework that makes even Fichte's account of the transcendence of the non-I inadequately transcendent.

We are able, then, to ask a new question: If the being of the self includes a "benevolence," as Ricoeur believes, then what role could the moral other play in the moral constitution of the self? Even if one answers "norms," as Ricoeur does, we must still wonder from whence norms gain their *moral* sense. Norms could be generated like other "objectivities" from rational calculation. "Truth" and "beauty" could also provide norms, that is, socially codifiable prescriptions, imperatives ("tell the truth," "seek the truth," "create beauty," etc.) no less than "moral goodness" ("be good," "do the good"). If one resorts to the self's alleged benevolent spontaneity for an answer, social morality would still be something of a luxury, a graciousness or charity, hardly worth fussing so much about as to risk one's equilibrium or social position, and certainly not one's life. At worst, social morality taken on in this way could just as easily slip into becoming an art, the art, say, of grand politics. I am not suggesting that the latter eventuality is Ricoeur's intent, conscious or otherwise, but it remains nonetheless a horizon of his thought.

In addition to receptivity, two additional capacities of the self are also said to be lacking their proper priority in Levinas: discriminations, also called "discernment" (339), and recognition of superiority. Here in chapter 10, the latter, recognition of superiority, is once again, as in chapter 7, treated in Gadamerian fashion, as recognition of the other's superior wisdom. The other's superiority is a function of knowledge, in the self and in the other, even if that knowledge is not wholly representational or self-transparent. Thus, an imperative such as "Thou shalt not kill"—which for Levinas is at once the moral significance of the "face" and the initial impact of the alterity of the other—would not come to the self by reversing the natural order, reversing, that is to say, the self-aggrandizing thrust of a desire to persevere in being. Rather, it would presuppose a prior capacity in the self able to recognize the other's superiority, a capacity embedded, incarnate in the self, which under the force of the sociality would become "conviction."

Ricoeur writes: "As for the master who teaches, does he not ask to be recognized in his very superiority? In other words, must not the voice of the Other who says to me: 'Thou shalt not kill,' become my own, to the point of becoming my conviction, a conviction to equal the accusative of 'It's me here!' *["me voici!"]* with the nominative 'Here I stand'?" (339). To see how Ricoeur's rhetorical question is a real one, and to answer it in the negative, we must again note a difference in level. What Ricoeur takes to be prior is a capacity to recognize an alterity as superior in one way or another, that is, the superiority of moral attributes, attributes recognized as and by personal wisdom. Levinas, in contrast, takes the impact of the alterity of the other to occur as moral transformation, the implosion and precedence of moral exigency on the self's otherwise self-serving interests. One would not first sovereignly recognize moral attributes, rather, one undergoes them, suffers morally. But following an existentialized version of philosophy's transcendental route, for Ricoeur, in contrast, there must always first be self-reflexivity, a capacity in the sense of a base, ground, or zero-point, from which and out of which and into which otherness is correlated. For Levinas, in contrast, such an insistence on recognition, or on recognizing the priority of recognition, misses accounting for the prior impact that is at once the impact of alterity as such and moral obligation.

No matter what it may and should become in addition or subsequently, for Levinas encounter with alterity is not from the first a matter of attributes and recognition. It is a matter of transcendence, of "contact" with alterity as such. For Ricoeur, following Heidegger and much of the Western philosophical tradition, transcendence is modulated and muted by the priority of thought and its dialectic, in this case articulated as receptivity. That is to say, for reasons compelling to a logic unable or unwilling to see limitations in its own circularity, and in Heidegger's case exalting such circularity into the rarified and exclusive atmosphere of "authentic" "thinking" (*Denken*), transcendence is only transcendental, the external only immanent. In this way thought never exceeds its own reach, and makes of its self-fulfillment a virtue and standard. To perform this reduction and at the same time to overlook its reductiveness, Ricoeur relises on Heidegger's concept of forestructure, in this case foreknowledge. As part of his critical effort to moralize Dasein, Ricoeur will reinterpret foreknowledge as "attestation" and "conviction," striving at this price to avoid an unwonted amorality, the amorality of "resolution" (*Entschluss*) as Heidegger conceives it. Still, conviction remains for Ricoeur (as resolution remains for Heidegger) an epistemological capacity, the accumulated result, as it were, of recognition of the other's superior wisdom, knowledge, teaching, mastery, and the like.

For Levinas, in contrast to Ricoeur, as we have seen, recognition of the other as superior—*morally* superior—is recognition of alterity as such. Alterity, in other words, in the most radical sense possible, that is, as unassimilated transcendence, can only "appear" to the self as moral alterity, the alterity of moral command. It is hence a puncturing of the self's capacities of self-identification all the way, a puncturing of the self's synthesizing powers, whether active or passive, hence a "recognition" mediated neither as knowledge nor as foreknowledge. The self is "more passive" in relation to such moral transcendence "than the passivity of receptivity," as Levinas has repeatedly written. This does not, however, make the encounter with the alterity of the other a stupidity or ignorance, as Ricoeur critically suggests. Nor is it fair to suggest, as Ricoeur does by misreading a citation from *Totality and Infinity* (see 337), that for Levinas the self's separation is an ignorance. Actually, it is neither the case that the self alone is ignorant nor that the encounter with the other is a knowledge. Rather, to express the matter directly, encounter with alterity precedes and conditions knowledge. What is prior to knowing is not ignorance but the priority of moral priority. What has priority over knowing and conditions knowing is subjectivity as moral responsiveness, subjectivity as subjection to the other in a humbling of powers and capacities, a reorientation of the self's natural for-oneself—its *conatus*— into a for-the-other. Contra Ricoeur, neither spontaneous benevolence nor conviction can be at the origin of morality, since to recognize and then internalize moral superiority one would first of all have to encounter and engage the moral. Levinas's reply to Ricoeur, then, is to appeal to an aboriginal priority.

Ricoeur's critique continues: not only can the Levinasian self not recognize superiority, it cannot distinguish or discriminate one other from another. "[I]t is in each case for the first time that the Other, a particular Other, says to me: 'Thou shall not kill'" (336). Ricoeur obviously misconstrues the radical alterity of each concrete other in Levinas, taking it to mean a reduction of all others, all persons, to the same pure alterity and to nothing but that pure alterity. A strange faceless world that would be indeed. An adequate Levinasian reply would follow the same line as we have already seen above regarding the recognition of superiority. That is to say, Ricoeur's strange picture of Levinas comes from promoting a category mistake, actually a conflation, into a criticism. But Ricoeur goes a step farther with the lack of discrimination charge than with the charge of lack of recognition. He argues that not only is there a lack, but that in addition it represents an internal flaw because Levinas's own works present multiple figures of the other. Levinas would thus be preempted, his answer—the plurality of others—being taken as more evidence for the problem. "Who will be able to distinguish," Ricoeur asks rhetorically, "the master from the executioner, the master who calls for a disciple from the master who requires a slave?" (339). In addition to inventing figures of his own, Ricoeur names several different figures that appear in Levinas's texts. Especially emphasized, however, is the difference between the positive figure of the so-called "master of justice" found in *Totality and Infinity* and the more radical and negative figure of "the offender" (338) found in *Otherwise than Being or Beyond Essence*. What is alleged to follow is that in addition to not being able to distinguish between various good figures, all of whom forbid murder, according to Ricoeur's reading Levinas's self cannot distinguish good from bad figures, or even bad from worse figures such as the offender, the executioner, and the master who enslaves. Leaving aside a point that might have been used to strengthen his contention, namely, that even "Thou shalt not kill" has various levels of meaning,[5] Ricoeur discerns in Levinas's alleged failure to provide the self with a capacity to discriminate a fatal "reversal."

It is because of the self's inability to discriminate that Ricoeur detects in the difference between *Totality and Infinity* and *Otherwise than Being or Beyond Essence* a "strange reversal" (340, f45). "I perceive," he writes, "a sort of reversal of the reversal performed in *Totality and Infinity*" (340). The self assigned to be responsible, thereby reversed of its natural being by morality in *Totality and Infinity*, by being reversed once again in *Otherwise than Being or Beyond Essence*, so Ricoeur contends, is thereby returned, contra Levinas's own intent, to its original position. Levinas thereby undoes his own efforts, or circles back to his starting point. I cite Ricoeur:

> The assignment of responsibility, stemming from the summons by the Other and interpreted in terms of the most total passivity, is reversed in a show of abnegation in which the self attests to itself by the very movement with which it removes itself. (340)

It is true that for Levinas the passivity of the moral self of *Totality in Infinity*, having initially reversed its power, having had its for-self converted into responsiveness to and for the other, becomes in *Otherwise than Being or Beyond Essence* a self "substituting" itself for the other, a for-the-other's for-itself. Thus, one might say along with Ricoeur that its first reversal into responsive passivity is reversed again into a substituting activity. Ricoeur invokes Levinas's term "testimony" (340), from *Otherwise than Being or Beyond Essence*, where the moral self in its encounter with the other is said to testify to that other, in order to suggest critically that Levinas has reverted to what Ricoeur, without the unnecessary detour of a reversed reversal, calls "attestation." "Is this [Levinas's] testimony so far removed," he asks, "from what we have constantly called attestation?" (340).

In his very next sentence, however, Ricoeur answers his own criticism and exposes his own rhetoric: "To be sure," he writes, "Levinas never speaks of the attestation *of self*, the very expression being suspected of leading back to the 'certainty of the ego'" (340). This difference, emphasized by italics, is precisely to the point, precisely Levinas's resounding answer. To be for-the-other all the way to taking responsibility for the other's for-itself is still to be for-the-other. One is testifying not to oneself but for the other, washing the other's hands not one's own. Levinas has said:

> Ethical testimony is a revelation that is not a knowledge. Must one still say that in this mode one only "testifies" to the Infinite, to God, about which no presence or actuality is *capable* of testifying. The philosophers said there is no present infinite. What may pass for a "fault" or the infinite is to the contrary a positive characteristic of it—its very infinity. (*EI*, 108)[6]

Testimony, radical as it can become, up to the point of substitution, stepping in for-the-other, is testimony *of* and *for* the other's moral height, the other's alterity. In contrast, Ricoeur's attestation always remains self-attestation, attestation of and to the self's moral righteousness, of and to the self's part in the play that reflection, at a distance, recognizes as moral encounter.

Thus, there is no surreptitious reversal of reversal in Levinas's account, but the intensification of an original reversal. Levinas's account is not a reflection at-a-distance on-the-distance of an already given morality, a reflection compressing its distances, to be sure, by means of hermeneutical circling, reducing the other to the self, to the oneself *as* another, as in Ricoeur's title. Rather, Levinas's ethics aims to go closer to morality than hermeneutics dares to go or can go. It aims to give voice not to the hermeneutical "this *as* that," but to what makes the *as* structure possible, the unlikeness at the root of likeness, the uniqueness at the root of similarity. The emergence of transcendence "*as*" morality is at once the emergence of transcendence and the emergence of morality, in a contact "closer to the self than the ego," as Levinas expresses it. "The self, a hostage," Levinas writes, "is already substituted for the others. 'I am an other,' but this is not the alienation Rimbaud refers to. I am outside of any place, in myself, on the hither side of the autonomy of auto-affection and identity resting on itself." Or, as if once again in direct response to Ricoeur: "The ego is not entity 'capable' of expiating for the others: it is this original expiation." "In this sense the self is goodness, or under the exigency for an abandon of all having, of all *one's own* and all *for oneself*, to the point of substitution" (*OBBE*, 118).[7] Ricoeur will have none of this compression. When Ricoeur remarks that "[i]t remains that, through the form of the accusative, the first person is indirectly involved and that the accusative cannot remain 'nonassumable' " (340), he has only projected a development onto its condition, that is, projected the self-reflective self proper to his own account onto Levinas's more radical account.

This sort of reductive projection, reflection reflecting itself, with its insistence on erasing residues, has had a long history in philosophy, and is perhaps its most consistent patrimony. Ricoeur's is but the latest instance of a long bottom line of "transcendental conditions," from Kant's "I think" to Husserl's "I represent" to Heidegger's "issue of being," all insisting on their rights and authority. All owe their allegiances and alleged necessity, however, to the internal and circular requirements of a transcendental epistemology—precisely the "totality that," as Ricoeur has written, "my own investigation has never assumed or even come across" (335). Ricoeur can never come across this totality precisely because all his investigations operate within it, unwittingly conforming to its contours. Levinas's thought, in contrast, articulates this totality by exceeding and rupturing it—from a moral angle, a height.

Hyperbole

Of course, Ricoeur is well aware that the central movement of Levinas's philosophy is a rupture, breach, or break with totality. Because this break is indeed impossible within the parameters—being and non-being—of the Parmenidean-Hegelian heritage, it is all the greater of a break, if one can qualify an absolute break in this manner. Though Levinas speaks of a "more" in a "less," he is certainly not limiting himself to a mathematical or quantitative model. The appearance of language such as this, and other peculiar formulations and grammatical deformations, imposing what Levinas himself often calls an "abuse of language," is no accident. For what can it possibly mean to be outside the all? To be otherwise than being? Beyond essence? The entire thrust of Levinas's thought is precisely to articulate the sense of such exteriority, an exteriority "impossible" from within that which it exceeds. The sense or significance of such an exteriority only comes, so Levinas contends, from ethics, that is, from appreciating rupture as moral impingement, moral command, "received" by a self overwhelmed and transformed—reversed—by moral obligation, charged and overcharged with moral responsibility for-the-other. The only irreducible alterity, irreducible to the self, is moral transcendence.

Now, for Ricoeur the same matter, breaking with totality, obviously has quite a different look. Standing within a seamless totality, the problem with

Levinas's thought is precisely its excess. For Ricoeur this excess is reflected in a language of exaggeration, indeed, of hyperbole. Because it is empty, however, speculative in the Kantian sense, it is sustained only by that language—mere words, "sound and fury." Now, the way hyperbole sustains itself is to always outdo the force of its own expressions in a linguistic self-overcoming that by its own logic extends to the point of the "scandalous" (338). The scandal originates, however, in three related errors (whose basic contours were first articulated in chapter 7). First error: exaggerating the sameness of the same. Or, in the register appropriate to the present inquiry: exaggerating the separation of the self. Second error, which follows from the first: exaggerating the alterity of the other. Third error, following from both: exaggerating the difference separating same and other, self and other person. These three errors are responsible for twisting Levinas's language, and Levinas's language is nothing but twisted. To repeat a citation given above regarding "irrelation": "Because the Same signifies totalization and separation, the exteriority of the Other can no longer be expressed in the language of relation" (336). We know Ricoeur's objection because we have already encountered it. Not only reality but (if one can separate these two) language also, and the requirements of meaningful communication (if one can separate these three) will not allow any radical breach: "[M]ust not language contribute its resources of communication, hence of reciprocity . . . ?" (339). "In short," he continues, "is it not necessary that a dialogue superpose a relation on the supposedly absolute distance between the separate I and the teaching Other?" (339). The requirements of language and communication, so Ricoeur contends, should force Levinas to abandon his impossible philosophy, just as they force him to unwittingly reverse himself while enunciating it, and force him to end in scandal. But they don't.

What on earth, then, is Levinas up to? Insofar as language and communication, like being, require relation and reciprocity, and no meaning can make sense outside of language and communication, are not Levinas's writings simply babble, meaningless noise, ranting? How can he write book after book, article after article? From whence does Levinas's work derive its force of persuasion for an impossibility, for an impossible break? Ricoeur's answer is direct. What Levinas is up to is "the systematic practice of *excess* in philosophical argumentation" (337). In a word, his writings and their central "break effect" (337), are a product of hyperbole. The whole force of Levinas's impossible philosophy comes from the strategic use of hyperbole. I will cite Ricoeur at some length:

> It appears to me that the break effect related to this thought of absolute otherness stems from the use of *hyperbole*, one worthy of

> Cartesian hyperbolic doubt.... By hyperbole, it must be strongly underscored, we are not to understand a figure of style, a literary trope, but the systematic practice of *excess* in philosophical argumentation. Hyperbole appears in this context as the strategy suited to producing the effect of a break with regard to the idea of exteriority in the sense of absolute otherness. (337)

Levinas's entire philosophy, then, is but an "effect," the product of clever staging, an elaborate show, display, or mask. To take it seriously would be to be duped. Of course Ricoeur's criticism recalls Hegel's 1807 polemic, entitled *"Faith and Knowledge,"* against Jacobi (and Kant and Fichte) whom he accuses of "empty shouting," of wanting "to replace philosophical Ideas with *expressions and words* which are not supposed to give knowledge or understanding."[8] They recall also Parmenides' theogony, his warning against taking the path of non-being: "a way wholly unknowable. For you could not know what is not—that is impossible—nor could you express it."[9] Levinas's talk of the self's extreme passivity, the other's extreme exteriority, and the extreme exigency of their ethical bridge, are hyperboles masquerading as truth, a "strategy suited to producing the effect of a break," but only an effect, like a stage effect, one must suppose, since such a break is impossible a priori.

The first and primary hyperbole is that of the radically separated self. The second and conditioned hyperbole is that of the radically exterior other. "To the hyperbole of separation, on the side of the Same," Ricoeur writes, "replies the hyperbole of epiphany on the side of the Other" (337). The logical motif from chapter 7 is here transposed to the level of rhetoric: "Separation has made interiority sterile... since the initiative belongs wholly to the Other.... Hyperbole, in *Totality and Infinity,* culminates in the affirmation that the teaching of the face reestablishes no primacy of relation with respect to the terms" (337–338). Having begun with a hyperbolic rhetoric masking an impossible irrelation in *Totality and Infinity,* there is nothing to stop, and everything to encourage an even more excessive, even more hyperbolic rhetoric in *Otherwise than Being or Beyond Essence.* Indeed, since the entire force of Levinas's thought is said to derive from the strategic deployment of excessive language, and since such a deployment would suffer, as does all figurative rhetoric, from diminishing returns over time (analogous to the phenomenon of sensory fatigue), the rhetorical ante must be constantly increased.

"Levinas's *Otherwise than Being,*" Ricoeur writes, "employs even greater hyperbole, to the point of paroxysm" (338). The "reversal of the reversal" noted earlier regarding the difference between *Totality and Infinity* and *Otherwise than Being or Beyond Essence,* according to which an initial responsibility extends so far as to become a withdrawal or retraction into the self, is in fact no reversal at all but rather a collapse, exhaustion, or "paroxysm" resulting from overexaggeration. "As retraction," Ricoeur writes, "the assignment of responsibility adopts the figure of hyperbole, in a range of excess never before attained" (338). Two instances of such excess, carved out of Levinas's complex analyses, are paraded for quick view. Ricoeur points first to the Levinasian self's temporality, its "past more ancient than any past of memory" (338), and second to the excessive imposition of responsibility, "'that is justified by no prior commitment'" (338; OBBE, 102). Tempting and instructive as it would be to respond to these particular instances by recontextualizing them, we will instead hold our sights on the broader criticism that makes them possible.[10] Commenting on the excess of *Otherwise than Being or Beyond Essence*, and linked to the earlier criticism regarding discrimination, Ricoeur continues:

> After this, the language becomes more and more excessive: "obsession of the Other," "persecution by the Other," and finally, and especially, "substitution of the I for the Other." Here, the work reaches its paroxysm: "Under accusation by everyone, the responsibility for everyone goes to the point of substitution. A subject is a hostage." (OBBE, 112)
>
> This expression, the most excessive of all, is thrown out here in order to prevent the insidious return of the self-affirmation of some "clandestine and hidden freedom" maintained even within the passivity of the self summoned to responsibility. The paroxysm of the hyperbole seems to me to result from the extreme—even scandalous—hypothesis that the Other is no longer the master of justice here, as is the case in *Totality and Infinity*, but the offender, who, as an offender, no less requires the gesture of pardon and expiation. (338)

Levinas's attempt to exceed the limits of philosophy thus ends in scandal, in the "scandalous hypothesis" of the indistinction of teacher and offender, of good and evil, both taken up by a responsibility so exaggerated that it is no less responsible for the one than for the other, indeed, a responsibility never responsible enough for either. How to respond?

It is obvious that Ricoeur neglects to acknowledge the clear distinction Levinas draws between the morality of the face-to-face, with its excessive obligation and responsibility, and the normative demands of justice, where offenders are punished and teachers rewarded. Without excusing or justifying the distortion of Levinas's thought that this neglect produces, we might say that it is due to Ricoeur's overly narrow focus on Levinas's account of the morality of the face-to-face relation (which in Levinas precedes but also requires justice). But even at the level of morality, without invoking the distinction between morality and justice, the Levinasian response to Ricoeur's charge of verbal excess must be to affirm the excessiveness of morality itself while denying its merely rhetorical or calculative status. That is to say, the Levinasian answer is to reaffirm the deeper significance of what appears to be merely an abuse of language. Shouting, after all, is not always empty for being shouting. When the wounded cry out, are we not there to help them, because their cries are cries of pain?

The excess of morality is no less moral for being excessive. Indeed, the opposite is true: because of its excess morality is moral. The very sign, as it were, of morality is its excess, the surplus of goodness over being, or, from another angle, the deficiency of being in relation to the good. It is to Levinas's credit, then, that his thought does not shrink from this excess, lets no one off this hook. Because the alterity of the other cannot be encompassed by the self, because there is no set of all sets, as it were, no totalization of the infinite, the self cannot—should not—rest in the complacency of self-esteem. Bad conscience, Levinas will say, is better than good conscience. Good conscience is not good enough. One never has done enough, and never will, unto death. "Responsibilities increase," Levinas wrote in *Totality and Infinity*, "to the measure that they are taken on." They increase, but they are never finished, never done. Corresponding, as it were, to the excess of morality is the excessive language of ethics.

In discussing the proper function of exaggeration in rhetoric, Richard Weaver in *The Ethics of Rhetoric* (1951) distinguishes between exaggeration as caricature and exaggeration as prophecy. The former, which is disreputable, "mere wantonness," "seizes upon any trait or aspect which could produce titillation and exploits this without conscience."[11] Levinas as much as Ricoeur would disparage such an abuse of language. But there is a proper use of exaggeration, used by the biblical prophets, and used by the true rhetorician, that is, the rhetorician who couples persuasion with truth (the truth that requires persuasion). "The exaggeration which this rhetorician employs," Weaver writes, "is not caricature but prophecy; and it would be a fair formulation to say that true rhetoric is concerned with the potency of things."[12] Although Levinas does not use the Aristotelian language of potency and actuality to express the relation of morality to being, the parallel is clear. The exaggeration Ricoeur points to in Levinas's writings is not, as he would have us believe, empty caricature, mere effect, the result of mistaking the impossible for the possible. It is rather the language proper to ethics, not equivalent to morality or to prophecy, but close to them in wanting to give a genuine account of the imperative exhortative force of the priority of the "ought" over the "is." With Ricoeur's criticism in mind (and without reducing it to a caricature). I will cite one more passage from Weaver:

> What he [the literalist] fails to appreciate is that potentiality is a mode of existence, and that all prophecy is about the tendency of things. The discourse of the noble rhetorician, accordingly, will be about real potentiality or possible actuality, whereas that of the mere exaggerator is about unreal potentiality.[13]

Levinas, then, is attempting to articulate neither being nor non-being, nor becoming, but rather a "real potentiality or possible actuality," the priority of goodness over being, and the insatiable desire of the self that responds to this call. To do so he must be a "noble rhetorician," not because moral exigency, and the exhortative language it puts into play, is a gloss on being, a decoration or luxury, but because morality makes greater demands than being, cuts deeper than being.

The greatness of Levinas's ethics—and the "glory" of morality itself—is to have put no stop to morality. The human is not the measure, but is measured by morality. So what if humanity proves again and again that it is insufficient to the demands of morality, is that the "fault" of morality or of us ourselves? Are we to revise morality to suit our need for satisfaction, for self-satisfaction, for the benefit and consolation of what Ricoeur calls "the good life"? Would that be truthful? Who is really more philosophical, more the philosopher: the one who measures morality by the truth of an unsurpassable reflexivity, or the one who measures truth by the radical transcendence of morality? Which moral philosophy is more correct, the one that ends with balanced accounts, with the satisfaction of knowing, firmness of conviction, or the one that ends in infinite debt, required to give all while more still is demanded, agitated by bad conscience? Levinas answers with the latter, Ricoeur with the former.

To bridge this portion of our exposition, confined to the second subsection of chapter 10, with the next portion, which turns to the third subsection, where Ricoeur's basic effort is to remoralize Heideggerian *Gewissen*, let us note an oddity. At the start of the third subsection Ricoeur excuses and even condones with regard to Hegel the "excesses, transgressions, and hyperboles" (343) that just three pages earlier we have seen him condemning with regard to Levinas. Ricoeur acknowledges that in his quarrel with Kant's moral philosophy, Hegel resorts to an "artifice," a "strategy" that "misrepresents Kant," attacking Kant for a non-Kantian "'postulate' wholly invented" (343) by Hegel. Admitting this, Ricoeur then writes:

> The artifice of the Hegelian construction is not, however, to be deplored; as an artifice it takes its place among the excesses, transgressions, and hyperboles of all sorts that nourish moral reflection, and perhaps, philosophical reflection in general. Moreover, the fact that this is a vision *of the world* that is mobilized by moralism is of the greatest importance. (343)

How peculiar. The very things for which Levinas is taken to task, namely excess and a strategy of hyperbole, when set in motion by Hegelian moral thought, are all of a sudden the very stuff by which "moral reflection, and perhaps philosophical reflection in general" are nourished! It seems that Ricoeur thus admits, along with Richard Weaver, precisely what we have been insisting upon in Levinas's defense. It seems that Ricoeur here agrees, contra his own criticism of Levinas, that rhetorical exaggeration is neither camouflage nor adornment, but required by "moral reflection" and "philosophical reflection in general." So be it.

Conscience

The first pages of the third subsection of chapter 10 are given over to a reinterpretation and reappropriation of Hegel's critique of Kantian morality, and Nietzsche's critique of the moral order more generally. Without entering into his argumentation, the innovative outcome of both examinations for Ricoeur is to "to step outside the poisoned circle of 'good' and 'bad' conscience" (347). Heidegger, to whom Ricoeur devotes the remaining pages of his book, is enlisted for the same service. But there is more to Heidegger. In line with the previous analyses of Hegel and Nietzsche, Ricoeur first shows that Heidegger's ontological account of Dasein's conscience also demoralizes conscience. Dasein's authentic self-appropriation guided by conscience is neither "good" nor "bad" in a moral sense. The "voice of conscience" is simply a call from Dasein to itself. It is a call at once "from" Dasein and "above" Dasein insofar as Dasein calls itself to more fully be its own being, to be its own being from the top down, or from the bottom up. While Ricoeur eagerly takes over Heidegger's ontology he is dissatisfied with his demoralization of conscience. To rectify the latter, he assimilates the ontological movement of Dasein, attested to by conscience, to his own notion of the moral self moved by the desire to live well ("aiming at the 'good life'"). In the following I will review these developments in greater detail before turning to Levinas's role and response.

In its movement to be itself, Dasein cannot be its own basis. This failure results not simply, as has been indicated, because Dasein sporadically "falls" away from its own proper task of being itself into the anonymity of a "they-self" *(das Mann-selbst)*, but, more deeply, because even when it strives resolutely to be itself fully, its oncoming death coupled with its engagement in the larger context of an always already ongoing historical being, make its task of being itself essentially impossible to complete. Dasein is always too late to fully be itself, even if its highest calling is nonetheless to make the attempt. Heidegger uses the term *guilt (Schuld)*, as we have seen, to characterize this fundamental failure in Dasein, its inability to be the basis it nonetheless must strive to be. The first point of Ricoeur's *explication de texte*, then, is to show that for Heidegger Dasein's "guilt" is ontological rather than moral.

Ricoeur's second point is to argue, against Heidegger, that having grounded Dasein in the ontological in this way, he is incapable of showing how in the depths of its being Dasein can be a moral being. The issue that Dasein is, that to which the "voice" of its conscience calls it, is an exigency to be, not an exigency to be good. "Ontology stands guard on the threshold of ethics.... Unfortunately," Ricoeur writes, "Heidegger does not show how one could travel the opposite path—from ontology toward ethics" (349).

Before moving to Ricoeur's positive solution to this latter problem, let us remark in passing something nowhere mentioned in chapter 10, namely, that both of Ricoeur's points regarding Heidegger are Levinas's too, and that they were articulated and emphasized by Levinas long before the appearance of *Oneself as Another*. The first point, regarding the amorality of Dasein, is one upon which Ricoeur, Levinas, *and Heidegger* agree. Of course, Ricoeur and Levinas evaluate it critically, in contrast to Heidegger, who in the name of ontology (the "ontological difference") insists upon and celebrates the amorality of Dasein's conscience and guilt. Morality is ontic; Heidegger's interest—the interest of "thinking"—is ontological.[14] Regarding Ricoeur's second point, that starting in ontology one cannot get to ethics, this too has been Levinas's longstanding criticism of Heidegger, and more broadly his criticism of the entire Parmenidean-Hegelian tradition of philosophy. Despite this double agreement, in his discussion of Heidegger it is only when Ricoeur turns his own positive alternative, which is at the same time the culmination of *Oneself as Another*, that he invokes Levinas for criticism. I am drawing attention to Ricoeur's unacknowledged adherence to Levinas's reading of

Heidegger both to contextualize Ricoeur's criticism of Levinas, and to emphasize one last time the almost inestimable importance Levinas's thought of alterity has for Ricoeur.

Moving to the positive, the following citation succinctly encapsulates what Ricoeur takes to be the innovative outcome and the culminating contribution of his critical reinterpretation and reappropriation of the ontologized conscience of Heideggerian Dasein.

> To this demoralization of conscience, I would oppose a conception that closely associates the phenomenon of *injunction* to that of *attestation*. Being-enjoined would then constitute the moment of otherness proper to the phenomenon of conscience, in accordance with the metaphor of the voice. Listening to the voice of conscience would signify being-enjoined by the Other. In this way, the rightful place of the notion of *debt* would be acknowledged, a notion that was too hastily ontologized by Heidegger at the expense of the ethical dimension of indebtedness. (351)

Conscience, then, instead of being a listening to the voice of being, is a listening to the voice of the other. In the face of Levinas's thought, this innovation is hardly earth shattering. Ricoeur's earlier definition of "'ethical intention' in chapter 7 (*"aiming at the 'good life' with and for others, in just institutions"* [172]) returns now rewoven into the very fabric of selfhood. "Benevolent spontaneity" is now attestation. The social dimension of morality, for which the self's receptivity prepares, is now characterized as conscience enjoined by the injunction of others to produce a self with conviction. These three terms, attestation, conscience, and conviction, summarize what we earlier called the "Hegelian" movement of Ricoeur's account of moral selfhood: starting with an already moral self, attesting to itself (self-esteem), one then turns to moral injunction as the impact of alterity, as conscience enjoined by others (self-respect), which results in a self holding its moral charge as conviction (justice). Such is the overall result of Ricoeur's studies, and his picture of moral selfhood. With regard, more specifically, to Heidegger's voice of conscience, Ricoeur's innovation, as we see in the citation above, is fairly obvious: the voice of conscience, its injunction, comes not from Dasein but from others. It is here, at such close quarters, as it were, that Ricoeur wants to distance himself from Levinas.

On the last pages of *Oneself as Another* Ricoeur argues against Levinas in two ways. First, it is because Levinas fails to understand social morality within the larger context of attestation-conscience-conviction that he has obscured the proper role of conscience and thus, owing to this obfuscation, mistaken itfor the hyperbolic and violent voice of the "master of justice." Ricoeur asks rhetorically: "Is it not because the state of [social] morality has been dissociated from the triad ... then hypostatized because of this dissociation, that the phenomenon of conscience has been correlatively impoverished and that the revealing metaphor of the voice has been eclipsed by the stifling voice of the court?" (352). At bottom, this criticism is but a final restatement, now from the perspective of Ricoeur's conclusions, of his earlier criticism (in the second subsection of both chapters 10 and 7) that having exaggerated the initial separation of the self, Levinas has so amplified the alterity of the other, and its moral force, that he has drowned out any appreciation for the self's prior moral capacity to receive moral alterity. By exaggerating the isolation of the self and the alterity of the other, or, to say this in another way, by not recognizing Ricoeur's triad of attestation-conscience-conviction, Levinas has both "impoverished," and "eclipsed" the conscience, and concomitantly turned the other's injunction into a "stifling voice of the court." We have already responded to the basic ground upon which this criticism rests.

Explaining Levinas's alleged error, Ricoeur reinforces his criticism by supplementing it with an aspect borrowed from Jacques Derrida's well-known critical essay of 1964 on Levinas: "Violence and Metaphysics: An Essay on the Thought of Emmanuel Levinas.";[15] Following Derrida, Ricoeur attributes the alleged Levinasian "reduction of the voice of conscience to the verdict of the court" (351) to the *violence* inherent in all interactions.

> It is because violence taints all the relations of interaction, because of the power-over exerted by an agent on the patient of the action, that the commandment becomes law, and the law, prohibition: "Thou shalt not kill." It is at this point that the sort of short-circuit between conscience and obligation takes place, from which results the reduction of the voice of conscience to the verdict of the court. (351)

Curiously, even ironically, Ricoeur chooses at precisely this juncture to enlist one of Levinas's spiritual teachers, Franz Rosenzweig, using the centerpiece of his *Star of Redemption*, the nonlegal nonprohibitory commandment to love, against Levinas, to indicate that commandment need not be interpreted as law and prohibition. The irony is that this is exactly Levinas's point, indeed the point we raised against Ricoeur's earlier insistence on the normative character of social morality.

Because the face of the other is for Levinas command without law, he opposes Kant, and hence opposes Ricoeur's earlier efforts, in chapter 7, to conflate alterity and normativity. Here, at the end of chapter 10, at the conclusion of *Oneself as Another*, it is again exactly because the face of the other commands ("Thou shalt not kill") *without* making this command a law, that Levinas argues for the priority of obligation over what Ricoeur now identifies as conscience. There is thus no "short-circuit between conscience and obligation," as Ricoeur suggests, but rather an absolute priority given to an obligating other who evinces responsibilities in the self, indeed, who evinces a responsible self. And it is because the self made responsible can never be responsive enough, as we have seen, that Levinas will not hesitate to support "bad" conscience (the conscience that has never done enough) over the complacency of "good" conscience.[16] The latter, which Levinas opposes, is precisely what Ricoeur supports in giving primacy to self-esteem and "the optative of living well" (352). This is why Levinas and Ricoeur are so far apart when it comes to the fundamentals of their respective ethical theories. Violence does not reduce Levinasian command to law. Indeed, the break which the alterity of the other effects upon the self is only violent from the point of view of the refusal coming from a *conatus* absorbed with itself, with its own possibilities, however historically rooted. For the moral self, opened up for-the-other, such a break and its "violence" is precisely a *pacific* call to responsibility from an unsurpassable height. If this is violence (which it is not) it is certainly not violation. It is, in any event, preferable to the indifference of complacency.

Unlike the first criticism in subsection three, Ricoeur's second and final criticism, found on the very last pages of *Oneself as Another*, is new—but at the same time it seems to us to be surprisingly weak. Levinas is accused of having reduced the multiple senses Ricoeur gives to conscience as the "voice of the other" to one sense: the otherness of other persons. Ricoeur first criticizes Freud (354) for reducing conscience by means of an "internalization of ancestral voices" (354). He then criticizes Levinas, on the other hand, for an externalization of conscience, for a "reduction, which seems to me to result," he writes, "from the work of Emmanuel Levinas as a whole, of the otherness of conscience to the otherness of other people" (354). "The model of all otherness is the other person" (354)—such is Ricoeur's final criticism of Levinas.

Though Ricoeur's "advance" over Heidegger was to treat the voice of conscience not as Dasein's own voice but as the voice of the other, in apparent contrast to Levinas, he insists upon "a certain equivocalness" regarding the alterity of the other persons who are the source of the injunction of conscience. "The ultimate equivocalness with respect to the status of the Other in the phenomenon of conscience," Ricoeur writes, "is perhaps what needs to be preserved in the final analysis" (353). First there is a large equivocation between an "anthropological reading" and a "theological reading" (353). Second, in addition to preserving the larger equivocation between anthropological and theological readings of conscience, Ricoeur wants also to preserve equivocations within each category. On the side the anthropological, Ricoeur points to the difference between grasping the voice of conscience as "parental and ancestral figures" (353), in one's head, as it were, and "another person whom I can look in the face or who can stare at me" (355), in the flesh. On the side of the theological, he points to the difference between a "living God" and "absent God—or an empty place" (355), as sources of injunction. Levinas's fault, then, is to have made the living person in the flesh, within the anthropological reading, "[t]he model of all otherness."

For Levinas, however, it is not a matter of reducing different figures of alterity to one figure. Rather, to say it again, the issue is to grasp the alterity that makes any and all figures of alterity other. And here Levinas would insist upon the priority of the alterity and injunctive force of the flesh and blood other. A "sculpted arm by Rodin," as Levinas puts it, can inspire the self to it moral obligations, true, but it can do so only because of the originary priority of the flesh and blood other. Regarding the anthropological readings, then, it seems that there can be no question that unless one is to sink into infinite regress (an error, by the way, for which Ricoeur faults Freud), then the injunctive force of "parental and ancestral figures" must of necessity be modeled on the injunctive force of the alterity of living persons "whom I can look in the face or who can stare at me," as Ricoeur puts it. All internalized exterior figures, that is to say, were once—whether developmentally or historically, whether fully or partially—*external* exterior figures. An internalized paternal or ancestral figure carries injunctive force, furthermore, precisely because one knows of the injunctive force of real living parents and progenitors, or, more broadly, of real living others. Here again we wonder why Ricoeur neglects Part IV of *Totality and Infinity*.

Regarding equivocations within a "theological reading," the injunctive force of God, or "the absent God—or an empty place," Ricoeur is right: Levinas does indeed insist that for an "adult religion" relationship with God occurs *through* moral relations with others. Not only the desire for goodness elicited by the other, but the demand for justice elicited by others, are manifestations of God's presence—and absence—in history. "[T]he universality of the Divine," Levinas writes, "exists only in the form in which it is fulfilled in relations between humans."[17] The moral reconditioning of the self, leading to the demand for redemptive justice for all humankind, is the way, as Levinas expresses this movement, "God comes to the idea." Doctrinal positions within theological disputes have no dogmatic authority when it comes to God's injunctive force. "There can be no 'knowledge' of God," Levinas writes, "separated from the relationship with men" (*TI*, 78). It can be said unequivocally, regarding the larger distinction between the theological and the anthropological, that Levinas's thought has no room for moral injunctions coming to conscience directly from

God, unmediated by a human and humane sociality. To require such mediation does not, however, reduce God to humanity: "The Other is not the incarnation of God, but precisely by his face, in which he is disincarnate, is the manifestation of the height in which God is revealed" (*TI*, 79).

If Ricoeur's stand regarding the relation between self and God is otherwise, and it is not at all certain in *Oneself as Another* where Ricoeur stands on his own concluding challenge to Levinas,[18] then Levinas's response would be to unequivocally reject that stand as idolatry, pointing to all the horrors of Western history, especially in the twentieth century, that stem from a faith alleged to be directly and unilaterally ordered by God. "The comprehension of God taken as a participation in his sacred life, an allegedly direct comprehension," Levinas will insist, "is impossible, because participation is a denial of the divine, and because nothing is more direct than the face to face, which is straightforwardness itself" (*TI*, 78). What, then, of the God who exceeds morality, Kierkegaard's God who "suspends the ethical"? Levinas rejects Kierkegaard's famous and influential interpretation of the story of Abraham's near-sacrifice of Isaac. "Perhaps," Levinas responds, "the ear Abraham had for hearing the voice which brought him back to the ethical order was the highest moment of this drama."[19]

NOTES

1. Though Ricoeur acknowledges "borrow[ing] an expression dear to Levinas" (22), Kathleen Blamey translates *"me voici"* as "It's me here," instead of the standard for Levinas translations, "Here I am." *Me voici* is a French translation of the biblical Hebrew *hineni*; see Genesis 22:1, 22:7, 22:11, and Isaiah 6:8.

2. Hans Georg Gadamer, *Truth and Method,* trans. Garret Barden and John Cumming (New York: Seabury, 1975); hereafter referred to as *TM.*

3. Emmanuel Levinas, *Totality and Infinity,* trans. Alphonso Lingis (Pittsburgh: Duquesne University Press, 1969); hereafter referred to as *TI.*

4. *TI*, 254–285; also see chapter 9, "The Metaphysics of Gender," in Richard A. Cohen, *Elevations: The Height of the Good in Rosenzweig and Levinas* (Chicago: University of Chicago Press, 1994), 195–219.

5. In Judaism, for instance, the prohibition against murder applies to killing one's fellows, to be sure, but it is at work, too, in prohibiting one person from greatly embarrassing another, or denying food and security to travelers, or taking away someone's job, or making a rash halachic ruling, or withholding halachic expertise. These actions strike so deeply against the other that they are "tantamount" to murder, though of course they are not "literally" murder.

6. Emmanuel Levinas, *Ethics and Infinity*, trans. Richard Cohen (Pittsburgh: Duquesne University Press, 1985); hereafter referred to as *EI*.

7. Emmanuel Levinas, *Otherwise than Being or Beyond Essence*, trans. Alphonso Lingis (The Hague: Martinus Nijhoff, 1981); hereafter referred to as *OBBE*.

8. G. W. F. Hegel, *Faith and Knowledge*, trans. Walter Cerf and H. S. Harris (Albany: State of New York University Press, 1977), 119–120.

9. Translated by John Mansley Robinson, in John Mansley Robinson, *An Introduction to Early Greek Philosophy* (Boston: Houghton Mifflin Co., 1968), 110.

10. For an account of Levinas's theory of time and intersubjectivity, see Cohen, *Elevations*, chapter 6, "On Temporality and Time" (133–161), and chapter 4, "Rosenzweig contra Buber: Personal Pronouns" (90–111); for an account of the relation of morality to contracts, see chapter 8, "G-d in Levinas: The Justifications of Justice and Philosophy" (173–194).

11. Richard Weaver, *The Ethics of Rhetoric* (South Bend: Regnery/Gateway Inc., 1953), 19.

12. Ibid., 19–20.

13. Ibid., 20.

14. That the shift from the ontic to the ontological *does* have a moral dimension has been noted by several commentators. See e.g., Richard A. Cohen, "Dasein's Responsibility for Being," *Philosophy Today* 27, no. 4 (Winter 1983): 317–325.

15. Jacques Derrida, *Writing and Difference*, trans. Alan Bass (Chicago: University of Chicago Press, 1978), 79–153.

16. See Emmanuel Levinas, "Bad Conscience and the Inexorable," trans. Richard A. Cohen, in *Face to Face with Levinas,* ed. Richard A. Cohen (Albany: State University of New York Press, 1986), 35–40.

17. Emmanuel Levinas, *Difficult Freedom: Essays on Judaism*, trans. Sean Hand (Baltimore: Johns Hopkins University Press, 1990), 137.

18. In the final section of the introductory chapter of *OA* (23–25), Ricoeur explains why he refrains from including his two concluding Gifford Lectures in the book: "I have presented to my readers arguments alone, which do not assume any commitment from the reader to reject, accept, or suspend anything with regard to biblical faith. It will be observed that this asceticism of the argument ... leads to a type of philosophy from which the actual mention of God is absent and in which the question of God, as a philosophical question, itself remains in a suspension that could be called agnostic, as the final lines of the tenth study will attest" (24). In contrast, the unity of Levinas's philosophy, which includes God, disputes the necessity for Ricoeur's asceticism and agnosticism.

19. Emmanuel Levinas, "Existence et ethique," in *Noms propres* (Montpelier: fata morgana, 1976), 109 (my translation).

EIGHT

Between Conviction and Critique
Reflexive Philosophy, Testimony, and Pneumatology

Eric Crump

With the publication of Paul Ricoeur's *Oneself as Another*, Pamela Sue Anderson notes that many readers may be "astonished" at Ricoeur's assertion of agnosticism, "both resolute and, however uncharacteristic of him, vehement."[1] She cites two texts from *Oneself as Another*. The first asserts a methodological agnosticism, enabling a preservation of the integrity of both philosophical discourse as autonomous and meaningful belief (*croyance*) apart from the security of a philosophical foundation. Ricoeur states that his principal reason for excluding the final Gifford lectures from publication in *Oneself as Another*,

> which may be debatable and even perhaps regrettable, has to do with my concern to pursue, to the very last line, an autonomous, philosophical discourse. The ten studies that make up this work assume the bracketing, conscious and resolute, of the convictions that bind me to biblical faith. I do not claim that at the deep level of motivations these convictions remain without any effect on the interest that I take in this or that problem, even in the overall problematic of the self. But I think I have presented to my readers arguments alone, which do not assume any commitment from the reader to reject, accept, or suspend anything with regard to biblical faith. It will be observed that this asceticism of the argument, which marks, I believe, all my philosophical work, leads to a type of philosophy from which the actual mention of God is absent and in which the question of God, as a philosophical question, itself remains in a suspension that could be called

agnostic, as the final lines of the tenth study will attest. It is in an effort not to make an exception to this suspension that the sole extension given to the nine studies conducted within the dimension of a philosophical hermeneutics consists in an ontological investigation that involves no ontotheological amalgamation.[2]

The second citation occurs within a discussion of the dialectic between the phenomenological discourse of passivity as the flesh or one's own body, the otherness of other people in the relation to intersubjectivity, and the conscience as the relation of the self to itself, and speculative discourse with its metacategory of "otherness." "The main virtue of such a dialectic is that it keeps the self from occupying the place of foundation."[3] For Ricoeur, the phenomenon of the conscience attests to an ultimate, irreducible equivocalness with respect to the metacategory of the other on the strictly philosophical plane.[4]

Perhaps the philosopher as philosopher has to admit that one does not know and cannot say whether this Other, the source of the injunction, is another person whom I can look in the face or who can stare at me, or my ancestors for whom there is no representation, to so great an extent does my debt to them constitute my very self, or God—living God, absent God—or an empty place. With this aporia of the Other, philosophical discourse comes to an end.[5]

For Anderson, Ricoeur's position concerning agnosticism and attestation in relation to the aporia of the other involves "a certain degree of self-deception in claiming to confront radical suspicion."[6] His reliance upon attestation as "the assurance—the credence and the trust—of *existing* in the mode of selfhood"[7] calls into question, Anderson contends, his assertions concerning the agnostic character of philosophical discourse. Though briefly entertaining the possibility of Ricoeur's own designation of his agnosticism as methodological, the primacy of attestation, within which suspicion is not merely the contrary of attestation, but that which inheres as "the path *toward* and crossing *within* attestation,"[8] is seen as profoundly affecting the status of the "so-called" autonomy of philosophical discourse:

Far from an autonomous discourse, philosophy gives any final priority concerning the Other to the domain of belief. Despite Ricoeur's claim to leave his philosophy open to doubt, he appears far from any religious scepticism, and he seems much closer to Descartes' certainty (even as guaranteed by God) and Hegel's absolute knowledge than he wants to admit. In other words, I conclude by challenging the idea of an *autonomous* philosophical discourse in Ricoeur since belief remains the ultimate, however, covert, foundation for attestation—for his hermeneutical method of truth.[9]

In other words, Anderson's suspicion is that, despite Ricoeur's protests to the contrary, the primacy of attestation signifies that Ricoeur's philosophical discourse is covertly determined by religious belief/conviction and theological discourse.

It is questionable, however, whether the senses of the term *agnosticism* in the citations from Ricoeur can be conflated in the manner in which Anderson claims. The second citation concerns a specifically intraphilosophical agnosticism, familiar to the tradition of French reflexive philosophy and its method of immanence.[10] The first citation utilizes agnosticism in the context of philosophy in relation to non-philosophy, its other, namely, religious faith and its discourse. It is this latter sense of the term *agnosticism* that Anderson chiefly has in mind.[11] Clarification of the senses in which agnosticism is used, or even the question of the relation between them, depends upon a prior clarification of what is meant by philosophy, specifically, Ricoeur's understanding of philosophy as a hermeneutics of the "I am." And an evaluation of Anderson's challenge toward Ricoeur's advocacy of the autonomy of philosophical discourse also requires a prior clarification of the sense of philosophy. In particular, since an asceticism of philosophical argument is claimed to mark, Ricoeur believes, all his philosophical work, one must explicate his understanding of philosophy in terms of the development of his thought.

This article shall attempt to clarify the sense of the autonomy of philosophical discourse in Ricoeur in relation to the overall structure of the relation between philosophy and theology in the development of Ricoeur's thought by noting the oft overlooked influence from two persons in the French Reformed tradition, primarily Roger Mehl and Pierre Thévenaz.[12] Secondly, Ricoeur's hermeneutical philosophy of the "I am" will be explicated as an *approfondissement* of the French reflexive philosophical tradition.[13]

ESCHATOLOGY AS THE HORIZON FOR PHILOSOPHICAL REFLECTION

Ricoeur claims that Roger Mehl's *La Condition du philosophe chrétien* is the "first great work in the French language where the new Reformed theology confronts the pretensions and the vocation of philosophy"[14] and articulates a positive attitude toward philosophical reflection on the basis of a radically Christocentric theology. The context for the book is the famous controversy in French philosophy and theology concerning the question "Is there a Christian philosophy?"[15] For Mehl, it is impossible to unite the affirmations of theology and philosophy in a synthetic framework that could be called a "Christian philosophy" *(philosophie chrétienne)*. The relation between faith and reason cannot be that of two modes of knowledge within the genus of knowledge. They are not two possibilities within the neutral homogeneity of a formal order that would envelop both. Mehl contends that both philosophy and theology would rightly protest against such a synthesis. The problem is

> to discover not a philosophy of Christian structure, but a philosophy of Christian intention. . . . This means that we shall be more interested in the philosopher than in the philosophy; and that when we approach philosophy itself, it is the *work* rather than the *system* that we shall consider in it: we shall deal with the Christian's condition in so far as he engages in philosophical activity.[16]

The condition of the Christian philosopher can only be clearly delineated if the pretensions of philosophy as system have been disrupted through critique in light of the eschatological character of God's self-revelation in Jesus Christ, which situates philosophical reflection under both judgment and promise. Revelation gives significance to philosophical reflection as work in light of situating the person of the philosopher as Christian in respect to the dialectic relation between fall and redemption. For Mehl, revelation as eschatological is considered as the term that, "remaining exterior to all philosophical work, moreover, not possibly being incorporated in this work, constitutes the judgment of this work."[17]

For Mehl, there are three major pretensions in the history of philosophy for collusion between philosophical reflection and dogmatics. The first pretension is for philosophy as metaphysics to serve as a necessary prolegomena to Christian dogmatics. It can serve as the ancillary preparation of the comprehension of revelation neither in terms of a continuity in form between the two affirmations within the genus of the true nor in terms of an overlapping identity of "matter" or content of the affirmations made. The notion of truth is fragmentary, and it "is impossible to establish an ascending hierarchical order of truth from the objective truths of science to the revealed truths of the gospel through the intermediary of truth pertaining to value."[18] Despite the fragmentation of the different sectors of truths, for the believer, the unity of truth exists only as a promise.

> It suffices us to know by faith that, in the order of things to come, all that is hidden will be revealed, that all things will take on their exact meaning, that all human activities will find their accomplishment, and that the truths we have reached will be unified. It is in this eschatological perspective that the problem of truth must be set.[19]

The second pretension is more subtle. The philosopher, in recognizing the primacy of revelation and the discontinuity between what reason claims to know of God and what God reveals of God's-self, can still claim that metaphysics necessarily intervenes in order to make possible the understanding of revelation. This pretension is the claim to elucidate in a systematic development the sense of revelation as "already given." To be sure, there is precisely a comprehension of revelation, but Mehl argues that this comprehension is not of a philosophical order. "The work of Christian dogmatics is, in a sense, a work of reason, but this reason must remain a reason proper to faith."[20] Dogmatic comprehension is entirely to be distinguished from philosophical or metaphysical comprehension in light of the eschatological foundation of faith.

The third pretension is to think that faith renders possible a spiritual philosophy in light of the renewing of the understanding or mind, so that there could be a "Christian state of philosophy":

> Already prevented from yielding its full fruit even when it stoops to things below it, our wounded reason is indeed still more so, when it attempts to raise itself to God. In order that it may succeed in this, in the measure permitted by its natural perfection, grace must first purify it, dress its wounds and guide it towards an object of which it is no longer worthy; but as soon as grace does this, it is indeed the withered reason itself, which revives under grace, the same reason, but healed, saved, therefore in another state, which sees and proves. Its knowledge is therefore truly natural, its philosophy even though christianized is a true philosophy.[21]

Despite the coherence of this position, Mehl contends that, according to the New Testament, the renewing of the mind remains a promise through the new creation of the human in Christ Jesus as an eschatological reality. The human cannot assert the restoration of the integrity of a primordial state. It is only true outside of ourselves (*extra nos*) in Christ and only through faith. The promise of the new creation will become a manifest reality only at the Parousia. "Thus we are forbidden to speak of the new human otherwise than in an eschatological perspective."[22] That which truly characterizes the present reality of the Christian is the condition of being a *homo viator* who is engaged in the movement toward the "new human" between the times of judgment and promise.

The renewal of understanding signifies that the intellectual activity of the Christian is called to give signs of this hidden reality, otherwise philosophy would remain solely the work of the "old" human, "nothing but a homage to the Prince of this world, travestied with the name of God, as extremist orthodoxies have always believed and as Barthianism in its revolutionary initial stages narrowly escaped thinking too."[23] Though hidden, the renewing of the mind is at work and bears fruit, "without our even being able to credit its empirical manifestations with normative or probatory value."[24] For Mehl, the work of the philosopher as Christian does not consist in inserting Christian theological propositions in his/her presuppositions, whether avowed or implicit, to be exempted from rational criticism. The eschatological relation between faith and reason is less in the themes, in philosophy itself as work, than in the philosopher as person. One could also say that the relation is manifest in its *allure*, its intention, its aims or motives.

This eschatological relation is one of tension, a relation *hors série*, one marked by the exceptional character of an absence of a common measure. This nonlogical relation lies at the root of the relation between philosophy and revelation, such that the pretentious relations of compromise, synthesis, and subordination between philosophy and faith are disallowed. The eschatological relation, hence, "renders at the same time to dogmatics its own dimension, its own intelligence, and to philosophy its autonomy, its rationality, its risk, its hope."[25]

The eschatological relation permits the requisite distinction between philosophy and theology. It also allows for a possible dialogue between theologian and philosopher with both enjoying equal freedom and dignity. The possibility of dialogue is grounded in the distinction, since to distinguish does not necessarily mean to separate.[26] For Mehl, philosophy, historically in its dialogue with theology, has benefited in an "indirect and somewhat oblique manner" from theology, for example, the appreciation of the problem of time. Likewise, theology has benefited from and has need of philosophy in terms of the development of a hermeneutics, a conceptuality, and a critique of philosophical discourse as a methodical exigence within theology. Like the aforementioned pretensions of philosophy, theology itself can be subject to the temptation of not recognizing its own need for philosophical reflection, resulting in a complete abstaining from philosophical reflection, whereas the real problem is in knowing how to use it.

> All Christian philosophy—and it is why it remains indiscernible to historians and to philosophers—appears to reside in this decision of the Christian to attest in philosophy the reality of the renewal of the mind.... Let us not call Christian a philosophy using Christian data or even suggestions—such a philosophy can remain profoundly pagan; but let us call Christian the philosophy—whatever its assertions—of a person who knows that the Kingdom is at hand, that all things will be made new, and who is preparing him/herself through philosophical reflection for the coming of that Kingdom—in short, the philosophy of a person whose thought feels the eschatological tension.[27]

In the preface to the first edition of *History and Truth*, Ricoeur states, with regards to the essay "The History of Philosophy and the Unity of Truth," that hope with an eschatological intention has an impact in philosophical reflection in the manner of an actual rational feeling, a regulative feeling capable of purifying both historical skepticism and fanaticism. Skepticism is that which refuses to inquire after meaning, and fanaticism is that which declares meaning and its closure prematurely. "[W]hat eschatological language calls hope is recaptured reflectively [for philosophy] in the very *delay* of all syntheses, in the *postponement* of the solution to all dialectics."[28] The philosophical dimension of the impact of hope preserves the idea of openness through the virtues of limitation and affirmation. Negatively, it shatters the hubris of philosophical systems or philosophies of history (or both in the case of Hegel) to claim monistic closure, but retains the interest of reason in the unity of truth. Positively, the impact of hope in philosophical reflection protects and affirms the specificity and singularity of distinctive philosophical and other visions of the world, namely, pluralism in distinction from a purportedly meaningless relativism. He also declares that he feels that it is possible to overcome the mutual exclusion involved in the apparent mortal contradiction between the eschatological and the philosophical. "Yet I feel that it is possible to convert this mortal contradiction into a living tension, that is to say, to live this contradiction—to live Christian hope philosophically as the directive principle of reflection—for the conviction of the ultimate unity of truth is the very Spirit of reason."[29] Ricoeur's craft as a historian of philosophy is marked by this tensive "dual affinity."

> Yet the methodological rigor of the history of philosophy does not seem weakened by linking the rationality of the historian's craft to the mystery of eschatology. For the subjective motivation of a craft is one thing, and the methodical structure which secures its autonomy another. The twofold affinity, by which I here define the median or intercalary situation of the history of philosophy, merely concerns the spiritual economy of man tormented by problems. This dependence within the order of spiritual motivation does not prevent the history of philosophy from achieving its own independence in elaborating its own problematic and its own methods.... This should be enough to show that a discipline may be dependent on the spiritual economy of man who exercises it, and autonomous as to its problems and its methods.[30]

Both the distinction between spiritual motivation of the philosopher as person and the methodological autonomy of the discipline of philosophy, and the twofold virtues of the impact of hope, are rooted in a further distinction in light of the relation between philosophy and its other, nonphilosophy. This more fundamental distinction is that between philosophy and nonphilosophy, understood as that which is anterior to philosophy precisely as the source of philosophy. The rationality of philosophy, when separated from its source(s), can only collapse into deceitful and violent rationalizations.

> Here philosophy seems to be well guarded against itself by nonphilosophy. This presents us with a perplexing situation as to the possibility of identifying philosophy with the search for a "point of departure." It seems that in order to be independent in the elaboration of its problems, methods, and statements, philosophy must be dependent with respect to its sources and its profound motivation. This fact cannot fail to be disquieting.[31]

Philosophy does not have its own (*propre*) object. It reflects upon experience in all its dimensions: scientific, ethical, aesthetic, political, et al. "Philosophy has its sources beyond itself"[32] and, as Jules Lachelier put it, "[i]t is the office of philosophy to *understand* all, even religion."[33] For Ricoeur, the "timid" hope of philosophical reflection is situated within the confines of the methodological autonomy of philosophical rigor and in the vicinity of its nonphilosophical sources. This "timid hope" is seen by Ricoeur as an extension of the *docta ignorantio* taught by Xenophanes:

> There never was nor will there ever be any man who has certain knowledge about the gods and about all things that I tell of. And

even if he does happen to get most things right, still he himself is not aware of this. Yet all may have shadows of the truth.³⁴

Ricoeur utilizes further this eschatological configuration of philosophy in his *De l'interprétation: essai sur Freud*. In the course of a philosophical interpretation of Freudian psychoanalysis, Ricoeur proposes a reflexive dialectic between archaeology and teleology within the limits of reflexive philosophy. He refers to

> the overdetermination of the symbol, which cannot be understood outside the dialecticity of the reflection which I propose. This is why all discussion which treats my double interpretation of religious symbols as an isolated theme necessarily retrogresses to a philosophy of compromise from which the incentive for struggle has been withdrawn. In this terrible battle for meaning, nothing and no one comes out unscathed. The "timid" hope must cross the desert of the path of mourning. This is why I will not stop on the threshold of the struggle of interpretations and do so by giving myself this warning: outside the dialectic of archaeology and teleology, these interpretations confront one another without possible arbitration or are juxtaposed in lazy eclecticisms which are the caricature of thought.³⁵

He acknowledges, however, that such an approach cannot solve the question of the radical origin of religious symbolism; it can through an enlargement of reflexive thought serve "merely to give us a frontier view of this symbolism."³⁶

> I shall not practice that crafty method of extrapolation. I declare quite clearly that I have no means of proving the existence of an authentic problematic of faith from a phenomenology of spirit, more or less borrowed from Hegelian phenomenology; I even admit quite willingly that such a problematic exceeds without doubt the resources of a philosophy of reflexion, that the anterior dialectic has immensely enlarged, without at the sametime shattering it in as much as it remains from beginning to end a method of immanence.³⁷

The reflexive dialectic between archaeology and teleology is situated within the horizons of creation and eschatology manifest in religious symbolism. Creation is the horizon of archaeology and eschatology is the horizon of teleology.

> I am not unaware of the fragility of this relationship, *in a philosophy of reflection*, between the figures of spirit and the symbols of

the sacred. From the viewpoint of the philosophy of reflection, which is a philosophy of immanence, the symbols of the sacred appear only as cultural factors mixed in with the figures of spirit. But at the same time these symbols designate the impact on culture of a reality that the movement of culture does not contain; they speak of the Wholly Other, of the Wholly Other than all of history; in this way they exercise an attraction and a call upon the entire series of the figures of culture. This is the sense in which I spoke of a prophecy or an eschatology. It is solely through its relation to the immanent teleology of the figures of culture that the sacred concerns this philosophy; the sacred is its eschatology; it is the horizon that reflection does not comprehend, does not encompass, but can only salute as that which quietly presents itself from afar.[38]

Several interrelated issues are raised in this discussion and require further clarification. The first concerns the nature and status of a "philosophy of reflection." A subsequent issue is the relation between reflexive philosophy and a phenomenology of the sacred, in which the symbols of the sacred simultaneously "exercise an attraction and a call" as distinct from cultural figures and yet can only appear as one amongst many cultural figures. We shall take as our guiding question here the question of the relation between reflexive philosophy and phenomenological in order to characterize Ricoeur's philosophical program as rather that of a "post-Husserlian Kantian" following the suggestion of Jean Greisch.[39] This is a more apt designation of Ricoeur's position than that of being a post-Hegelian Kantian that Anderson highlights. Anderson overestimates the significance of the impact upon Ricoeur of the French reception of Hegel in the 1930s in the work of Alexander Kojève, Jean Hyppolite, and Eric Weil.[40] Though Ricoeur adopts at certain points Weil's language of "post-Hegelian Kantianism," Ricoeur himself notes that

> [m]y first formation had been rather from the German side with K. Jaspers and E. Husserl .... As a student, I belonged to a generation which had not as yet pursued the great Hegelian work with perseverance, which took place chiefly under the impulsion of Alexander Kojève, Jean Wahl, Jean Hyppolite, down to the actual period of translators. I knew at first the university Kant. But it was a very French Kantianism, constructed moreover with liberal borrowings. Unfortunately, students today are not aware of almost all of F. Ravaisson, E. Boutrous, J. Lachelier....[41]

While many expositions of Ricoeur highlight and focus upon his philosophical program as a synthesis of phenomenology and hermeneutics,[42] or in passing note the influence early in his career of Husserl, Gabriel Marcel,[43] and Karl Jaspers, most discussions neglect the crucial and pivotal influence of the French reflexive philosophical tradition. It should not be forgotten that Ricoeur was initiated into reflexive philosophy by Léon Brunschvicg through the completion in 1934 of his *diplôme d'études supérieures* on the problem of God in the thought of Jules Lachelier and Jules Lagneau.[44]

> In fact, the true benefit of this passage by Lachelier and Lagneau was elsewhere. Through them, I found myself initiated and in face incorporated in the tradition of French reflexive philosophy, akin to German Neo-Kantianism.[45]

> On the one side, this tradition goes back, through Émile Boutroux and Felix Ravaisson, to Maine de Biran; on the other side, it inclined towards Jean Nabert who had published in 1924 *L' Expérience intérieure de la liberté*, a work which situated him somewhere between Bergson and Léon Brunschvicg.[46]

Ricoeur's work has always been marked by a productive dialogue in and through a tensive pluralism of philosophical positions.[47] And he has retained the import of the French reflexive tradition as a constitutive dimension in his philosophy. In response to the question concerning the characteristic presuppositions of the philosophical tradition that acknowledges himself as belonging to, he describes them in the following manner:

> [I]t is in the line of a *reflexive* philosophy; it continues in the movement of Husserlian *phenomenology*; it wishes to be a *hermeneutic* variant of that phenomenology.[48]

Pierre Thévenaz's militant philosophical development likewise situates itself in the tensive dialogue between reflexive philosophy and phenomenology, with a radical primacy conferred upon reflexive philosophy. This development shall cast light on Ricoeur's own *approfondissement* of the reflexive tradition, in which the phenomenological and hermeneutic moments are simultaneously the realization and transformation of reflexive philosophy.[49]

PIERRE THÉVENAZ AND REFLEXIVE PHILOSOPHY

Experience, according to Thévenaz, always gives to philosophical reflexion its decisive motives and salutary warnings.[50] Experience as a radical shock (*expérience-choc*) and its capacity for contestation can initiate and motivate reflection. For Thévenaz, all true experience puts reason into question in such a way that reason becomes a question for itself: *quaestio mihi factus sum*. The results of philosophical inquiry are incessantly put into question, and this critical interrogation marks the proper status of reason as "the ascending progress of philosophy insofar as reason consents to remain open and disposable with regard to experience."[51]

Thévenaz further contends that philosophical reason, when confronted with the proclamation of the Gospel, finds itself placed into radical question. Philosophy, though it came into being the moment it began to contest itself, experiences an intensification when confronted with the claim that it, as the wisdom of the world, is only folly before God (I Cor. 3:19). Reason could find itself tempted with the possibility of either revolt (as in an absolute rationalism) or abdication (as in *sacrificium intellectus*), but it as reason cannot avoid the disconcerting question of its own possible foolishness. Even if reason brackets God, it has still not suppressed the radical philosophical aporia of its own possible foolishness. In light of the imputation of folly, being affronted with the possibility of folly, reason itself undergoes an experience of ignorance, a "radical ignorance of itself," "powerless in knowing and in proving to oneself whether it is folly or not."[52] Its fundamental aporia is beyond both error and Cartesian doubt.[53]

For Thévenaz, however, this fundamental aporia is not a reason for despair as if it were an absolute impasse; rather, this impasse possesses a negative fecundity for the possibility for reason's beginning an adventure of research— "the consciousness of an aporia is not an aporia of consciousness."[54] The consciousness of the fundamental aporia is the consciousness of the crisis of reason as the suspension of the supposed "naturalness" and self-evident "good sense" of reason.

> However, the imputation of folly or the aporia of reason reveals at once this world of "sense" and the "self-evident." There is meaning, there is rationality, certainly, but it is not self-evident: rationality is not "natural." In effect, there is an impasse precisely because the reference to an established (hence, accessible) sense is removed. Until now one willingly thought that the progress of knowledge would realize itself insofar as very natural, but rationally unfounded evidences would at last be brought to light and submitted to critique. But all this work, by which science constituted itself for centuries against the "wholly naturalness" of initial experience, itself rests upon the radical, fundamental, ontological "wholly natural" that no one experience or audacity of reason had ever either called into question or appear to do so.

The foundation of natural evidences could be contested because of a more fundamental "wholly natural" sustained the enterprise: the very being of reason.[55]

With the imputation of folly, reason that had served as the critical foundation of the progress of science, enters into a state of crisis in which its "naturalness" is no longer given. Reason as the naturally evident principle of critique now finds itself in a state of crisis in which its naturalness is called into question. Reason undergoes a radical reduction; now its sense must be founded, for suddenly it cannot rely upon a nature. "The sense is not inscribed in things or in the nature of reason; it is to be inscribed. Reason is not given; it is to be procured as such."[56] But, if reason does not have an evident "nature," then folly cannot be inscribed "by nature" in the essence of reason. Instead, if folly remains possible and reason remains to be discovered, then the sense of folly imputed to reason should be sought in the "folly" of the sense of reason that calls itself "natural," the sense that is reputed to be the secure guarantee of all its activity.[57]

For Thévenaz, the "folly" of this sense of reason is termed the "autism of reason." Autistic reason supports itself upon its so-called natural evidences, not encountering the experience that truly puts it into question and in crisis projects it outside of itself, without that which is truly other. It "is subjective by the simple fact of being itself, of only being self. Lacking the other, it has alienated itself in itself."[58] The autocritique of reason, even its most conscious radicalization of itself, is not sufficient in itself to overcome the autism of reason, precisely because the autism of reason is its self-sufficiency, its "autarchy." For Thévenaz, the autarchy of reason is distinct from the autonomy of reason; it is the alienation of the autonomy of reason "when it is the refusal of every external instance and the entire putting into question of reason, when it attempts to found reason upon itself or not to found it at all, it betrays a heart of autism."[59] Autistic reason is a prisoner of itself. Its "captive thought" (II Cor. 10:5) retained the "true captive" (Rom. 1:18): it is there the "injustice." It believed itself too righteous (cf. Eccl. 7:16)."[60]

For Thévenaz, the Christian experience of the Gospel certainly was a decisive shock, but fundamentally it was only the occasion for reason to emerge from itself, to escape autism. The experience of crisis is now a philosophical experience, which emerges in light of its astonishment at the radicality of its crisis.

> Whoever says crisis of consciousness says the seizure of consciousness. In suspending itself in this manner in the void, through the *epoche* of sense, in placing itself thus between parentheses itself, reason necessarily directs its attention upon itself consequently.

> It is astonished, but it is astonished above all at being what it is. Its sense itself, this sense which proceeded in such a manner from itself that it had not even noticed, is astonishing: why sense rather than folly? Reason is called thus to correct itself and, as it is on a new plane, to begin anew. It is towards a new consciousness of itself that it is called first of all.[61]

It is called toward a new consciousness of itself in which rationality is not self-evident to itself and the possibility of folly is not excluded. In the suspense of the epoche, reason is called "to find the sense of its folly and to find the folly (possible) of its sense."[62]

In the suspension of its so-called "natural sense" reason finds itself situated. The situation of its beginning (*situation de départ*) is neither a first truth or certitude nor any longer a principle to which deduction clings; rather, its initial situation is the contingency of a prereflexive experience that is nontransparent to itself.

> The initial situation is then the moment where the philosopher has recognized that he is at work, where he proceeds to pass to the consolidation of an experience again precarious or to the amplification of a yet embryonic consciousness. The situation of departure is then an essentially problematic, I mean, interrogative, questioning situation. It is the moment of the "putting into question" of experience, on the one hand, and of philosophy, on the other hand. Putting into question in the double sense of a question which begins to be formed, an interrogation which begins to take consciousness of itself and, on the other hand, of a contestation of lived experience, or putting it between parentheses, or of philosophy instigating a malaise, an impatience, an appeal, or an exigence to found itself.[63]

The initial situation also plays a permanent role in the ulterior philosophical reflection of reason, whose assurance rests on the awareness of the situation and is yet marked by incertitude through being put into question.[64] The explicative putting into question of the situation of reason involves the fundamental question of the relation between the sense (or intelligibility) of the situation and the self-reflexivity of reason.

The phenomenological and reflexive methods are used by Thévenaz in order to explicate the "situation of reason." Under the condition of the phenomenological reduction, noematic analysis progressively explicates the consciousness of the situation in light of the primacy of intentionality's anteriority. Intentionality affirms the primacy of consciousness *of* something over consciousness of oneself, the priority of intentionality *ad extra* over the *ad intra* of reflexion.⁶⁵ But, for Thévenaz, while intentionality remains the chronologically first structure of consciousness, reflexion is the ontologically first structure of consciousness.

> Reflexive analysis has a proper conception of reflexion, but perhaps a feeble, or insufficiently elaborated, notion of being; while phenomenology has an apt conception of being, but a too objectivist or insufficient conception of reflexion. It is in mutually enriching each other that these two methods could trace a new field for philosophical thought. The first would establish the immediate and explicit relation to the self; the second the relation to the object. Not that they are simply complementary and have divided into two juxtaposed sectors the total area of consciousness.... We say, on the contrary, that phenomenological intentionality should enclothe itself in the reflexive structure of consciousness, which, because it is more radical, has a sort of ontological primacy in relation to it.⁶⁶

The reflexive method is the movement from the comprehension of the situation to the self-understanding of reason as being-situated. For Thévenaz, the reflexive method is a more radical "reduction" in that its "reduction is no longer a methodical artifice of reason, manipulated by it, but it has become the condition even of reason."⁶⁷

The explication of the situation in light of the radical experience of the suspension of sense also involves the phenomenological bracketing of the atavisms of reflection or traditional attitudes, religious and philosophical. Part of this bracketing is the methodical bracketing, for Thévenaz, of claims concerning the God of the Gospels or Christian truth for reasons of method. The methodical bracketing expresses a methodical indifference towards positive affirmations concerning revelation as well as negative, rationalistic critiques. Thévenaz insists upon not collapsing the distinction between a skeptical putting into question and a methodical putting between parentheses. "This indifference of method is only methodical, hence, provisional, and this shall be, ... [rather] to wander anew than to transform it into a systematic and definitive *indifferentism*."⁶⁸

In light of the experience of the fundamental aporia, the benefit of the phenomenological reduction for Thévenaz lies in the reductions of the senses of the various forms in which the autism of reason can present itself.⁶⁹ Reason can be autistic either as an absolute/unconditioned point of view, as an instrumental organ of objectivity, as assimilative of reality into itself, or as divine, that is, self-sufficient. These forms are either evident or camouflaged forms of *la raison divine*. Thévenaz contends that the experience of the radical reduction exposes the excessive divine pretensions of the unconsciousness of autistic reason. The purification of reason's pretensions, through the phenomenological reductions and the reduction of reflexive analysis, allows for the emergence of the humility of reason, a reason conscious of its condition, its humanity. For Thévenaz, philosophical reason is that of "philosophy *sans absolu*."[70]

A philosophy *sans absolu* is the mark of a philosophy of concrete reflexion that assumes the situation as its permanent condition. Through the conscious assumption of its condition, reason is engaged autonomously in its condition. The unconsciousness of its condition in the autism of reason is the major temptation of reason, its "bad faith." Neutrality and indifference, traditional marks of the freedom and sovereign mastery of reason, are, for Thévenaz, the expressions of the autistic refusal of the condition of reason. For Thévenaz, such neutrality and indifference cannot charaacterize the engagement of human reason in its condition. For an unconditioned reason, a reason not deabsolutized, lucidity upon itself and the world is only possible through disengagement through skeptical doubt and neutrality, and its "objectivity" is proportional to its degree of disengagement. Thévenaz contends that such a proposed lucidity, that itself relies upon "a perfect translucidity in oneself" (*une parfaite translucidité à soi-même*), rests upon an unconsciousness of self. Rather, he proposes that the progressive explication of the reflexive consciousness of the condition of reason should discover as authentic a lucidity of reason "where one is lucid towards oneself, there where one locates exactly it interior opacities. A lucidity bound to the condition is, on the contrary, a lucidity upon the non-transparency of this condition."[71]

Besides the possibility of indifference/neutrality, there are other permanent forms of temptation for a human reason in condition, such as that of rationalization and its inverse, the abdication of the *sacrificium intellectus*. Also even a nonimperialistic reason can harbor traces of absolutism by demarcating zones of influence where faith and reason each maintain their absoluteness in isolation behind barriers, without being contested by the other. Lines of demarcation as professed signs of humility and modesty could in fact be inevitable masks of an unrepentant will to power of an enclosed absolutism.[72] For Thévenaz, the most crafty temptation of the autarchy of reason's pride is to dissimulate itself under the modesty of limits. Yet the deliberate acceptance of such a temptation would signify the regression of philosophy insofar as reason would not consent to remaining open and disposable with regard to experience—in this case, the experience of those who believe. Such a decision would once again signify the forgetfulness of the condition of reason.

For Thévenaz, the condition of reason is not restrictive in the sense that it determines, stipulates, or legislates to reason. The de-absolutization of reason as something unconditioned does not imply the total conditioning of reason. Nor does it imply the absolutization of the condition: "[T]he condition of reason does not become an absolute which stipulates to it. The condition of reason is the description neither of an objective situation that determines reason nor of a simply subjective situation."[73] Even to speak, as Thévenaz does, of the "Christian condition of philosophical reason," does not mean that reason is placed heteronomously under external stipulations. Instead of being a stipulation to which reason must capitulate, Thévenaz understands the Christian condition as an appeal coming from the total experience of a believing human being. "An appeal does not stipulate [ne conditionne pas]; it precisely appeals, it calls for a free decision."[74] This free decision is a response in light of reason's endeavor to understand the appeal. "The decision marks the decisive moment in the acceptance of the condition, the moment where consciousness emerges in an action, in an activity, testifies by acts, by its engagement itself that it is conscious and that it has a response to give."[75]

Does this mean that philosophical reason qua philosophical knows that it is before God *(devant Dieu)*? This is a question that Ricoeur posed in the conclusion of his preface to Thévenaz's work.[76] Thévenaz's posthumously published *La condition de la raison philosophique* would respond in the negative. A philosophical reason, de-absolutized of its purported ontological guarantees of being directly related to God, is not divine. Furthermore, for Thévenaz, it is the experience of the believer that acts upon philosophical reason in condition as an appeal to exceed itself *(appel à se dépasser)*. "It is not a matter of it elevating itself to or entering into a direct relation with God; it is not a matter any longer of surpassing itself towards a superhumanity. Rather, it takes notice that it is in the human or towards the human that it is called to exceed itself."[77] For reason, the human experience of the believer is an appeal to enlarge experience in a transforming dilation or amplification of the awareness of its condition. "Reason, in doing this, . . . does not rejoin faith, replace it, and its direction or vocation does not become dictated by faith."[78] The relation between faith and reason as an appeal from one to the other is not that of *un conditionnement*. The appeal from faith to reason is not an appeal for the conversion of reason, but rather the appeal for the conversion of reason to "reason in condition *(en condition)*." If there is no direct relation from philosophical reason to God, Thévenaz contends that one cannot speak of a faith of reason.[79] Reason's explication of its condition allows it to take account of that which is given in this condition, namely, "the indispensable mediation of the human experience of the believer."[80]

RICOEUR AND THE HERMENEUTIC TRANSFORMATION OF REFLEXIVE PHILOSOPHY

Thévenaz's articulation of an autonomous philosophy *sans absolu* in relation to Christian faith is likewise affirmed by Ricoeur in what he terms a "philosophical approach," an autonomous way between abstention and capitulation. Ricoeur understands that approach to be that of approximation, in which the work of philosophical discourse situates itself in proximity to kerygmatic and theological discourse. Ricoeur maintains that

> [t]his work of thought is a work starting with listening and nevertheless within the autonomy of responsible thought. It is an incessant reform of thinking, but in the limits of simple reason. The conversion of the philosopher is a conversion within philosophy and to philosophy according to its own internal exigencies. If there is only one *logos*, the *logos* of Christ asks of me nothing less, in the capacity as a philosopher, than a more whole and more perfect putting into work of reason, nothing more than reason, but *all* of reason [*raison entière*].[81]

Yet, in distinction from Thévenaz, Ricoeur presents an *approfondissement* in terms of a hermeneutic transformation and realization of reflexive philosophy. While Thévenaz spoke of human experience as the indispensable mediation in the relation between faith and reason, for Ricoeur, language becomes the privileged, but not exclusive mediation: "Whatever ultimately may be the nature of the so-called religious experience, it comes to language, it is articulated in a language, and the most appropriate place to interpret it on its own terms is to inquire into its linguistic expression."[82] The major development beyond Thévenaz is the systematic explication of language in its myriad forms as belonging to the human condition and drawing the implications of its *Sprachlichkeit* for a hermeneutic transformation of reflexive philosophy, whose initial situation is the fullness of language such that the condition of reason is hermeneutic.

Ricoeur contends that this linguistic turn itself is an implication of reflexive philosophy when a philosophy of reflexion is no longer conceived as a philosophy of consciousness. Ricoeur's proposal, that reflexion can and should be hermeneutic, is an appropriation of Jean Nabert's understanding of the relation between act and sign.[83] What Ricoeur proposes

> attaches itself again to reflexive philosophy; it is connected to the philosophy of Jean Nabert, to whom I dedicated of old my

> *The Symbolism of Evil.* It is with Nabert that I have encountered the most concise formulation of the relation between the desire to be and the signs in which desire expresses itself, projects itself, and explicates itself. With Nabert, I firmly hold that to understand is inseparable from understanding oneself, that the symbolic universe is the milieu of self-explication. This means, on the one hand, that there is no longer any problem of meaning if signs are not the means, the milieu, the medium, thanks to which an existing human being seeks to situate itself, project itself, and understand itself; and, on the other hand, in the inverse sense, that there is no direct apprehension of the self by itself, no interior apperception of signs. Briefly, my hypothesis of philosophical labor is that it is concrete reflection, that is to say, the *cogito* mediated by the whole universe of signs.[84]

For Ricoeur, the mediation between the intelligibility of the situation and the self-reflexivity of rational reflexion occurs through the exteriority of signs; and it is a mediation that can and should be (and, in Ricoeur's subsequent work, is in fact) analogically extended from signs to symbols, to discourse, to discourse as work (*oeuvre*), to texts, and actions (*sensée* as a text). Understanding something and understanding oneself are both semiotically mediated, and reflexion is the bond between the comprehension of signs and that of oneself. More specifically, reflexion is "the appropriation of our effort to exist and our desire to be through works which testify of this effort and of this desire."[85]

Yet the indirectness of the mediation of reflexion through signs is necessitated, not only due to the self-attestation of the self in the detour through works, but also because of the reality of the various masks consciousness can assume as false consciousness. Immediate consciousness is first of all "false" consciousness, and "it is always necessary to rise by means of a corrective critique from misunderstandings to understanding."[86] The necessity of a corrective critique also arises in the case of the phenomenon of testimony with its trial-like character. The phenomenon of testimony in which an attestation of something is pronounced by someone likewise raises the possibility of false witnesses. In the case of religious testimony, the possibility of false witnesses raises also the possibility of false gods.

And it is with the limit phenomenon of religious testimony that the limits of a philosophical approach of reflexive philosophy as hermeneutical can be discerned, such that testimony represents the limit that "should be applied to words, works, actions, and to lives which attest to an intention, an aspiration, an idea at the heart of experience and history which nonetheless transcend experience and history."⁸⁷ For Ricoeur, following Jean Nabert, testimony is a limit case where "the greatest interiority of the act [as reflexive] corresponds to "the greatest exteriority of the sign."⁸⁸ The understanding of testimony represents the point of departure for the promotion and dilation of self-understanding of the most interior self through the open attention toward external signs that testify to the absolute in its appearances. In the phenomenon of testimony there is the mutual promotion of exteriority and interiority through the mutual dependency of the interiority of the act and the exteriority of the sign.

For Ricoeur, this mutuality between exteriority and interiority necessitates that a reflexive philosophy as a philosophical hermeneutic has to be "an ellipse with two foci that mediation tends to conflate but which can never be reduced to a unified central point" of identity.⁸⁹ The exteriority of testimony mediated through signs also disallows the primacy of interiority at the expense of exteriority and the resulting conflation of the desire for God with the desire for self-understanding⁹⁰ (and, for Thévenaz, the autarchy of reason). The two foci are two interpretive acts, the act of understanding of oneself and the historical understanding of the signs of the disclosure of the self-disclosure of the absolute. Furthermore, the two foci are both of the nature of judgements and acts (since judgments are the traces of acts).

> The correlation of judgments with judgment, of criteriology with trial, only expresses, in judicial terms, the relation of two *acts*: the act of a self-consciousness which divests (*se dépouille*) itself and tries to understand itself, the act of testifying by which the absolute is revealed in its signs and its works. In the same way as the act of original affirmation is enclosed in the discourse of predicates of the divine, testimony, understood as the action of testifying, is enclosed in the story of the witness to which we also give the name of testimony. If, at the level of judgments of a correlation, at the level of acts one can speak of reciprocity. The promotion of consciousness and the recognition of the absolute in its signs are reciprocal.⁹¹

This reciprocal promotion, for a philosophical hermeneutic of testimony with its elliptical foci, is the milieu within which the philosophical approximation of autonomous reason takes place. But the reciprocal promotion between reason and the testimony of faith can only occur if the distance between them is and remains irreducible precisely in terms of their difference. "The mutual promotion of reason and faith, in their difference, is the last word for a finite consciousness."⁹² The intersection between the acts of faith and reason in the interpretation of the phenomenon of testimony and its external signs entails the reciprocal promotion of each in its respective autonomy. Perhaps the recognition of their irreducible difference is the reason why there can only be a philosophical approach, an approach that draws near. Perhaps for a philosophy of simple reason that begins with language that attests its nonphilosophical sources and motivates reflection, the faith attested in testimony is its promised land; "but like Moses, the speaking and reflecting subject can only glimpse this land before dying"[93] in the new birth of faith. A simple reason that in its philosophical hermeneutic of testimony apperceives the pneumatological divide between the two and acknowledges the I of faith's testimony that "I believe that by my own reason or strength I cannot believe in Jesus Christ, my Lord, or come to him. But the Holy Spirit has called me through the Gospel, enlightened me with his gifts, and sanctified and preserved me in true faith, just as he calls, gathers, enlightens, and sanctifies the whole Christian church on earth and preserves it in union with Jesus Christ in the one true faith."[94]

NOTES

1. Pamela Sue Anderson, "Agnosticism and Attestation: An Aporia concerning the Other in Ricoeur's *Oneself as Another*," *Journal of Religion* (1994): 65.

2. OA, 24.

3. Ibid., 318.

4. For Ricoeur, the philosophical discussion on conscience and the "agnostic" claims made therein are distinct from the theological discussion of the testimony of conscience as a figure of the "summoned subject," responding self. Ricoeur did not include the final Gifford lectures in OA.

5. OA, 355. Cf. RF, 82.

6. Anderson, "Agnosticism and Attestation: An Aporia concerning the Other in Ricoeur's *Oneself as Another*," 75.

7. Ricoeur, Sa, 350 [302].

8. Ibid.

9. Anderson, "Agnosticism and Attestation: An Aporia concerning the Other in Ricoeur's *Oneself as Another*," 76.

10. Jean Nabert, *Elements for an Ethics*, Preface by Paul Ricoeur and trans. William J. Petrek (Evanston: Northwestern University Press [Studies in Phenomenology and Existential Philosophy], 1969).

11. Anderson, "Agnosticism and Attestation: An Aporia concerning the Other in Ricoeur's *Oneself as Another*," 76.

12. Roger Mehl was Ricoeur's friend and colleague in the Protestant Theological Faculty at the University of Strasbourg. Ricoeur wrote a review of Mehl's *La Condition du Philosophe chrétien* (Neuchatel/Paris: Delachaux & Niestlé S. A. [Série Theologique de L'<<actualité protestante>>], 1947 [*The Condition of the Christian Philosopher*, trans. Eva Kushner (Philadelphia: Fortress Press, 1963)]), published in *Christianisme social* 56 (1948):551–557.

Pierre Thévenaz (1913–1955) was from 1948 till his death a Swiss professor of philosophy on the Faculté des Lettres de l'Université de Lausanne. He also was in charge of *Revue de Theologie et de Philosophie de Lausanne* beginning in 1951, founded and directed the collection *Être et Penser* from 1943 until his death, and collaborated on the *Cahiers suisses of Esprit*. Ricoeur published a review, "Un philosophe protestant: Pierre Thévenaz," in *Esprit* that also was the preface to Pierre Thévenaz's posthumous collection of essays, *L'Homme et sa Raison*, Tome I: *Raison et Conscience de Soi* (Préface de Paul Ricoeur; Neuchatel: Éditions de la Baconnière [Être et Penser–Cahiers de Philosophie, 46], 1956.

13. It is difficult to state succinctly what is proper to the French reflexive philosophical tradition as a whole. Each of the figures in this tradition are quite distinctive in their own right and the characterization of French reflexive philosophy depends on the figures chosen. For instance, in his well-known encyclopedia article on *philosophie réflexive* [republished as "La philosophie réflexive," in *L'expérience intérieure de la liberté et autres essais de philosophie morale*, Préface de Paul Ricoeur (Paris: Presses Universitaires de France [Philosophie Morale], 1994): 397–411], Jean Nabert confines his attention to Maine de Biran (1766–1824), Jules Lachelier (1832–1918), Jules Lagneau (1851–1894), and Brunschvicg (1870–1944), whose orientation follows a method of immanence. Nabert does not include in this portrait of reflexive philosophy those who have been associated with the philosophical "spiritualism" of the movement "Philosophie de l'Esprit" founded by Louis Lavelle in conjunction with Rene LeSenne. On the differences between the two "reflexive" orientations, see Gilbert Varet's article "Spiritualisme et philosophie réflexive," *Revue des sciences philosophiques et théologiques* 74 (1990): 23–34.

For further treatment of reflexive philosophy in France, one may profitably consult: Gabriel Madinier's *Conscience et Mouvement: Étude sur la philosophie française de Condillac à Bergson* (Paris: Presses Universitaires de France, 1938), *Conscience et Signification: Essai sur la réflexion* (Paris: Presses Universitaires de France, 1953), *Vers une philosophie réflexive* (Neuchatel: Éditions de la Baconnière [Être et Penser–Cahiers de Philosophie, 50], 1960); Paul Ricoeur, "Commémoration de Centenaire de Mort de Jules Lagneau: "Le jugement et la Méthode Refléxive selon Jules Lagneau," "*Bulletin de la Societé française de Philosophie* 88 (1994): 120–138.

14. Ricoeur, "La condition du philosophe chrétien," in *L3*, 235. This review essay was originally published in *Christianisme social* 56 (1948): 551–557.

15. The controversy had its origin in a series of lectures at the Institut des Hautes Etudes de Belgique given by the great French historian of philosophy, Émile Bréhier, in 1928, subsequently published as "Y a-t-il une philosophie chrétienne?" *Revue de métaphysique et de morale* 38 (1931): 133–162. Étienne Gilson, Bréhier's fellow historian of philosophy at the Sorbonne, responded to Bréhier's negative answer to the question on the occasion of a meeting on March 21, 1931 of the Société Française de Philosophie. His address was entitled "La Notion de Philosophie chrétienne" [*Bulletin de la Société française de Philosophie* 31 (1931): 37–39, 73–82.

16. Roger Mehl, *La Condition du philosophe chrétien*, 25 [28–29].
17. Mehl, *La Condition du philosophe chrétien*, 28.
18. Ibid., 48 [53].
19. Ibid., 51–52 [57].
20. Ibid., 111 [119].
21. Étienne Gilson, *Christianisme et philosophie* (Paris: Vrin, 1936): 37–38.
22. Mehl, *La Conditon du philosophe chrétien*, 149 [159].
23. Ibid., 155 [165].
24. Ibid., 157 [167].
25. Ricoeur, "La condition du philosophe chrétien," in *L3*, 242.
26. Cf. Eberhard Jüngel, "Der menschliche Mensch: Die Bedeutung der reformatorische Unterscheidung der Person von ihren Werken für das Selbstverständnis des neuzeitlichen Menschen," in *Wertlose Wahrheit: Zur Identität und Relevanz des christlichen Glaubens. Theologische Erörterungen III* (München: Chr. Kaiser Verlag [Beiträge zur evangelischen Theologie; Bd. 107], 1990}: 165–196.
27. Mehl, *La condition du philosophe chrétien*, 197.
28. Ricoeur, *HT*, 12.
29. Ibid., 7.
30. Ibid., 9, 10.
31. Ibid., 14.
32. Ricoeur, "Philosopher après Kierkegaard," in *L2*, 34: "La philosophie a toujours affaire à la non-philosophie, parce que la philosophie n'a pas d'objet propre. Elle réflechit sur l' expérience, sur toute expéience, sur le tout de expérience: scientifique, éthique, esthétique, religieues. La philosophie a ses *sources* hors d'elle-même."
37. Jules Lachelier, *Oeuvres de Jules Lachelier,* II (Paris: Librairie Félix Alcan, 1933): 205: "C'est l'office de la philosophie de tout *comprendre*, même la religion." Cf. Louis Millet, *Le symbolisme dans la philosophie de Lachelier* (Paris: Presses Universitaires de France [Bibliothèque de Philosophie Contemporaine], 1959).
34. Ricoeur, *HT*, 14. Cf. Leon Brunschvicg's presentation and estimation of the significance of Xenophanes in *La Raison et la Religion* (Paris: Presses Universitaires de France [Bibliothèque de Philosophie Contemporaine], 1964):

64–66 and *Le Progrès de la Conscience dans la Philosophie Occidentale*, I (Deuxième éd.; Paris: Presses Universitaires de France [Bibliothèque de Philosophie Contemporaine], 1953): 4–6.

35. Ricoeur, "Une Interprétation philosophique de Freud," in Ci, 175–176.
36. Ricoeur, *DF*, 504.
37. Ibid.
38. Ibid., 508.
39. Jean Greisch, "La métamorphose herméneutique de la philosophie de la religion," in *Paul Ricoeur: Les métamorphoses de la raison herméneutique. Actes du colloque de Cerisy-la-Salle 1er–11 août 1988*, sous le direction de Jean Greisch et Richard Kearney (Paris: Les Éditions du Cerf [<<Passages>>]): 319–334, especially 316.
40. Pamela Sue Anderson, *Ricoeur and Kant: Philosophy of the Will* (Atlanta: Scholar's Press [American Academy of Religion–Studies in Religion, no. 66], 1993): 8–32, esp. p. 8 ("Yet I contend that Ricoeur's first essays reflect a definite grounding in Cartesian/Kantian orthodoxy, at the same time as this background is modified somewhat by Ricoeur's engagement with Hegel and later the post-Hegelian critics").
41. Ricoeur, "Entretien avec Paul Ricoeur: Questions de Jean-Michel Le Lannou [sur: comment la pensée de P. Ricoeur se situe-t-elle dans al tradition française en philosophie?]" *Revue des sciences philosophiques et théologiques* 74 (1990): 91.
42. E. g., Don Ihde's *Hermeneutic Phenomenology: The Philosophy of Paul Ricoeur* (Evanston: Northwestern University Press [Studies in Phenomenology and Existential Philosophy], 1971).
43. Paul Ricoeur, "Gabriel Marcel et la Phénoménologie [confèrence suivie d'une discussion avec G. Marcel et autres]" in *Entretiens autour de Gabriel Marcel: Colloque autour de G. Marcel au Centre Culturel de Cérisy-la-Salle, 1973* (Neuchâtel: Editions de la Baconnière [Langages], 1976): 53–74, 75–94.
44. *RF*, 15 ["Je reconnais aujourd'hui la marque de l'un de ces armistices dans le mémoire de maitrise que je consacrai—durant l'année universitaire 1933–1934—au *Problème de Dieu chez Lachelier et Lagneau*. Que des penseurs aussi épris de rationalité et soucieux de l'autonomie de la pensée philosophique aient ainsi fait à l'idée de Dieu, à Dieu même une place dans leur philosophie, me satisfaisait intellectuellement, sans que ni l'un ni l'autre de ces maîtres m'invitât à commettre un amalgaime quelconque entre la philosophie et la foi biblique. C'est pourquoi j'ai parlé d'armisitce plutôt que d'alliance. D'ailleurs, ces incursions précoces du côté du Dieu des philosophes sont pratiquement restées sans lendemain, en dépit des imprudentes promesses qu'on eut lire dans le préface de la *Philosophie de la volonté* et dont je vais dire un mot plus loin."].
45. Ricoeur, "<<Le jugement et la méthode réflexive selon Jules Lagneau>> Commemoration du centaire de la mort de Jules Lagneau," *Bulletin de la société française de philosophie* (1994): 122.

46. *RF*, 15–16.
47. Ibid., 18 [8].
48. Ricoeur, "De l'interprétation" in *Dta*, 25. Cf. Paul Ricoeur, *Cc*, 235.
49. Ricoeur, "De l'interprétation" in *Dta*, 25–26.
50. Our discussion of Thévenaz shall primarily restrict itself to the posthumously published, unfinished text, *La Condition de la raison philosophique* (1960). The editors note in their "Avertissement" that it had been formerly announced as forthcoming, to be entitled *Introduction à une philosophie protestante*. It remains the torso of Thévenaz's most sustained and systematically framed reflections. For a developmental presentation and theological evaluation of his thought, including a bibliography of primary sources and secondary discussions, see Bernard Hort, *Contingence et Interiorité: Essai sur to signification théologique de l'Oeuvre de Pierre Thévenaz* (Genève: Éditions Labor et Fides [Lieux Théologiques n° 14], 1989).
51. Thévenaz, *La condition de la raison philosophique*, 20.
52. Ibid., 44.
53. Ibid.
54. Ibid., 46: " . . . *la conscience d'une aporie n'est pas une aporie de la conscience*, . . . " Cf. Thévenaz, "Crise de la raison et critique de la raison," in *L'homme et sa raison*, t. I: *Raison et conscience de soi*, 167–186.
55. Ibid., 49.
56. Ibid., 50.
57. Ibid., 51.
58. Ibid., 52.
59. Ibid., 55.
60. Ibid., 58.
61. Ibid., 68–69.
62. Ibid., 62.
63. Ibid., 76.
64. Ibid., 103.
65. Cf. Ricoeur, "Entretien avec Paul Ricoeur," *Revue des Sciences philosophiques et théologiques* 74 (1990): 88.
66. Thévenaz, "Réflexion et conscience de soi," in *L'homme et sa raison*, I:120.
67. Thévenaz, *La condition de la raison philosophique*, 82.
68. Ibid., 86.
69. Ibid., 94–101.
70. See Thévenaz, "La philosophie sans absolu," in *L'homme et sa raison*, I: *Raison et conscience de soi*, 187–207.
71. Thévenaz, *La condition de la raison philosophique*, 139: " . . . l'on est lucide sur soi-même, là où l'on repère exactement ses opacités intèrieures. Une lucidité liée à la condition est au contraire une lucidité sur la non-transparence de cette condition.

72. Ibid., 141.

73. Ibid., 119: "... la condition de la raison ne devient pas un absolu qui la conditionne. La condition de la raison n'est ni la description d'une situation objective qui détermine la raison, ni la description dune situation simplement subjective."

74. Ibid., 142: "Un appel ne conditionne pas: précisement il appelle, il fait appel à une décision libre."

75. Ibid., 144: "La décision marque le moment où la conscience débouche dans une action, dans une activité, témoigne par des actes, par son engagement même qu'elle est consciente et qu'elle a une réponse à donner."

76. Ricoeur, "Préface," in *L'homme et son raison*, I: *Raison et conscience de soi*, 23.

77. Thévenaz, *La condition de la raison philosophique*, 147.

78. Ibid., 149.

79. Thévenaz here would be in diagreement with Karl Jasper's *Philosophial Faith and Revelation* [*Der philosophische glaube angesichts der Offenbarung* (München: R. Piper Verlag, 1962)].

80. Thévenaz, *La condition de la raison philosophique*, 169.

81. Ricoeur, "La liberté selon l'espérance," in *Ci*, 394.

82. Ricoeur, "Philosophy and Religious Language," in *FS*, 35. See also Ricoeur, "De l'interprétation," in *Dta*, 29.

83. See Ricoeur, "L'acte et le signe selon Jean Nabert," in *Ci*, 211–221.

84. Ibid., 169.

85. Ibid., 21.

86. Ibid., 22: "... il faut toujours s'épar une critique corrective de la mécompréhension à la compréhension."

87. *EBI*, 119–120.

88. Ibid., 148.

89. Ibid., 143.

90. Cf. Ricoeur, "Emmanuel Levinas: Thinker of Testimony," in *FS*, 116.

91. Ricoeur, "The Hermeneutics of Testimony," in *EBI*, 151.

92. Ibid., 153.

93. Ricoeur, "Existence et herméneutique," in *Ci*, 28: "... mais, comme Moïse, le sujet parlant et réfléchissant peurt suelement l'apercevoir avant de mourir."

94. Martin Luther, "The Small Catechism," in *The Book of Concord*, ed. and trans. Theodore G. Tappert (Philadelphia: Fortress Press, 1959), 345.

NINE

At the Limit of Practical Wisdom
Moral Blindness

David Pellauer

In his Gifford Lectures, now published as *Oneself as Another*, Paul Ricoeur concludes his investigation into the meaning of selfhood with a surprising and complex reflection on the theme of what in English we would generally call ethics. In fact, we need to be careful of our language here because what Ricoeur calls ethics is in some important ways just one moment in the larger scheme of his ethical reflections. It refers to the teleological moment that underlies and interacts with what he identifies as the subsequent deontological or normative and then the practical dimensions of his theory. I want to begin by taking this theory for granted in order to test it from another perspective, one that Ricoeur also regularly recognizes in his writings. That is, I want to look for its limits, or at least one of them, to consider what difference it may make.

We may consider this concern for limits to reflect the Kantian dimension in Ricoeur's thinking, what he himself has sometimes characterized as a kind of post-Hegelian Kantianism. I take it that by this designation he means to indicate that he wishes to allow for a temporalized version of something like a Kantian model of reasoning, one that might reflect something such as Hegel's *Phenomenology* but without a Hegelian claim to attain absolute knowledge.[1] We may also see this concern for limits as directly resulting from Ricoeur's typical method of argumentation in terns of a dialectic of opposed terms. The goal for such a dialectic most often is to discover or articulate a mediating term that connects the two poles, allowing us to move in either direction from one extreme toward the other. However, sometimes he also begins from the middle term, and the goal then is to discover the polar structure that situates this initial term.[2] In either case, there is no Hegelian *Aufhebung* that would lift us above or out of this polar structure. This lack of sublating transcendence ending in an atemporal Absolute may be another reason Ricoeur prefers to refer to himself as still a Kantian, albeit a post-Hegelian one.[3] It is also why I believe it has been so difficult, not to say almost impossible for him to address directly the ontological dimension of his thought since being is that which lies beyond the polarities, so to speak.[4]

However, that topic is not what is at issue here. Instead, I want next to review briefly the background that brings Ricoeur to his ethical reflections in *Oneself as Another* in order to have some basis for considering what I am proposing as at least one of its limit cases: moral blindness.[5]

The purpose of *Oneself as Another* we are told is threefold. It is first intended "to indicate the primacy of reflective mediation over the immediate positing of the subject" (1, trans. altered). This in itself is a major project that may be traced back as far as Ricoeur's earlier essays "Heidegger and the Question of the Subject" and "The Question of the Subject: the Challenge of Semiology" in the *Conflict of Interpretations*,[6] as well as to his writings on Freud, where this work can itself be seen to have been anticipated, if only obliquely, in the weighting of the subjective pole in the method of description and analysis used in *Freedom and Nature: The Voluntary and the Involuntary*.[7] From a broader perspective, however, we can also see this concern for the subject, now become the self, as part of the larger challenge within twentieth-century French philosophy to the Cartesian tradition, since central to this portion of Ricoeur's argument is what he calls the "shattered *cogito*." Earlier, in his Freud studies, he had spoken only of a "wounded *cogito*."[8] Now the Cartesian *cogito* points at best to an idea of perfection, something like a Kantian regulative idea that we never fully instantiate.[9] At worst, it is an empty, sterile truth from which nothing follows except by the addition of something beyond the *cogito*.[10] In either case, the *cogito* loses it privilege of being the foundation for philosophical and personal knowledge, one indication why the question of selfhood is so crucial for attempts to move beyond the Cartesian framework in a way other than by simply inverting its central claims; for example, by asserting an anti-*cogito*.

The second large step in his argument turns on concept of identity in relation in particular to the idea of personal identity. Here, Ricoeur makes a distinction between what he calls *idem*-identity and *ipse*-identity in relation to what it means to be a self. The former sense points to what is always the same, the latter to something more like a narrative identity, that is, the identity of a character who remains identifiable as the same character through the ups and downs of a story that unfolds over time. It is this latter kind of identity that is central to personal identity, although there is also an aspect of *idem*-identity to who we are owing to the fact that ours is an embodied existence marked by a largely stable character. Character here means that set of lasting dispositions by which a person is recognized, or as Ricoeur puts it, it is the "what" of the "who" (122).[11] To put what is at issue another way, our identity as selves has to be discovered in a manner similar to the way we discover the identity of a character in a narrative, and since this identity always bears the stamp and limits of an interpretation, we can also call it the key to a hermeneutic of selfhood in contrast to any claim to an immediate intuition of or coincidence with something such as a pure Cartesian ego. Such an account is also not meant to give in to the anti-*cogito*—the denial of subjectivity and selfhood—that Ricoeur sees in much contemporary philosophy, a striking example of which is found in Nietzsche. So with this framework of apparently opposed positions, we once again have an attempt to find a mediating position, situated between and linking two extremes, which are themselves only approachable asymptotically starting from the mediating term.

The interpreted self discovered through reflection answers the question of practical wisdom. It answers the questions: Who is speaking, Who recounts him- or herself, and Who is the moral subject to which actions can be imputed? In effect, with the addition of considerations arising from the philosophy of action, the self as a being capable of action is seen to be an agent who is responsible for his/her actions. Corresponding to the first three of these questions, then, is a shifting series of analyses that starts from the philosophy of language, moves on to the philosophy of action, and finally ends up at the question of personal identity as narrative identity, with the results already indicated. It is on this basis that the introduction of consideration of the ethical and moral determinations of action leads us to that point where we can raise the limit question of what bounds this complex network of interrelated concepts that are held together by something more like an analogical unity than by any ultimate foundation.[12] For the interpreted self is itself embedded within a larger dialectical framework, complementary to that of selfhood and sameness, a dialectic of self and the other than the self, where this otherness too is an ingredient constitutive of selfhood in its fullest sense. It is at this level that the ethical-moral element most naturally enters into play, although it clearly has roots in the earlier levels in such factors as our ability to ascribe our actions to ourselves and our capacity to bind ourselves for the future through our ability to make and in most cases keep promises.[13]

Narrative is again what provides the linking step from the narrated self, arising from the consideration of action theory, to moral theory. It does so because the narration of action, of the self's action, whether by oneself or another, leads to an extension of the practical field both temporally and spatially. What is more, narrative, for Ricoeur, is never ethically neutral, thereby adding another connector to the series of steps being traced. In a story—the question of whether it is history or fiction is not directly relevant here—action and character are intimately linked, albeit in a tensive manner that corresponds to the tension between concordance and discordance in the dynamic that emplots any story.[14] "The person, understood as a character in a story, is not an entity distinct from his or her 'experiences'" (147), but these include experiences that extend over longer spans of time than those actions usually considered by action theory, which tends to favor examples such as raising one's arm or picking up a pencil. This extension over time and over complex chains of actions amounts to an expansion of the field of practice, now understood as corresponding to such complex forms of action as can be narrated, with their successes or their failures, their turns for the better or the worse, their unintended consequences. At its limit, this practical field can amount to the story of a life, of a community, or of history as a whole, a point that is important for any discussion of moral blindness and its possible cure. For the moment, though, it will suffice to note that our ability to experiment with narrative already gives us a way of mapping and exploring this practical field. But then maps always have edges and this is another reason it is important to look for the limiting cases, if only to recognize where those edges or boundaries lie.

A final connector from narrative selfhood to moral reflection, as I have already indicated, lies in our ability to make promises. Ricoeur sees this ability as important because it is one way of achieving a kind of fragile concordance out of all the many heterogeneous elements that can appear in and be brought together in a narrative—among them: characters, situations, reversals and surprises, points of view, and a more or less successful sense of an ending. Hence, for Ricoeur there is no methodological break in the move that introduces moral considerations into his reflections on selfhood, although at the same time there will be an aspect of novelty that is not reducible to what went before. It is the question of "who?" that accounts for the continuity, while it is predicates such as "good" and "obligatory" that indicate the new element that comes on the scene at this point.

Once again, Ricoeur's argument is complex and multifaceted, particularly given his efforts to locate it in relation to other contemporary thinkers such as John Rawls, Michael Walzer, Karl-Otto Apel, and Claude Lefort, to name only a few. Even more encompassing is his use of the philosophies of both Aristotle and Kant as the means of setting forth his position. For a more detailed analysis of how this works, we would need to attend carefully to how Ricoeur in fact pays close attention to the central texts of these two thinkers without concerning himself about "Aristotelian or Kantian orthodoxy" (170). Here, it must suffice to summarize this complex structure as follows. It can again be divided into three steps that link a teleological and a deontological moment to a third, practical moment where the questions raised by actual hard cases and conflicts call for practical wisdom as a means of resolving these difficulties while also holding the whole structure in a fragile equilibrium. Once we see this point, we can also trace these three moments in the reverse direction, thereby confirming the coherence of the dialectic in question.[15]

The process forward from the teleological level begins with what Ricoeur calls the "ethical intention." The groundwork for the aspect of intentionality at work here was already present in the self's very ability to intend to act and to intend itself in ascribing its actions to itself, even if this occurs only indirectly through reflection. When this basis capacity to intend to do something becomes an ethical intention, Ricoeur sums it up as "aiming at the 'good life' with and for others, in just institutions" (172), where the good, as something lacking, something to be attained, is what contributes the teleological thrust to the model. In turn, this idea of a good life as something to be attained can be said both to presuppose and to give rise to self-esteem insofar as the evaluations of actions reflect back upon their agent. Ricoeur treats self-esteem largely in terms of the reflexive aspect of self-evaluation of one's own actions. He does so in order to point out that this sense of self-esteem, so understood, remains abstract without a reference to others who also convey the evaluations of an agent's actions to the person in question, thereby again underscoring the basic underlying dialectic of *Oneself as Another*. Finally, this reference to individual others whom we may encounter face to face is itself incomplete if we do not take into account the existence of our relations to others constituted through and mediated by institutions.

An initial insight into our relation to others can be seen, following Aristotle, at the level of friendship, that is, at the level of the face-to-face relation to another individual, where our solicitude for this other shapes and guides this relation. Through this relation, my self-esteem can be complemented by the self-respect that comes from living according to my best intentions, it is also here that the problem of reciprocity begins to appear insofar as genuine friendship is not unilateral. Furthermore, once the question of reciprocity is evident, we may say that the question of equality also enters the scene, although it is not yet clear what is to count as equality or who is to count as an equal. Here, we can see beyond the positive case Ricoeur is tracing, the negative possibility of moral blindness as that which does not see the other as equal and perhaps does not "see" the other at all. However, to stay within the parameters of Ricoeur's presentation, next it is necessary to recognize that face-to-face relations with all other persons are impossible. As the number of others increases, we are led in the direction of increasing anonymity of the other and to relations mediated by institutions where we may never meet others face-to-face or even be aware of their individual existence as other than a possible fellow participant in or victim of such institutions. Here is where the question of justice arises, as was indicated in the application of the adjective "just" to institutions in the original formulation of the ethical intention, although once again we can say that it has been already anticipated before we get to this point.[16] Corresponding to this movement, but also already implicit at the level of friendship, is the question of the norm and how it "ought" to shape our behavior. This is why Ricoeur says that it is at this second level that obligation is added to the teleological aim of the first level with its ideal of the good.

It is worth noting in passing that for Ricoeur "what fundamentally characterizes the idea of an institution is the bond of common mores and not that of constraining rules" (194). This is a point meant to allow us to distinguish the legitimate use of "power in common" from domination and hence not always to have to demonize power, even while we can acknowledge its links to the possibility of evil. More important, though, is the face that this willingness to recognize the reality of power helps us better to understand why, when we get to the level of actual moral existence and the conflicts that inevitably arise (cf. 249f.), any solution is necessarily a fragile one and subject to amendment. It is also why, I believe, Ricoeur can characterize human action overall as inevitably tinged with a tragic dimension. I shall return to the possible significance of this morally necessary willingness to be ready to change and this inherent tragic aspect of human existence when we take up the question of the implications of moral blindness for making sense of this threefold structure of ethics, morality, and practical wisdom.

Practical wisdom is what is called for on the third stage of our traversal across this structure, as this is where actual conflicts arise. This can happen, for example, owing to disagreement about what are to count as primary social goods. It can also be due to historical and cultural differences regarding the priority and evaluation of such goods, as well as because of the inherent difficulties of politics, where politics is understood to be concerned with the distribution of such goods and, more important, of political power. Likewise the question of the ends of "good" government, or even that of the legitimacy of any particular form of government can give rise to dispute. In Ricoeur's reading of Kant, who serves as the emblem of the deontological level, just as Aristotle does for the teleological one, neither the emphasis on the autonomy of the will nor the rule of universalization applied to the maxims of the categorical imperative is seen to be capable of resolving these conflicts. It "is because the categorical imperative generates a multiplicity of rules that the presumed universalism of these rules can collide with the demands of otherness, inherent in solicitude" (262).

It is the golden rule, understood in terms of Gabriel Marcel's notion of availability (*disponibilité*), that serves as the mediating term here that makes possible the practical wisdom that resolves the conflict.[17] Practical wisdom, we are told, "consists in inventing conduct that will best satisfy the exception required by solicitude, by betraying the rule to the smallest extent possible" (269). At the level of justice, this amounts to discovering the equitable solution.[18] It also means not turning this solution in turn into a rigid rule—the road back from practical wisdom to reformulated or new normative rules is not that immediate or that direct. However, it is not my intention here to stay within the boundaries of this fascinating, complex structure to explore its details and possible implications. Instead, I now want to start from its limits, or at least from one of its limits, what I am calling "moral blindness." By this notion, I mean the fact that we do not even "see" that there is a moral question, conflict, or dilemma, so the question of practical wisdom does not even arise. Hence, it is not a matter of the wrong description of some moral fact. Moral blindness is rather the failure to even recognize that there is a moral fact or state of affairs to be investigated and evaluated.

Someone may ask, what then is the point, since there is nothing to decide. But what I have in mind is the apparent fact that people have not always recognized as ethical situations—that is, situations that call for ethical decisions and action—situations or states of affairs that we today take for granted as being such situations or states of affairs and as having ethical overtones. Again, what is at issue is not that today we think or even know that people in the past were wrong about some ethical issue we judge correctly today. It is rather that people have come to see that there is an ethical issue where no such issue was previously seen. Tied to this is the assumption on my part that without such recognition that there is an ethical issue, the question of action, of just action does not arise, even if whatever is or is not done in such a situation does obviously have consequences, consequences that from a subsequent point of view, once the moral blindness has been removed, "cured" if you will, may be judged harshly as blameworthy or condemnable from an ethical point of view. They may, of course, also be recognized in some cases as actions or consequences that are worthy of praise, although I suspect that this is the less likely case. It is those cases where we have come to recognize a previously unseen injustice that most often seem to have been revelatory of what I am calling overcoming moral blindness.[19]

As an example of what I mean by such moral blindness, I propose the case of slavery. That is, I cite slavery as illustrative of a phenomenon that we would like to believe everyone would condemn today as morally reprehensible. Yet we also know that this was not always the case. Indeed, for most of human history as we know it just the opposite judgment seems to have been predominant. But to see better how slavery may serve as an example of what I am calling moral blindness, we need to go even farther. From the perspective of moral blindness, it is not that some people in the past believed slavery to be legitimate that is telling; it is rather that in thinking about slavery, when they did so, in overwhelming numbers they did not consider it to involve an ethical issue at all in the sense that here was a phenomenon that called for an ethical decision, or an application of practical wisdom, or that raised questions of justice and injustice. I admit that I am oversimplifying here and that there are a number of preliminary cautions that need to be acknowledged. Slavery is a complex phenomenon with a long, and again a complex, history. We cannot simply identify, say, slavery as it existed in the United States with slavery as it existed in the ancient worlds of Greece and Rome. Nor from the point of view of historical research can we say that at a particular moment in the past no one was against slavery. History finds it difficult, for example, to recover the slaves' point of view since they were unable to leave documents that speak to this point. It is just that from the point of view of today, we wonder why those who we know did question slavery were such a small minority and why they made such little impact. Similarly, slavery may even still exist. Many have claimed that it has not completely disappeared.[20]

My task here is not to analyze the case against slavery or its history. It is to find an example that gives force to what I am calling moral blindness in a way that suggests how such a notion is indicative of the limits of the analysis of the moral dimension of selfhood Ricoeur has presented as a basis for thinking about questions of justice and of practical wisdom. Why is this useful? Why, following Ricoeur's own maxim, should we look for the limits? As an answer, I propose that we consider what recognizing such a limit may add to the back and forth traversal that characterizes Ricoeur's dialectical mode of reasoning. Since we have already made the forward traversal, let us follow Ricoeur on the path back and see what illumination recognition of the phenomenon of moral blindness sheds on what we have seen Ricoeur has already said.

At the level of practical wisdom, as we have seen, even within the limits of moral reflection, conflicts are inevitable. The moral life is marked by a tragic dimension. But even if we acknowledge that conflicts are inevitable, we have also to recognize that they don't always occur. One reason is our moral blindness. We don't see that a conflict exists. In the worst case, even when a victim or victims may cry out, we do not hear them or "see" them as victims. Their suffering does not count because we do not see it as real suffering. There is pain, yes; hunger, yes; but not "real" suffering in the sense of something morally or ethically relevant. We can even do this to ourselves. That is, we can be morally blind to our own moral conflicts and shortcomings.

So what does our recognition of moral blindness tell at this first level? First of all, that while Ricoeur's theory as we have it in *Oneself as Another*, even when complemented by his insightful essays in *Le Juste*, can recognize the inevitability of moral conflicts calling for practical wisdom, and can even suggest why such conflicts can and will occur, it cannot foretell which conflicts will occur, nor is it sufficient to account for why they happen when they do. His comments on the limits of politics can be taken as supporting this conclusion. For example, within the realm of political discussion, there is always the danger of a monopolistic usurpation that will determine the order of priority among the competing demands of the recognized spheres of justice. Beyond this, we have already mentioned the dangers involved in controversy over the ends of government and in crises of legitimacy. Yet none of these possibilities may take place—or indeed they may, but when they do they do not exhaust the list of what conflicts may in fact occur in this realm, even when we inductively seek to construct a typology of possible conflicts derived from actual cases of conflict. History has the capacity yet to surprise us. I would make the same point about Ricoeur's comments on the limits of an ethics of argumentation, where the danger of unexamined convention seems ineradicable.[21] This latter discussion is particularly significant at this point because it is directed more to the deontological level than to the discussion of practical wisdom, but it can also be seen as overlapping the sphere of practical wisdom and hence serves as one indication that carries us back to this middle region of Ricoeur's ethical theory.

Before returning to that region, however, let me propose as a first conclusion that recognition of moral blindness at the level of practical wisdom suggests a practical maxim, not a deontological rule, that we try to keep in mind that we may be missing what is important, and that we ought to be willing to look for it. A second lesson is that we must guard against too easy an assumption that we will know evil or injustice when we see it, even when we suffer it. If we have learned anything from those working with victims of family violence and violence directed against women, it is that often the victims blame themselves and they do so in a way that denies that there is a problem of justice at issue because they are "blind" to this fact. To put it another way, recognizing moral blindness as a limit of ethical reflection can teach us that we don't always recognize the victim. At the same time, we need to add that neither does it teach us how always to recognize injustice, a victim, a moral hard case; such recognition, once it has occurred, does, however, counsel us to try to "open our eyes," to be willing to have "our eyes opened."

What happens when we return to the level of deontological morality? Ricoeur has already recognized that the one-sidedness of specific norms, together with the question of when and how any norm applies, along with the lack of unity, points us both to the need for practical wisdom and back to the most original ethical affirmation. I do not see that the recognition of moral blindness adds a lot here other than to reinforce our sense of the limits of what is attainable on this level. In a positive sense, this indicates just how thorough moral philosophy has been on this level—I would even grant this to those who prefer a utilitarian or consequentialist approach to the question of normative ethics, it is just that in both cases Ricoeur's analysis underscores the narrowness of such an approach. This is well indicated in *Oneself as Another* by his reading of the tension in Kantian formalism and his critique of attempts to solve everything with an ethics of argumentation (274–283).

Particularly telling in this sense is Ricoeur's critique of the criterion of universalization as it functions in Kant's thought. He focuses on this criterion in terms of the kinds of restrictions it imposes on the kind of coherence to which a system of morality can aspire (276). I believe that thinking about moral blindness suggests another possibility as well, especially if we do not limit ourselves to the Kantian texts. This has to do with the possible claim that the idea of equality overcomes that of moral blindness. That is, we may be tempted to think that if we were only to treat everyone equally, there will be no irresolvable problem. Ricoeur's whole argument, along with those of many contemporary moral theorists, is meant to acknowledge the fact that things are not so easy in practice, even within the bounds of a dialectic of ethical/moral reflection. However, our acknowledging the possibility and even the reality of moral blindness that have been overcome. We don't in fact always recognize people as equals and moral theory cannot account for this. I am not referring here to those cases where we deliberately refuse to acknowledge others as equals to us, cases where moral judgment is recognized as applicable and where praise or blame is appropriate and called for. I mean those more difficult cases where moral theory does not even recognize such a failure on anyone's part, those cases, for example, where only those who "count" are acknowledged as worthy of treatment as equals, however formally proportional or distributive their treatment may be in practice. The problem is that the question of equality in a broader sense does not even arise. Thus, if we use Kant's own language and say "act in such a way that you always treat humanity, whether in your own person or in the person of any other, never simply as a means, but always at the same time as an end,"[22] recognition of our moral blindness teaches us that we need to ask not only what a person is, but *who*.[23] Here we come back to the central thesis of *Oneself as Another*.

However, to continue our reverse traversal of its dialectic of moral reflection, can we save the notion of equality as a solution to moral blindness if we return to the most basic level, that of our most original ethical affirmation? I think not, at least not apart from the back and forth movement of dialectical reflection. What we would like to be able to say is that the notion of equality is present from the very beginning, as is the imperative to discover its actual scope of application. Moral blindness as a fact of experience says that this may not be the case. One can talk of equality, can "have the idea," and still overlook the ethical other.[24]

We can find a parallel case of what is at issue here in Chaim Perelman's well-known discussion of justice. He too makes a division between a formal and an applied level. "To everyone," he says, "the idea of justice inevitably suggests the notion of a certain equality."[25] This leads him to define "formal or abstract justice as *a principle of action in accordance with which beings of one and the same essential category must be treated in the same way*."[26] But as he quickly adds, "The application of formal justice calls for the prior establishment of the categories regarded as essential,"[27] and as he acknowledges this is not easy to do. Our discussion of moral blindness suggests that this notion of difficulty should also be complemented with one of incompleteness and, furthermore, that neither the fundamental level of ethical affirmation nor the three-stage dialectic as a whole can tell us how to recognize such completeness or incompleteness. But perhaps it also teaches us that, in moving back and forth among these stages we can in fact learn to recognize the importance of this question of completeness and to seek its implications and consequences at each level, even while attempting to expand the basic dialectical polarity.

I further believe when we return to the level of primary ethical affirmation having touched the limit of moral blindness at the level of practical wisdom, we may also see that the question of the nature of the good is not fully settled by this primary affirmation or even by recognition of a fundamental ethical intention. In a purely formal sense, we can say that the idea of the good is that of an end that integrates lesser ends. What our experience of moral blindness can teach us is that our notion of such a primary good may not be as integrative as we would like to think, either abstractly and formally or concretely. This is an insight whose lesson we need to carry back to the higher levels of the norm and of practical wisdom. At the deontological level we again have reason not to be too quick to claim that we fully understand what is universal in the universalization of obligation implied in the norm. At the level of practical wisdom, we may discover a deeper sense of prudence about the adequacy of our solutions, however equitable they may seem. In particular we need to be attentive to the time frame in question. Are we dealing with a portion of a lifetime, or a whole life? Is it the life of an individual or of a group of individuals—or a whole community or even humanity as a whole? Do our considerations apply to a short span of time or, somehow, in intention at least, to the whole of history.

Overall, then, what can we say in conclusion of our discussion of how recognition of moral blindness contributes to our understanding of Paul Ricoeur's ethical reflections in *Oneself as Another* and in the work he has continued to publish since that work? Three things, I believe. First, as Ricoeur himself often reminds us, it is good to look for the limits and to recall that they are limits. Even at the level of practical wisdom, our solutions, however equitable they may be, are fragile—and are limited. Nor, if we accept Ricoeur's model of dialectical reflection, can we ever in fact escape such limits, even though we can attempt to broaden them and may succeed in doing so; a humbling thought.

Second, testing the limit helps to keep the dynamic aspect of the overall dialectic alive. We must not think we have reached the end when we have reached the level of practical wisdom. We may still not see all that there is to see. Similarly, if we trace our way back to our primary ethical affirmations to revise or broaden them, neither can we rest there, satisfied with our good intentions. They are too abstract and incapable by themselves of resolving actual moral conflicts, injustices, or unnecessary suffering.

Third, we may also learn to recall that there is a place for reflection on evil as well as on good at all three levels of the dialectic. Ricoeur briefly recognizes this in *Oneself as Another*, but he does not dwell upon it,[28] although it is a theme that runs through all his work. Therefore, allow me to end by suggesting that what reflection on moral blindless can ultimately teach us is that in the deepest sense evil is not equivalent to an incapacity or unwillingness to do the good or to find the just solution within some established moral order. It can also be a failure to see the problem, in the sense of a failure to see that there is a problem, even before we ask for a description or an evaluation of that problem. This is a failure that does not seem reducible to some incapacity on our part, at least not to some necessary incapacity, since history tells us our moral blindness can be and at times has been overcome, at least in part. But because evil is a failure to see for which we are finally responsible, this is why it is condemnable and why we can and will be held accountable for it.[29]

NOTES

1. Cf., for example, *CI*, 412; *FP*, 527; "Biblical Hermeneutics," *Semeia* 4 (1975): 139–142.

2. Cf., for example, *CI*, 336, where in taking up the topic of demythization, he says that "the philosopher cannot be content with a superficial eclectic juxtaposition of the two modalities of demythization. He must construct the relationship between them." In the following essay on the myth of punishment, he notes that he intends to "develop this aporia in two directions" (ibid., 357).

3. See the chapter "Should We Renounce Hegel" in *TN3* for a good statement of why he believes he must resist what he calls the "Hegelian temptation," albeit not without a certain note of regret.

4. His statement at the end of his essay "Existence and Hermeneutics" is well known. Having concluded that "existence as it relates to a hermeneutic philosophy always remains an interpreted existence," he goes on to add that "in this way, ontology is indeed the promised land for a philosophy that begins with language and with reflection; but, like Moses, the speaking and reflecting subject can only glimpse this land before dying" (*CI*, 24). The ontological theme does recur regularly in his subsequent work, however, often in the last chapter, and in recent years he has begun to address it more directly in a number of important essays. Cf., for example, *RM*, 259–313; *OA*, 297–356; "From Metaphysics to Moral Philosophy," *Philosophy Today* 40 (1996): 443–458; "Pour une ontologie indirect: l'être, le vrai, le juste (et/ou le bon)" (unpublished); "Multiple étrangeté" (unpublished).

5. I admit that there is a figurative as well as a conceptual aspect to this notion as I understand it at this point, so another approach to the same issue may be possible through what we might call moral deafness in parallel to moral blindness. Assuming a similar case can be made for this limit case, how the two may or may not cohere is a topic that may be worth pursuing. In fact, the notion of moral blindness goes back some years in my thinking now to conversations with my wife when she was working on her essay on moral callousness. Mary D. Pellauer, "Moral Callousness and Moral Sensitivity: Violence Against Women," in *Women's Consciousness, Women's Conscience: A Reader in Feminist Ethics*, ed. Barbara Hilkert Andolsen, Christine E. Gudorf, and Mary D. Pellauer. (Minneapolis: Winston Press, 1985), 33–50.

6. CI, 223–266.

7. Paul Ricoeur, FN. Cf. the analysis of this methodology of weighting one pole over the other in Don Ihde, *Hermeneutic Phenomenology: The Philosophy of Paul Ricoeur* (Evanston: Northwestern University Press, 1971), 14–20.

8. FP, 420–430, esp. 428; CI, 173.

9. Such a reading is not inconsistent with the notion of a teleology of the subject presented in FP if we understand it to be a *telos* that can only be approached asymptotically.

10. Paul Ricoeur, "The Crisis of the *Cogito*," *Synthese* 106 (1996): 57–66.

11. Cf. Ricoeur's earlier discussion of character as an aspect of the involuntary in FN, 355–373.

12. It is the analogical unity of our ways of acting that leads Ricoeur to favor an interpretation of being in terms of action rather than of truth or validity when he finally turns to the ontological dimension of this whole discussion. OA, 297–356; see also Paul Ricoeur, "From Metaphysics to Moral Philosophy," trans. David Pellauer, *Philosophy Today* 40 (1966): 443–458.

13. Ricoeur agrees with Hannah Arendt that it is the possibility of forgiveness that compensates for our failure always to keep our promises.

14. Paul Ricoeur, TN, 3 vols. See esp. chap. 3 of vol. 1: "Time and Narrative: Threefold Mimesis" (52–87).

15. In "Les trois niveaux du jugement médical," *Esprit* no. 227 (décembre 1996): 23–33, Ricoeur starts from this reverse direction in order to consider how although questions of applied medical ethics usually begin from individual situations of patient care, they also lead back to the teleological level and the question of the good life by way of such considerations as the "medical contract" to provide care to all who need it and the need to attempt to universalize precepts once they are recognized, a point that raises the issue of the limits of any codification of medical practice regarding its ethical dimension in the threefold sense Ricoeur articulates.

16. We recall that Aristotle holds that "if people are friends, they have no need of justice," but also that "the justice that is most just seems to belong to friendship." *Nichomachean Ethics*, trans. Terence Irwin (Indianapolis: Hackett, 1985), 1125a27–28, 208.

17. Cf. Paul Ricoeur, "Ethical and Theological Considerations on the Golden Rule," in FS, 293–302, for a fuller discussion of the significance of the golden rule.

18. Ricoeur has been pursuing the question of justice and its relation to equity in a number of essays published subsequent to OA. See Paul Ricoeur, LJ; "Les trois niveaux du jugement médical"; "Justice et verité" (unpublished).

19. The questions of how, when, or why such curing of moral blindness occurs or has occurred are difficult and beyond the purview of this essay. In

the cases where we recognize this has happened, however, we can turn to what insight the historian can give us, but this will always be subject to the limits of historical generalization. More general models, I believe, as hermeneutic, can only claim the kind of adequacy typical of any interpretation.

20. The front page of the *New York Times* for 20 January 1997, for example, includes a story "The Ritual Slaves of Ghana: Young and Female."

21. Ricoeur points out, for example, how proponents of an ethics of argumentation tend to formulate their analyses of what counts as an acceptable argument in terms of "an interpretation of modernity almost exclusively in terms of breaking with a past thought to be frozen in traditions subservient to the principle of authority and so, by principle, out of reach of public discussion" (OA, 287).

22. Immanuel Kant, *Groundwork of the Metaphysic of Morals*, trans. H. J. Paton (New York: Harper Torchbooks, 1964), 96.

23. His emphasis on the question *who* means that Ricoeur's ethical reflection is mainly concerned about ethical questions at the level of human relations. I do not see this as excluding questions having to do with such issues as the rights of animals or of the earth itself in ecological ethics, however. Ricoeur's own favorable comments about the work of Hans Jonas support this (e.g., OA, 272; LJ, 65). It is just such questions have to be seen as derived from the human level where ethical issues first arise.

24. It may be worth noting in passing, given my earlier comment about a parallel limit case of moral deafness, that Emmanuel Levinas combines the two when he says that in seeing the "face" of the other we bear the injunction "Thou shall not kill." It is an open question whether Levinas really gives us a solution to what I am calling moral blindness, however.

25. Chaim Perelman, *The Idea of Justice and the Problem of Argument*, trans. John Petrie (London: Routledge & Kegan Paul; Atlantic Highlands, NJ: Humanities Press, 1963), 12.

26. Ibid., 16.

27. Ibid., 27.

28. OA, 215–218.

29. An earlier version of this essay in French was prepared for a conference entitled "La Sagesse Pratique: Autour de l'oeuvre de Paul Ricoeur," held at the Université de Picardie-Jules Verne, in Amiens, France on March 5–8, 1997. The French version of that essay will be published in the conference proceedings, edited by Jeffrey Andrew Barash and Miraille Delbraccio, in the series *Documents: Acts et Rapports pour l'Education* (Paris: Centre national de documentation pédagogique, 1998).

TEN

Response to Rawls

Bernard P. Dauenhauer

I
> In general, I only speak about authors that I can go along with far enough to be able to say that separating myself from them is costly to me but the cost is worth it because I have passed through the school of their opposition. Those with whom I do not have this relationship of productive conflict, I do not speak of. This explains many of my silences, which are due neither to ignorance, nor to contempt, nor to hostility.[1]

n this measure from *La Critique et la conviction*, Paul Ricoeur has clearly passed through the school of John Rawls's "opposition." Ricoeur discusses Rawls's *A Theory of Justice* not only in *Oneself as Another*.[2] He also deals with it in "Le cercle de la démonstration" and "John Rawls: de L'autonomie morale à la fiction du contrat social" in his *Lectures I* and "Une théorie purement procédural de la justice est-elle possible? A propos de la théorie de John Rawls" and "Après *Théorie de la justice* de John Rawls" in his *Le Juste*.[3] Rawls also figures prominently in some other essays of Ricoeur's. Among these is one that I will draw on extensively in this piece, namely his "Éthique et morale: visée théologique et perspective déontologique."[4]

In this paper, I want to concentrate on Ricoeur's critique of Rawls's well-known contention that in matters of justice there is a basic priority of the right over the good. After presenting Ricoeur's critique, I will then offer my assessment of its strength.

Rawls argues that, given the fact that democratic states today and for the foreseeable future are made up of citizens who hold a plurality of views about what constitutes a good life or about what goods we ought to seek, and given the fact that no society can encompass all goods, there must be a fair procedure for determining a society's political and legal structure according to which a citizen's rights and opportunities to exercise his or her freedom to choose among goods will be distributed or regulated. The political society as such is not to pursue any specific set of goods. Rather, it is to see to it that every citizen has a fair share of the basic goods needed to live a free life according to one's own lights and equal opportunity to exercise that freedom. Thus, there is a priority of the right, the proper distribution, over the good, the things that are distributed or pursued.

Rawls would have the proper distribution determined by fair beginning among representatives of the individuals who make up the society. The bargaining is what takes place behind the famous Rawlsian veil of ignorance, a veil that hides from the representatives exactly what share of these basic goods will go to which person. The outcome of the bargaining is an agreement or contract to accept two basic, ordered principles of justice. These two principles are: "Each person is to have an equal right to the most extensive total system of basic liberties compatible with a similar system of liberty for all" and "[s]ocial and economic inequalities are to be arranged so that they are both (a) to the greatest benefit of the least advantaged and (b) attached to offices and positions open to all under conditions of fair equality of opportunity."[5]

The priority of the right over the good means, Rawls says, that these two principles impose limits on permissible ways of life that citizens may pursue. It does not mean that justice has no concern for the good. But it does mean that the proper political conception of justice does not presuppose any particular comprehensive philosophical or religious doctrine. Nor is it formulated in terms of any comprehensive doctrine. This conception of justice is, rather, formulated "in terms of certain fundamental ideas viewed as latent in the public political culture of a democratic society."[6]

Rawls denies that his conception of justice is procedurally neutral. It need not ensure that all citizens have equal opportunity to advance just any conception of the good that they choose, for example, conceptions of the good that would violate either of his two principles. But his conception is neutral in aim. Neutrality in aim means "that the state is not to do anything intended to favor or promote any particular comprehensive doctrine rather than another, or to give greater assistance to those who pursue it."[7]

This conception of justice is not indifferent to all goods. It calls for the virtues of civility, tolerance, reasonableness, and fairness, that is, the virtues that make one a good citizen of a democratic state. Furthermore, a society that is ordered by Rawls's conception of justice is good for persons taken individually in two ways. First, it provides the good of having the capacity to be participants in fair social cooperation. Second, such a society secures for its citizens the good of justice and the social bases of the mutual self-respect. Thus, in securing the equal basic rights and liberties, fair equality of opportunity, and the like, political society guarantees the essentials of persons' public recognition as free and equal citizens. In securing these things political society secures their fundamental needs.[8]

These goods, however, are the fruit of the exercise of justice as fairness. They depend upon justice, not vice versa. In this sense, then, the just is prior to the good.

Ricoeur's basic question for Rawls and those who, like him, hold a fundamentally procedural conception of justice asks "whether this reduction to procedure does not leave a residue that requires a certain return to a teleological point of view, not at the price of repudiating the formalization procedures, but in the name of a demand to which these very procedures lend a voice."[9] His critique leads him to conclude that "a procedural conception of justice furnishes at most a rationalization of a sense of justice which is always presupposed. By this argument I in no way aim to refute Rawls, but only to develop the presuppositions he has which seem to me unavoidable."[10] Inasmuch as Rawls's formalization of the concept of justice presupposes some prior engagement on the pursuit of some good, justice ultimately belongs to a certain pursuit of a good and hence is not prior to it.

The position that Ricoeur himself defends, to which I will return shortly, is one that draws together the Aristotelian heritage of teleology and the Kantian heritage of deontology. He adopts by convention a distinction between the terms *ethics* and *morality*. Ethics refer to the aim of an accomplished, fulfilled life; morality refers to "the articulation of this aim in *norms* characterized at once by the claim of universality and by an effect of constraint."[11] Using this distinction, he proposes to defend "(1) the primacy of ethics over morality, (2) the necessity for the ethical aim to pass through the sieve of the norm, and (3) the legitimacy of recourse by the norm to the aim whenever the norm leads to impasses in practice."[12]

The point of departure for Ricoeur's critique in *Oneself as Another* of Rawls's theory is his reflection on the notion of distribution. Institutions deal with the distribution of shares. And justice is in its first instance applied to the distributions that institutions make.

The very notion of a just share, though, is riddled with ambiguity. First, is one to emphasize the separateness of my share from those of other individuals? Or is one to emphasize the bonds of cooperation that the division into shares is supposed to establish or reinforce? The latter emphasis would tend to stress a mutual indebtedness that both prompts and is the outcome of the division of shares. This can be called the communitarian emphasis. The emphasis on the separateness of shares, by contrast, would stress impartiality and a certain concern with disinterestedness in the making of the distributions. This can be called the liberal individualistic emphasis.

A second ambiguity springs from the tight connection between the notions of justice and equality. How is equality to be defined? Is it to be a simple or arithmetic equality in which all the shares are equal? Or is it to be a proportional equality in which there is an equality between a particular recipient and his or her share? As we learn from Aristotle, it is a matter for justice to determine whether or when shares are to be distributed arithmetically or proportionally.

In Ricoeur's view, the idea of the just tends to point in two opposite directions. It points both in the direction of a "good" solicitude for each member of the society, no matter how faceless, and in the direction of the "legal," to such a degree that justice appears to be indistinguishable from positive law.[13] To overcome these ambiguities, thinkers such as Rawls have been led to strip every teleological basis from the idea of justice and give it instead a completely deontological status. Rawls's way of pursuing this objective has been to completely formalize the concept of justice.

Rawls brings his deontological approach to justice into the institutional domain by adopting the fiction of a social contract made by representatives of individuals behind the veil of ignorance. Through the contract, the individuals are supposed to get beyond a primitive state of nature by entering into a state of law. The fictional contract is supposed to separate the just from the good. It is to do so by substituting a deliberative procedure for any prior commitment to a specific conception of a common good.

At the level of institutions, then, the Rawlsian contract occupies the place that autonomy holds at the level of individual morality. Freed from the particularizations of individual inclinations and desires, the contractors provide a law for themselves that is the law of freedom itself. This law of freedom, in turn, is to protect the individuals in their pursuit of their own interests and desires. Or, as Ricoeur puts it: "Rawls therefore fully assumes for his own purposes the idea of an original contract between free and rational persons, concerned with promoting their individual interests. Contractualism and individualism thus move forward hand-in-hand."[14]

The apparent motivation for Rawls's antiteleological orientation is his determination to oppose utilitariansim. He scarcely touches on Aristotelian teleology. The danger of utilitarianism is that it would endorse the sacrificing of some people for the sake of the overall betterment of the entire group. It would thus give legitimacy to practices that make some people scapegoats for the advantage of others. Rawls resists any rationale for scapegoats on the Kantian grounds that no unequal division of advantages should lead to the result that the least well off are sacrificed, are made the means for the well-being of others. The social contract is to preclude scapegoats.

To flesh out the implications of this contract and the conditions it presupposes, Ricoeur considers the answers Rawls gives to three questions. The first question is: "What would guarantee the fairness of a situation of deliberation from which agreement could result concerning a just arrangement of institutions?"[15] Rawls's answer is that all parties in the discussions leading to the contract would be equal in the following respects: (a) They would all know the fundamental motivations and passions that all people have; (b) they would all know the primary social goods that every reasonable person can be presumed to want; (c) they would all know what alternative conceptions of justice are available fro them to choose among; (d) they would all have access to all relevant information; and (e) they must all expect the contract to be observed regardless of whatever circumstances arise. According to this answer, Ricoeur says, "what the initial situation must annihilate, more than anything else, are the effects of contingency, due to nature as much as to social circumstances, so-called merit being placed by Rawls among these effects of contingency."[16] The process and outcome of the establishment of the contract are thus radically ahistorical.

The second question is: What principles of justice will the contracting parties choose? The Rawlsian answer is that the principles chosen will all be principles of distribution. These principles are to cover all the sorts of advantages that can be distributed. They are to cover both rights and duties and benefits and burdens. The principles are to disregard the diversity among goods and to make no evaluative ranking of them. The only relevant consideration is whether the distribution is fair, whether, that is, the contracting parties in the original position were all equal and all agreed to the terms of distribution, including how the inevitable inequalities were to be handled.[17] The second of the two principles that Rawls proposes is the famous "difference principle." This is an antisacrificial principle. It amounts to: "Whoever could be the victim must not be sacrificed even for the benefit of the common good. The principle of difference, in this way, selects the most equal situation compatible with the rule of unanimity."[18]

The third question asks about the reasons that the parties behind the veil of ignorance would have for preferring the Rawlsian principles to any version of utilitarianism. The Rawlsian answer is that his principles would lead to the maximizing of the minimum share. Since no one would know which share he or she would receive, it is in each person's interest to make sure that if he or she gets the smallest share, that share will still be the largest possible. In the condition of uncertainty about which share one will receive, decision theory would require that one agree only to a distribution in which the smallest share would be as large as one could make it, given that some unanimous decision must be reached.

The Rawlsian answers to these three questions lead Ricoeur to ask (a) to what extent can an actual historical society be obligated to observe the terms of an ahistorical contract, and (b) whether a purely procedural conception of justice can really break all links to a sense of justice that antedates it and that continues to be in play? Ricoeur's answer is that Rawls's conception of justice "provides at best the formalization of a sense of justice that it never ceases to presuppose."[19]

Rawls's answers to the questions, Ricoeur contends, lead to two important conclusions. First, Rawls's universalism has as its corollary principles of justice that are sheerly formal. The criterion of universality ensures that no empirical content can satisfy it, for it requires setting aside individual inclination in favor of rational will, it forbids treating others simply as means in the sphere of dialogue, and it eliminates teleological or utilitarian considerations from the institutional sphere. Kantian autonomy is to govern the three spheres. Each person is autonomous to the extent that inclination is excluded from the determination of what each is to do or aim for. The idea of the person as end in himself is the expression of autonomy in dialogical situations. And the freely joined contract is autonomy's equivalent at the level of institutions.

The second conclusion that Rawls's answers yield is that, unlike the principle of autonomy for which Kant claims legitimacy because it is a "fact of reason," the Rawlsian contract is a fiction. Why, Ricoeur asks, would the legitimacy of institutions have to depend on a fictional social contract designed to be the counterpart at the institutional level to autonomy at the individual and dialogical levels?

Ricoeur suggests that Rawls's position comes out of and reflects a context in which people have been "enslaved for millennia to a principle of domination transcending their will to live together."[20] They no longer realize that they are sovereign, not because some fictional contract makes them so, but because of a will to live together that they have now forgotten. Once this will is forgotten, then there is nothing but a fiction that can make the contract equivalent to autonomy and to the recognition of each person as an end and not a means. Indeed, Ricoeur continues:

> If now, by moving backward, we carry this doubt affecting the fiction of the contract back to the principle of autonomy, does

not the latter also risk finding itself a fiction intended to compensate for forgetting the foundation of deontology *in the desire to live well with and for others in just institutions*?[21]

To buttress this proposal, Ricoeur returns to the ambiguity that he pointed out concerning the distribution of shares. When closely examined, Rawls's purely procedural rules of distribution show that they obscure two things. They obscure the diversity among the goods to be distributed. Thus, Rawls enumerates as goods to be distributed such things as revenues, social advantages and burdens, honors and criticisms, and positions of authority or responsibility without making anything of the qualitative differences among them. Rawls's procedural rules also disregard the differences among individuals or groups in the contributions they make to a society's well-being and continued existence. These differences, as Aristotle saw, pose a substantial distributional problem.

Rawls is not troubled by his incorporation into his theory of the idea of primary social goods. These are the goods that are required for the pursuit of any other goods. They include elementary opportunities and powers, rights and liberties, wealth or income, and as a result of having these primary goods, the good of self-respect.[22] But, leaving aside the matter of self-respect, all of these primary social goods are open to diverse meanings and evaluations. Rawls's distributional principles cannot settle the conflicts that unavoidably arise from this diversity. Furthermore, not only are these goods evaluated differently. Each evaluation or estimation of any one of them bears the marks of the historical and cultural context of the estimation in question. Thus, each estimation, by its contextual limits, conflicts with the aim of universalism.[23]

Michael Walzer, Ricoeur notes, has taken into account the real qualitative diversity of goods and of the evaluations made of them. The upshot of his doing so is a shattering of the supposedly unitary principle of justice into separate spheres of justice. Among these spheres is that which governs membership in a political society, that which determines the needs of members that call for legal protection or assistance, that which determines what can be bought and sold, and that which covers the distribution of offices in the society.[24] Walzer's work thus raises, without claiming to solve, the problem of how we are to arbitrate the competition among spheres of justice and their interpretation in such a way that we can avoid, or at least reduce, the threat that the norms of one sphere will encroach indefensibly on those of another sphere. It is to this problem that Ricoeur's alternative to Rawls's theory is addressed.

As I indicated above, Ricoeur's critique of and alternative to Rawls's theory do not aim simply to overthrow it. He recognizes that Rawls's concern for universal principles, individual freedom, and fair procedures, especially in pluralistic contexts, is well placed. Nonetheless, he holds that Rawls's theory fails precisely because it insists on the priority of the right over the good. In its stead, Ricoeur argues for a position that recognizes

> 1. the priority of the ethical over the moral, 2. the necessity nonetheless for the ethical aim to pass through the sieve of the norm, 3. the legitimacy of recourse from the norm to the aim, when the norm leads to conflicts for which there is no other resolution than a *practical wisdom* which refers to that which, in the ethical aim, is most attentive to the singularity of situations.[25]

One will recall that Ricoeur, by convention, uses the term *ethical* for the goal of a life that is to be fulfilled by actions that are considered and the term *moral* for the obligatory side of actions. This is the side of norms, obligations, and prohibitions. It is characterized both by a demand for universality and by a sense of constraint.

Consider first Ricoeur's argument for claiming the priority of the ethical over the moral. He defines the ethical as "the aim for the good life, with and for others, in just institutions."[26] All three constituents of this definition have equal importance.

The good life is not something that one is commanded to seek. It is something that one wishes or hopes for. It is something that someone is concerned about either for oneself or for another.

Concern for the good life for oneself is rooted in self-esteem. There are two things that make a self worthy of esteem. The first is the capacity to choose, to prefer A to B, for reasons. This is its capacity to act purposefully. The second is its capacity to act effectively, to initiate. This is the capacity to interrupt the causal flow of nature and to introduce changes into the course of things, indeed to begin something new in the world.

Self-esteem is the reflexive moment of action. Through appreciating our actions and our capacity to perform them, we come to appreciate ourselves as the ones who bring them into being. We see that we can not only inaugurate something new but that we can also assess our deeds and order them in some hierarchy. Thus, we see that, unlike mere instruments or simple natural forces, we can organize our lives to pursue an ultimate aim, the aim for the good life.

The aim for the good life, though, is not an aim for something for oneself alone. It is to aim to live well with and for others. Self-esteem does not lead to egotism. Rather, it is intrinsically tied to solicitude for others. As Ricoeur puts it:

[S]olicitude is not added to self-esteem from the outside. Rather, *it unfolds the dialogical dimension that is implicit in self-esteem*. Self-esteem and solicitude can neither be lived nor thought without each other. . . . Self implies the other than self, so that one can say of someone that he esteems himself as another.[27]

Each self encounters other selves who, like him or her, can initiate new things and to whom responsibility for deeds can be imputed. But this reciprocity is of a distinctive sort. Each self is unique. The unsubstitutability of selves for one another is the basis for the solicitude a self has, not for just any selves, but for specific selves.

Reciprocity is not incompatible with some sorts of inequality. The inequality between child and adult, between student and teacher, or between apprentice and master can be admitted without negating reciprocity. Similarly, there can be inequality of health or strength. But these inequalities can be compensated for. The adult, the teacher, or the master deserves recognition for his or her superiority. But when he or she receives it, it is from a self that the recognition comes. Thus, reciprocity is restored. Similarly, when one finds another ill or weak and offers compassion, the inequality between them does not prevent gratitude and appreciation from restoring reciprocity. The solicitude that each person in any of these situations of inequality has for the other re-establishes an equality like that which obtains in true friendship.

The third part of Ricoeur's definition of the ethical aim refers to just institutions. For Ricoeur, "an institution [is] a system for dividing or distributing rights and duties concerning money and property, responsibilities and powers, and, in short, benefits and burdens. This *distributive* character of institutions, in the broad sense of distribution, is what poses a *problem of justice*."[28] An institution is a structure belonging to some historical community. It is irreducible to any form of interpersonal relations but is not fully dissociable from them. "What fundamentally characterizes the idea of institution is the bond of common mores and not that of constraining rules."[29]

Institutions provide a way of including more people in a community than interpersonal or face-to-face relations could. They also extend the efficacy of actions or practices over long spans of time. Through institutions and the distributions they make, the ethical aim is extended to include within the circle of concern many more people than could be encompassed by "I-you" relationships. Through them, "third parties" are included. With the inclusion of these thirds, the category of "each," as in "to each his or her own share." This "each" is not the impersonal "one." Rather, it is the participant in a system of distributions. It is here, with the "third," that the problem of justice appears most trenchantly. It appears in the form: Have you and I dealt justly with the third parties in our community?

Ricoeur defends his introduction of the notion of the just into the ethical aim, the aim of living the good life with others, by noting that one already finds what he calls the *sense* of justice in the mythical material worked over in Greek tragedies as well in religious traditions. This sense of justice supports, but is not exhausted by, legal systems. Furthermore, the sense of justice is tied to that of injustice. Indeed, the sense of injustice regularly appears before that of justice. That is, it is the complaint that *x* is unjust that usually gives rise to thought about what is truly just or unjust.[30] And so, Ricoeur concludes that initially "justice is still a virtue on the path toward the good life and ... the sense of the unjust precedes by its clarity the arguments of jurists and politicians."[31]

The second stage of Ricoeur's reply to the Kantian procedural deontological theories such as that of Rawls, or of Jürgen Habermas for that matter, focuses on the moral norm. For Ricoeur, one will recall, the stage of the moral is just one of the three constituents of the complete ethical aim.

The moral counterpart to the ethical aim for the good life is the demand for norms that are universal. This demand expresses the demand for rationality in conduct. Strictly speaking, Ricoeur says, we can only make sense of the demand for universality by taking it to be a formal rule. It does not tell us what to do. Rather, it establishes the criterion according to which we ought to assess the maxims of our actions. The maxims of our actions should be purified from all reference to desires or inclinations, to pleasure, or to happiness, in short, of all reference to that which is particular. So purified, the legitimate maxims will be those that hold good for all persons, at all times, and in all circumstances. Those who act only in accord with such maxims are autonomous.

Kant compensates for the emptiness of this purely formal demand for universality with his second version of his categorical imperative, which commands us to "act always in such a way that you treat humanity in your own person and that of the other, not only as a means but always also as an end in itself."[32] This second version introduces on the moral level an equivalent, namely respect, to solicitude on the ethical level.

In Ricoeur's view, what prodded Kant to add respect, and indeed the moral level in its entirety, to solicitude and the ethical level was violence. Kant, Ricoeur says, believed that the spontaneous relationship between people was that of violence or exploitation. Exploitation is built into the very structure of action, for in action the agent exercises a power that makes someone else a patient, and potentially a victim. This power exercised on another can be either physical or psychological. The point of the moral level, then, is to prevent the agent from making the patient a victim. In this sense, Ricoeur says, "*the moral . . . is the figure that solicitude takes on when confronted by violence and the threat of violence.*"[33] Kant's second formulation of the categorical imperative, then, is a formalization of the negative version of the Golden Rule, that is: Do not do to another what you would not want him to do to you.

Rawls, in Ricoeur's view, completes the formalization of the idea of justice by linking Kantian deontology to social contract theory through the fiction of an original distribution decided on behind a veil of ignorance. The two basic principles that would guide this distribution reflect the two sorts of Aristotelian rules for justice. Rawls's first principle is a formalization of Aristotle's principle of arithmetic equality. His second is a variant on Aristotle's principle of proportional justice. But, unlike Aristotle's principle of proportionality, neither of Rawls's principles makes reference to the worth of individual contributions to society.[34]

Ricoeur's fundamental criticism of Rawls's position is that Rawls takes his principles to be supported by what he calls our considered convictions. But, Ricoeur argues, these considered convictions, which, as Rawls himself recognizes, do not depend on his two principles of justice, themselves are convictions about what the Golden Rule amounts to. By adopting the point of view of the least favored, Rawls takes into account the fundamentally unjust distribution of benefits and burdens in every society we know of. True to the Kantian imperative to treat everyone as an end in himself, Rawls directs his sense of equity against these injustices. But, Ricoeur says, behind this imperative is the thrust of solicitude, which effects the transition from self-esteem to the ethical sense of justice.[35] This solicitude is a manifestation of our fundamental will to live the good life with others in just institutions.

The third stage of Ricoeur's alternative to the kind of Kantian universalism that Rawls espouses takes its point of departure from the conflicts that arise when one tries to apply a system of universal norms to concrete situations. All too often, there is a conflict between norms that is irresolvable by appeal to some other universal norm. We find ourselves confronted with a decision for which there is no unequivocal rule. Such was the situation Antigone faced. Situations of this sort show the tragedy often involved in action, tragedy that no set of norms can eliminate. For Ricoeur, the only recourse we have in such situations that is consistent with the solicitude we owe to others to one that eschews both legalism and arbitrariness. This recourse is one that harks back to the ethical ground from which morality springs.[36] For egress from the impasse that abstract norms of morality generate when they are applied to a significant number of concrete situations, we have no sensible alternative other than that of resorting to practical wisdom. "Practical wisdom consists in inventing conduct that will best satisfy the exception [to some moral rule] required by solicitude, by betraying the rule to the smallest extent possible."[37]

Ricoeur defends this position with the help of several examples. Consider first the often noted conflict between the concern to respect cultural differences and the concern to uphold universal human rights. What is at stake in this conflict is whether the proclaimed human rights are not themselves simply the manifestation of Western particularism.

Ricoeur rejects cultural relativism, which denies that there are any authentic universal norms. But he insists that it could only be at the end of long, open dialogue among members of different cultures that we could rightly claim to know just what these universal norms are. This dialogue, he says, has scarcely begun. He therefore proposes the admittedly paradoxical notion of

> *universals in context* or *potential or inchoative universals.* This notion gives the best account of [what Rawls calls] *the reflective equilibrium* that we seek between *universality and historicity.* Only a discussion at the concrete level of cultures could say, at the end of a long history still to come, what *putative universals ought to be accepted universals.*[38]

Meanwhile, we have only practical wisdom to guide us in our disagreements about what are really human rights and how we should deal with violations of them.

A second example that Ricoeur offers to resolve conflicts between moral norms comes from a discussion that has taken place within the organization Amnesty International. The question is: How should physicians practice medicine in high risk situations such as psychiatric confinements or prisons, to say nothing about their participation in the administering of capital punishment? The very situation is one that constitutes an attack upon the freedom or health of the inmates. Should the physician in such situations insist on following to the letter the requirements of the Hippocratic oath, even if he or she were to be dismissed by the officials for doing so? Or should the physician yield to the constitutive constraints of the system, making whatever exceptions to the oath that he or she finds compatible with self-respect, respect for others, especially the inmates, and respect for the oath itself?

In such situations, the physician need not and probably should not make the decision alone. He or she should seek the advice of friends and professional colleagues. Nonetheless, there is no rule that either the physician or the advisors can find that would wholly eliminate the clash between rules. They can only have recourse to practical wisdom to construct a line of conduct that is both properly solicitous for the well-being of the inmates and properly respectful of the rule enshrined in the Hippocratic oath. This practical wisdom, Ricoeur says, is "close to what Aristotle meant by the term *phronesis* (which is translated as prudence). The *Nicomachean Ethics* says that it is in the practical order what the unusual experience is in the theoretical order. This is precisely the case with moral judgment in situation."[39]

A third example that Ricoeur offers to defend his position takes up again the matter of the diversity among the goods that the society's institutions distribute. Though Rawls does distinguish primary social goods from other goods, he does not discuss in any detail either the diversity among these goods or between these and other important goods. Nor does he deal with diverse evaluations of the relative worth of each of these goods.

History, Ricoeur argues, shows that there is no immutable rule for ranking these several goods that is universally convincing. A society ranks them on the basis of a public debate, but the ranking is always contestable. Any particular ranking holds good for a people only for a certain historical era. It never attains the status of an irrefutable conviction that is accepted by all thoughtful people at all times.

This public debate, in Ricoeur's eyes, is the counterpart of the advice friends and professional colleagues give in private matters. It yields political judgment, which is always judgment in a situation. Participants in this debate cannot simply cite universal norms. They must exercise a practical wisdom that is communal rather than personal or individual. This practical wisdom aims for what Aristotle calls equity, which is superior to, or the perfecting of, abstract justice. Without the search for the equitable to guide the application of the universal norms that Rawls, or anyone, defends, we are in danger, we are in danger of sacrificing people to principles. We are in danger of disregarding the solicitude that we owe to others, a solicitude that gives rise to the very respect for them that the universal rules of justice are supposed to make manifest.[40]

The considerations that underpin the three claims that constitute Ricoeur's response to Rawls lead him to conclude that we must accept and live with the fact that there is an interminable dialectic between our ethical concerns and our quest for genuine moral norms. This dialectic cannot come to theoretical closure. Its outcome, rather, is practical judgment, the exercise of practical wisdom in some specific situation.[41]

How are we to assess Ricoeur's response to Rawls? Unquestionably, Rawls's ideal theory of justice has its attractions. If there is an ideal standard firmly in place, then we could not only assess our present institutional practices. We would also have a fixed star to guide the reforms we should make. Ricoeur's alternative provides no such security. Nonetheless, his critique of Rawls is compelling and his alternative rings true to experience. To support this assessment, I want to focus on one important feature of Rawls's position, namely its implications for a truly just democratic constitution.

In *Political Liberalism*, Rawls goes into some detail about how a just liberal constitution for a democratic state is to give expression to the two principles of justice that he has set forth.[42] The truly just democratic constitution must embody what he calls "constitutional essentials." These essentials are of two sorts. On the one hand, a just liberal constitution must contain the basic principles that specify the general structure of the government and the political process. Thus, it must delineate and allocate the legislative, executive, and judicial powers and specify how officials gain them. On the other hand, the constitution must make explicit the equal basic rights of each citizen as "the right to vote and participate in politics, liberty of conscience, freedom of thought and association, as well as the protections of the rule of law."[43]

Rawls recognizes that constitutional essentials of the first sort can be specified in several different acceptable ways. For example, some liberal constitutions might call for presidential government while others call for parliamentary government. But the constitutional essentials that deal with basic rights and liberties "can be specified in but one way, modulo relatively small variations. Liberty of conscience and freedom of association, and the political rights of freedom of speech, voting, and running for office are characterized in more or less the same manner in all free regimes."[44]

It is easy, Rawls says, to tell whether the principles of justice that specify citizens' equal basic rights and liberties are satisfied by a constitution. Whether they are or not is more or less visible on the face of the constitutional arrangements and the practices to which they give rise. Because these constitutional essentials can, "modulo relatively small variations," be specified in only one way, one can readily determine whether a constitution contains them. When they are present and when the citizens ratify the constitution, then, according to Rawls, these essentials are fixed once and for all. These fixed provisions allow the people to express "their reasoned democratic will, and indeed without these procedures they can have no such will."[45]

My criticism of this part of Rawls's position does not imply criticism of any particular provision of any constitution. Rather, my objection is to Rawls's claims about the clarity and unalterability of constitutional provisions.

Consider Rawls's claim about the clarity and unalterability of the freedom of speech provision in the light of the corresponding provisions in two other democratic constitutions, the Norwegian and the French. Article 100 of the Norwegian Constitution says:

> There shall be liberty of the Press. No person may be punished for any writing, whatever its contents, which he has caused to be printed or published, unless he wilfully and manifestly has either himself shown or incited others to disobedience to the laws, contempt of religion, morality, or the constitutional powers, or resistance to their orders, or had made false and defamatory accusations against anyone. Everyone shall be free to speak his mind frankly on the administration of the State and on any subject whatsoever.[46]

One can reasonably ask a number of questions about this article. For example, does it declare two freedoms, one of speech and one of the press, or only one? If two, then do they both have the same restrictions? What counts as proscribed resistance to the orders of the constitutional powers? And, not of least importance, what amendments of Article 100 would be permissible, given Article 112, which says:

> If experience shows that any part of this Constitution of the Kingdom of Norway ought to be amended . . . [s]uch amendment must never . . . contradict the principles embodied in this Constitution, but solely relate to modifications of particular provisions which do not alter the spirit of the Constitution.

Rawls notwithstanding, one would be hard pressed to say, just from the words of Articles 100 and 112, whether the Norwegian free speech provisions are equivalent to those in the United States First Amendment.

The French Constitution's free speech provisions are no more transparent than the Norwegian ones. They are, in fact, far more complex to state and give rise to no less difficult questions. First, the Preamble of the present French Constitution, adopted on October 4, 1958, says: "The French people solemnly proclaim their attachment to the Rights of Man and the principles of national sovereignty as defined by the Declaration of 1789, reaffirmed and amplified by the Preamble to the Constitution of 1946."[47] The Preamble of the Constitution of October 27, 1946 says:

> The French people proclaim anew that every human being, without distinction of race, religion or creed, possesses inalienable and sacred rights. They solemnly reaffirm the rights and freedoms of man and the citizen as set forth in the Declaration of Rights

of 1789, and the fundamental principles recognized by the laws of the Republic.[48]

The Declaration of the Rights of Man and of the Citizen says:

> Article 10: No one is to be importuned because of his opinions, even religious ones, provided their manifestation does not disturb the public order established by law. Article 11: Free communication of ideas and opinions is one of the most precious rights of man. Consequently, every citizen may speak, write and print freely: yet he may have to answer for the abuse of that liberty in the cases determined by law.

Rawls is surely not ignorant of the history of both Norwegian and French constitutional interpretation and jurisprudence. But it seems evident that questions such as those I raise can only be answered by considering that history, a history that is still unfolding. For example, in early September 1996, serious French political figures argued that French constitutional principles would not only allow but indeed would call for legal sanctions against Jean-Marie Le Pen and the French National Party that he leads for his racist speeches. Similarly, there is a history of interpretation of the United States First Amendment that also continues to unfold. Is "hate speech" constitutionally protected? Is it contrary to the First Amendment to limit the amount of money that one can spend for political advertising? There is no good reason to think that any of these histories is or should be at an end.

In sum, one learns several things from these examples of different constitutional ways of declaring a right to free speech. First, one can know what a constitutional provision amounts to in practice and hence what it actually means only if one knows the history of its interpretation. Second, no such history of interpretation is ever finished so long as the constitutional provision is in force. And third, particular constitutional provisions are regularly interpreted in the light of both prevailing circumstances and other constitutional provisions with their own histories of interpretation. In short, no constitutional provision's meaning, Rawls notwithstanding, is clear on its face. His ambition to have some constitutional essentials settled once and for all is misplaced.

It is truer to the historical character of all human doings, including political doings, to acknowledge that no constitutional provision can or should be treated as definitive. They are all responses to some particular set of circumstances. Inasmuch as they claim to be just prescriptions for future conduct, they are always subject to the test of how people fare who observe them. If experience shows that they do not contribute to what Ricoeur calls living the good life with and for others in just institutions, then they should be changed. Furthermore, precisely because of the historical character of human existence, no experience could ever show that any particular constitutional provision is definitively warranted. They are all always open to contestation in the light of what Ricoeur calls the ethical aim.

Rawls rightly stresses that constitutions are documents of exceptional importance. They aim to capture a group of people's sense of themselves as members of a durable political society. Framers and ratifiers of constitutions rightly seek to give them the preeminent status they need to retain power through all foreseeable circumstances.

Nonetheless, the framers and ratifiers are not omniscient. Neither they nor any interpreter can justifiably claim to pronounce the last word. Rawls's quest for universally valid principles of justice that resolutely resist taking into account any specific historical goods has led him to neglect the limitations on the validity of any particular constitutional provision and hence of any particular determinations of what justice demands.

Ricoeur's account, by contrast, gives us a far better way to understand both the impetus to establish constitutions containing universal norms, and the need for an interminable process of interpreting and modifying them. He situates the impetus to justice in dialectical tension with the pursuit of a common good. His tripartite dialectic corresponds (a) to a society's understanding, however inexplicit it may be, that it is held together by its members' union in pursuing some common goods, (b) to its becoming aware that there is a complex distributional question that calls for universal norms, and hence for something such as a constitution that specifies universal rights and obligations, and thus rules out "scapegoating," and (c) to its learning that this constitutional imperative can never be definitively satisfied and hence there is no alternative to an ongoing exercise of a practical wisdom that is action guiding in even the most complex and difficult situations. It is practical wisdom that must both adapt norms to particular circumstances and perceive when the norms themselves must be reworked. In short, Ricoeur provides a fine alternative to Rawls's insistence on the priority of the just over the good.

NOTES

1. Paul Ricoeur, Cc, 124.
2. John Rawls, A *Theory of Justice* (Cambridge: The Belknap Press of Harvard University Press, 1971), hereafter cited as *TJ*.

3. "Apres *Theorie de la justice* de John Rawls" deals with some of the modifications Rawls makes of his theory in writings subsequent to *A Theory of Justice*. Some of these modifications appear in Rawls's *Justice et democratie* (Paris: Éditions du Seuil, 1993). They are also found in his *Political Liberalism* (New York: Columbia University Press, 1993), hereafter cited as *PL*.

4. Paul Ricoeur, "Ethique et morale: visee theologique (sic) et perspective deontologique" in *Ragione Pratica Liberta Normativita*, ed. Marcello Sanchez Sorondo (Roma: Universita Lateranense, 1991), 353–366. Hereafter cited as *EMVT*. "Theologique" is surely a misprint for "teleologique."

5. *TJ*, 250 and 83. Rawls refines these two principles in *PL*, 291, but not in such a way that it affects Ricoeur's critique.

6. *PL*, 175.
7. *PL*, 193.
8. *PL*, 203.
9. OA, 228.
10. *LJ*, 88. See also OA, 236.
11. OA, 170.
12. OA, 170.
13. OA, 228.
14. OA, 230.
15. OA, 231.
16. OA, 232.
17. OA, 234.
18. OA, 235. See also *LJ*, 74 ff.
19. OA, 236. See also Paul Ricoeur, "Le cercle de la demonstration," in his *Lectures I*, esp. 220–223.
20. OA, 239.
21. OA, 239.
22. Chandran Kukathas and Philip Pettit, *Rawls: A Theory of Justice and Its Critics* (Stanford: Stanford University Press, 1990), 25.
23. OA, 251–252.
24. Michael Walzer spells out his theory in his *Spheres of Justice: A Defense of Pluralism and Equality* (New York: Basic Books, 1983).
25. *EMVT*, 353.
26. *EMVT*, 354. See also Ricoeur's argument for the priority of the ethical in OA, 171–202.
27. *EMVT*, 355.
28. *EMVT*, 356.
29. OA, 194.
30. OA, 198 AND *EMVT*, 356. One will recall that John Stuart Mill, in chapter 5 of *Utilitarianism*, broaches the issue of justice by first listing the things that generally strike us as unjust.
31. *EMVT*, 357.

32. *EMVT*, 358. Ricoeur's French version of Kant's second formulation of the categorical imperative differs from the usual English rendition, which is: "Act always so that you treat humanity whether in your person or in that of another always as an end, but never as a means only." But so far as I can tell, this difference does not affect Ricoeur's line of argument.

33. *EMVT*, 359.
34. *EMVT*, 360.
35. *EMVT*, 361.
36. *OA*, 241–248.
37. *OA*, 269. My insertion.
38. *EMVT*, 363. My insertion. See also *OA*, 283–286.
39. *EMVT*, 364. See also *OA*, 261–262.
40. *EMVT*, 365–366 and *OA*, 284–285.
41. *OA*, 287.

42. Rawls presents *Political Liberalism* as a political theory that is compatible with a number of comprehensive moral theories, though it itself is, unlike the theory he presented in *A Theory of Justice*, not a comprehensive theory. Because *PL* makes a more restricted claim than *TJ* does, my criticism of *PL* holds a fortiori for *TJ*.

43. *PL*, 227.
44. *PL*, 228.
45. *PL*, 232.

46. *The Constitution of the Kingdom of Norway,* English version, Norwegian Ministry of Foreign Affairs, 1992.

47. *The French Constitution*, bilingual edition (Paris: Ministere des Affaires Estrangeres, 1995), 5. Hereafter cited as *FC*.

48. *FC*, 63.

ELEVEN

The Right and the Good
A Solution to the Communicative Ethics Controversy

James L. Marsh

For many years it has seemed to me that ethical theory has been plagued by a series of antinomies: between "is" and "ought," "right" and "good," particular tradition and universal norm, concrete, individual other and reflectively justified norm, justification and application, deontology and teleology, self and other. Thinkers as diverse as Walzer, Nozick, Rawls, Habermas, Apel, Macintyre, and Taylor, each drawing in his own way on Aristotle, Kant, and Hegel, have contributed to and made moves to overcoming such antinomies. "The communicative ethics controversy" I take to refer to this general set of antinomies, even though specific thinkers may understand it to refer to more specific issues such as that of particular context versus universal norm. Who will put this ethical Humpty Dumpty back together again.?[1]

Enter Paul Ricoeur. Part of the significance of his *Oneself as Another* is his attempt to do precisely that, to integrate what has hitherto been split asunder. Ethical reflection is not the whole of his book, but rather constitutes the last part of a progressively deepening and widening inquiry into the self attempting to answer the following questions. Who is speaking? Who is acting? Who is interpreting herself as herself? Who is the moral subject of imputation? The first set of studies (1 and 2) answers the first question using the resources of the philosophy of language. The second set (3 and 4) answers the second question using the philosophy of action, and the third set (5 and 6) answers the third question basing itself of hermeneutics. The fourth set of studies (7, 8, and 9) answers the fourth question concerning the ethical. And a final study reflects on the ontological implications of selfhood.

The first four studies, then, focus on the "who" of language and action by means of inquiry into their "what," "why," and "how." Ricoeur here has recourse to reflective mediation over immediate positing of the self. Studies 5 and 6 reflect on the concordance and discordance between *idem* identity and *ipse* identity, between the self conceived as having a permanent, underlying core and the self as an affair of freedom. The last set of ethical studies emphasizes the dialectic between the self and other. All three dialectics are present throughout the book, but in each part a different dialectic is emphasized. Ricoeur's general claim is that selfhood on all levels implies otherness and vice versa.

The final set of ethical reflections crowns, completes, and renders concrete the inquiry into the self. Ricoeur defines the ethical perspective as "aiming at the good life with and for others in just institutions" (180). This definition has three components: the self as oriented to the good, solicitude as defining my life with others in community, and just institutions such as these mediate my life in community. The meaning of the good life progressively expands from the self to immediate others to just institutions. As I said above, the self is mediated by otherness, the good life of the self by immediate others and just institutions.

Ricoeur notes a distinction between ethics and morality. The former inquires into what is good, the latter into what is obligatory. The former takes its bearings from Aristotle, whose ethics is teleological; the latter is influenced by Kant, for whom morality is defined by teleological norm. Ricoeur here makes three general claims: he asserts the primacy of ethics over morality, the necessity for the ethical aim to pass through and be tested by morality, and the necessity to have recourse to teleological aim when norms lead to conflicts and antinomies, as they inevitably do. For example, Ricoeur notes the necessity at times to lie or not to tell the full truth to a person who is dying. One study each is devoted to each of these three theses, and this chapter will correspondingly have three parts and a final, concluding part of critical reflection. In all three studies Ricoeur proves his theses by reflecting on the tripartite character of the ethical life as the good of the self, as involved with others, and as mediated by just institutions (170–171).

THE PRIMACY OF ETHICS OVER MORALITY

The good life is the object of the ethical aim. As such the good is composed of actions that are defined by standards of excellence in different domains allowing us to characterize as good a doctor, an architect, or professor. These standards of excellence are themselves integrated into broader and deeper life plans that have a narrative unity, which Aristotle refers to as the end of man as such, his end as a man to live rationally, ethically, contemplatively. The content of the good life is "the nebulus of ideals and dreams of achievements with regard to which a life is held to be more or less fulfilled or unfulfilled" (179). Ricoeur notes a hermeneutical circle between life plan and major, particular decisions that carry it out such as the decision to marry or to enter upon a certain career. On the ethical level self-interpretation should lead to self-esteem; on a moral level self-interpretation leads to self-respect, but this is subordinated to self-esteem. Self-respect is self-esteem as that passes through the testing of the norm (171).

The apparent solitary, egological focus on the good life as grounding self-esteem is overcome, according to Ricoeur, when Aristotle reflects on friendship in order to develop his concept of solicitude, the "with and for others" aspect of ethical life. Friendship serves as a transition between the aim of the good life and justice, the virtue of human plurality in the political sphere. The fully happy man, rather than being self-sufficient, needs friends because they are essential to the exercise of virtue prior to human excellence. I cannot adequately be a friend to myself and thus have self-esteem unless I am friends with another, another self. "I cannot myself have self-esteem unless I esteem others as myself" (193). Friendship in the truest, fullest sense, that based on the good as opposed to mere utility or pleasure, is reciprocal and mutual. Friendship borders on justice, but it is not justice, because the latter governs institutions and the former interpersonal relationships (182–188).

If the good and happy man needs friends, it is because friendship helps him realize or perfect himself on the highest intellectual or moral level. Friendship in its intrinsic goodness and pleasure is to be fully conscious of myself as intellectual and free and generous.

Solicitude expands what we mean by ethical life. Solicitude is not added onto self-esteem from outside, but simply unfolds its dialogic aspects (180). Solicitude, the concrete care for the other as other, benevolent spontaneity, is developed by Ricoeur after treating the reciprocity of friendship. Solicitude has a more fundamental character than does obedience to duty, which character Ricoeur defines as benevolent spontaneity based on self-esteem. This disposition allows the benevolent and compassionate self to rectify the initial asymmetry involved in either receiving an injunction from a "master of justice" (Levinas) or offering sympathy toward one who is suffering. In the first case self-esteem is presupposed in receiving the injunction; in the second case self-esteem is enhanced insofar as the suffering other enables me to feel and to share her suffering. Mutuality as reciprocity, however, remains the norm in the light of which either asymmetry is judged inadequate (188–194).

Justice in institutions is based upon but goes beyond solicitude to concern itself with equality. "Equality... is to life in institutions what solicitude is to interpersonal relations" (202). Institutions are the structure of living together as this belongs to a historical community; this structure is irreducible to interpersonal relations and yet bound up with them in a remarkable way. The institution is the point of application of justice, and equality is the ethical content of justice. Equality here is proportional, not arithmetical, and, therefore, implies some legitimate inequality. Because of differences in merit between one person and another, some people may be entitled to a greater share of some good. Proportional equality is a relationship between two relationships of person and meriting of some good. For instance, if one person receives an A for performance in class and another a B for less adequate performance, both persons are treated equally in the class, but in a proportional and complex, not a simple and arithmetical, sense (201).

What basically characterizes an institution is the bond of common mores and not merely that of constraining rules; here, we recall our notion of the ethos of living together. Here also we mark the distinction between power in common, which comes from individuals acting together in community, and domination, the relation of the governed to those governing. Power is more fundamental than domination and grounds it as legitimate or illegitimate. More of this discussion later (194–196).

The just as proportional in institutions faces in two directions at once, toward the good, with respect to which it marks the extension of interpersonal relations to institutions, and the legal, the judicial system conferring upon the law commerce and rights of constraint. Justice is primarily distributive and is not primarily economic. Ricoeur in this study focuses on the former. It refers to the appointment of roles and tasks, advantages and disadvantages among the members of society. Justice as distributive allows us to reject both sides of a false debate between individualism and society. Society is always more than the sum of its members because its life is institutionalized. On the other hand, there is no separate, super entity above and beyond individuals. The key concepts of sociology refer to the probability that individuals will act in a certain way (197–201).

Ricoeur in the next chapter, chapter 8, deals with the transition from ethics to morality. Kantian universality is anticipated by the universality of the Aristotelian mean, and by such universal, human virtues and capacities as the abilities to initiate an action, to choose on the basis of reasons, and to estimate and evaluate the goals of action. Morality as Kant interprets it, on the other hand, reveals its links to the good life through Kant's insistence that nothing is unqualifiedly good except good will. Not only does "good" in this claim retain its teleological imprint, but we see a parallel between Kantian good will and Aristotelian rational desire. Moreover, morality becomes necessary in order to test and ratify what is genuinely good and just (203–205).

We enter the Kantian, normative problematic through the gate of universality, which develops through the three versions of the categorical imperative. The first emphasizes the autonomy of the will in relation to desire, the second unconditional respect for the other as an end in herself, and the third bringing about a kingdom of ends in a context of justice. Parallelism exists between autonomy, respect for others, and the kingdom of ends in the moral sphere and the self pursuing the good, solicitude, and just institutions in the ethical sphere (203–204).

Ricoeur argues here that there is a continuity between the first formulation of the categorical imperative stressing universality and the second and third versions in which plurality of persons comes into play. Underlying the prescription of universality is that of humanity, and the basic idea here is the person as an end in herself, as having unconditional value. Such unconditional value is experienced and known already on the ethical level, and is expressed imperfectly on that level as the Golden Rule: "Do not do unto others what you would not have them do to you," or "Treat others as you would have them treat you." The golden rule, for Ricoeur more than Kant, acts as a transition from solicitude on the ethical level to the second formulation of the categorical imperative to treat others as ends in themselves and not merely as means (218–227).

Moving to the domain of justice, Ricoeur regards Rawls's *Theory of Justice* as the most ambitious effort to free the deontological viewpoint of morality from the teleological perspective of ethics. At the same time Rawls's effort best illustrates the limits of that enterprise. In each of three key elements of his theory—an original position, in which particular life prospects and advantages of the participants are concealed behind a veil of ignorance; the two principles of justice, the first stating that each person is to have an equal right to the most extensive basic liberty compatible with a similar liberty for others and the second stipulating that social and social economic inequalities are to be arranged so that they are both reasonably expected to be to everyone's advantage and attached to positions and offices open to all; and the *maximin* argument for the two principles—Rawls strives for independence from teleology.

Yet each stage tacitly or implicitly implies some reference to teleology. In the original position, for example, all of the participants are aware of legitimate preferences for primary goods, one of which is self-respect. On the level of the two principles, the mutuality and reciprocity of the ethical level seems to be presupposed in the sense that distribution of rights and duties, benefits and burdens has to be fair. Moreover, the argument for the two principles, the *maximin* argument stating that each party would and should choose the arrangement that maximizes the minimum share, would seem at best to be a formalization of an ethical sense of justice that it never ceases to presuppose. One indication of this point is that Rawls appeals to a reflective equilibrium between his theory and our considered convictions expressing and rooted in a prior, lived sense of justice (228–237).

In spite of its proclaimed independence from teleology, deontology reveals its dependence on the ethical in at least three more ways. First, Kant's recognition of "the fact of morality" as a starting point for ethical reflection indicates that this fact is attested to and rooted in a recognition that only a good will is unconditionally good. Second, the person as an end in himself is initially lived in the community, and the Golden Rule is an initial thematization of that awareness. Finally, the social contract as a fiction founding institutions is fictional because of a will to live together, which communities may have forgotten (238–239).

The final stage in Ricoeur's argument is the return to the ethical after passing through the norm. What motivates this return is the conflict emerging from the one-sidedness of the norms themselves. The inadequacy of the norm requires recourse to a respect for the other based upon ethical self-esteem. The norm is not rejected but qualified, chastened, and situated in a broader ethical context. "Practical wisdom consists in inventing conduct that will best satisfy the exception required by solicitude, by betraying the rule to the smallest extent possible" (269).

In his treatment of ethical, prudential conviction Ricoeur reverses the path of his previous studies and moves from reflection on just institutions, in which Hegelian *Sittlichkeit*, minus *Geist*, is recovered as a kind of collective *phronesis*, through the interpersonal, in which telling the truth to the dying and abortion are reflected upon, to the autonomous, good-seeking self. One advantage of this procedure is that the self more clearly emerges at the end of Ricoeur's reflections as genuinely other to itself, mediated by other persons and just institutions. Also, a circle is inscribed in the three chapters insofar as Ricoeur moves from a relatively immediate ethical self through the detour of the norm to a self fully, explicitly, and concretely mediated by the other.

Sittlichkeit in Hegel's sense is, as I have said, recovered in a form of collective *phronesis*. We give the rule of justice a broader application than it has in Hegel insofar as it extends to collective deliberation about the distribution of power, its relation to domination, and the priorities among the primary goods as defined by Rawls: income, wealth, self-respect, liberty, and opportunity; the debate concerning the possible ends of good government such as "security," "prosperity," "equality," and "solidarity," and the process of legitimating institutions, policies, and practices in society. Collective *phronesis* involves reflecting in public on the political conceived as reflection on a set of practices relating to the distribution of political power in its relation to domination, reflecting in an open, democratic, dialogal, respectful manner on these issues, and avoiding any univocal imposition of the good on the people. There is, then, a principled indeterminacy in democratic theory and practice that Ricoeur, following Lefort, wishes to affirm (253–262).

In reflecting on interpersonal morality, Ricoeur considers first the question of telling the truth to the dying. Here, there are two possible extremes to be avoided: that of always telling the truth without taking into account the capacity of the person to receive it, and that of never telling the truth because we assume the person is too weak to receive it. Practical wisdom lies in inventing the behavior appropriate to the particular situation. Sometimes the truth should be told and sometimes not, depending on the circumstances. The choice is not simply arbitrary. One relevant distinction, which Ricoeur makes and Kant does not, is that between a sensible happiness proper to the lower faculty of desiring and a more reflective happiness taking the form of a deep giving and receiving between persons. The distinction allows us to deny any necessary incompatibility between happiness and suffering. At times I will withhold the truth totally, and at times I will use telling the truth as the occasion for communicatively giving and receiving and thus deepen the relationship with the person afflicted (269–270).

We can treat issues arising from the beginning of life similarly. Extreme positions to be avoided, according to Ricoeur, are a biologistic definition of the human person such that genetic heredity determines and constitutes the individual person from the moment of conception; and the opposite extreme of saying that only fully developed, rational individuals deserve respect. What should happen is that the notion of respect needs to be accompanied by a minimum ontology of development, which adds to the idea of capacity the notion of aptitude admitting of degrees of actualization. Corresponding to these degrees would be different rights and duties; the right not to suffer, the right to protection, which itself has different degrees of force or emphasis; the right to respect once something like exchange of preverbal signs, albeit asymmetrical, has begun between fetus and mother (270–272).

Such critical solicitude, once that has passed through the test of the moral norm and the conflicts engendered by it, is characterized by three features.

First, the differing positions call upon the same principle of respect, differing only in the amplitude of application. Second, the Aristotelian principle of the just mean is good advice; in this way the determination of a period of gestation during which abortion is permitted requires a highly developed moral sense. Third, moral judgment in this situation will be all the less arbitrary insofar as the decision maker has consulted the men and women deemed to be the wisest. Here, the decision made is not monological but flows from the plural nature of the debate. "In conclusion, one can say that it is to solicitude, concerned with the otherness of persons, including 'potential persons,' that respect refers, in those cases where it is itself the source of conflicts, in particular in novel situations produced by the powers that technology gives humans over the phenomena of life" (273).

In his reflection on autonomy, Ricoeur considers the tension between universality and particular context and traditions. He gives full credit to Habermas's theory of communicative action for recovering in one stroke the Kantian emphasis on autonomy, respect for the other and just institutions, and concedes validity to Habermas's argument as a form of justification. Habermas's approach is limited, however, insofar as he does not develop adequately the *phronesis* necessary to apply a universally valid norm. Once again Habermas's universality is not rejected but only qualified, chastened, and situated in a broader context.

Habermasian universality rooted in a communicative practice governed by criteria of truth, sincerity, and rightness, oriented to the better argument, forbidding any arbitrary exclusion of feeling, opinion, or value, and aiming at moral norms that are truly universal, constituted by all and applying to all, is legitimate as a process of justification. It requires, however, a complementary process of actualization and application that takes into account particular historical, communal, and individual contexts. What is also required is a reflective equilibrium between universality and historicity. Here, Ricoeur argues that the notion of universality in context or potential universal or inchoate universal best accounts for such reflective equilibrium.

The current discussion of human rights is an example. Basically, these rights can be regarded as well-argued derivatives from the ethics of argumentation as developed by Habermas and Apel. Such human rights have been ratified by every state, and yet the suspicion remains that they are simply the fruit of the cultural tradition of the West. Universalism and context overlap on a small number of fundamental issues such as those contained in the Universal Declaration of the Rights of Man and the Citizen. Yet they have been implemented effectively even in a partial way only in Western democracies. To the extent that the values in our culture are not shared by other cultures, the charge of ethnocentrism is directed toward these texts themselves, which nonetheless have been ratified by all the governments in the world.

One should resist this skeptical drift, replete with the danger of relativism, and affirm a paradox. One must maintain the universal claim attached to a few values where universal and historical intersect, and one must, on the other hand, submit the claims to a discussion, not merely on a formal level, but on the level of convictions embodied in forms of life. Every party must recognize that potential universals are contained in so-called exotic cultures, admit as possibly true the proposals that are foreign to us, and I would add, in a way faithful to Ricoeur's spirit, own up to the contradiction in the West and North between universals affirmed and concrete economic, cultural, and political imperialism that violates these. The tendency to subordinate Third World countries to First World well-being, the regular subversion or repression of democracy in Third World countries where that threatens First World priorities, and the use of international organizations like the U.N. simply to carry out the imperialistic aims of the First World, which demonstrably occurred in the Gulf war, are violations of genuine universal rights and values of the West such as respect for human dignity, democracy, and concern to treat the individual or collective other as an end in herself, not just a means to my well-being.

What is offensive about human rights talk is, I think, its ideological use and abuse by the West in its project of imperial domination and exploitation. Both Habermas and postmodernism miss different aspects of this point, the one affirming universal rationality but missing or at least not emphasizing enough its imperial use and abuse (Habermas, remember, supported the Gulf War) and the other legitimately bothered by imperialism and arrogant ethnocentrism but lacking, for the most part, any satisfactory account of rationality. Derrida's *The Other Heading* is an interesting exception to this claim, affirming the legitimacy of universals but critical of their abuse in the imperial project. Ricoeur, on the other hand, allows us to steer between the Scylla of a triumphalistic, Western modernism and universalism and the Charybdis of a skeptical, normless, postmodern relativism (284–290).[2]

Ricoeur summarizes his account by saying that "the practical wisdom we are seeking aims at reconciling Aristotle's *phronesis*, by way of Kant's *Moralitat*, with Hegel's *Sittlichkeit*" (290). One result is that autonomy has ceased to be self-sufficient and has become receptive to and dependent in various ways on the other taken in different senses: the friend, the community, the state taken as a set of institutionalized political practices. His project is very ambitious and very synthetic, a reflective attempt to overcome one-sidedness.

Having a similar orientation, I am in great sympathy and agreement not only with the general thrust of Ricoeur's argument but with many of its details. Nonetheless, I wish to raise a few questions concerning the scope and validity of his achievement. First, it may be that morality is present much earlier on the lived ethical level itself and not merely on a reflective, discursive level that emerges from the ethical level. Is there not in our everyday experience a lived sense of deontology and right that coexists with and relates to our striving for the good? Consider the spontaneous outrage I feel when a woman is raped or a black is viciously insulted. Would not Ricoeur's claim about the Golden Rule as arising on the ethical level, as well as his discussion of the original ethical fact, support this line of thought? Habermas also would support this argument insofar as communicative action is not only the discursive argumentation concerning validity claims but the lived, spontaneous praxis in the world that is already moral, oriented to and based upon validity claims.[3]

Second, even if one disagreed with the above philosophical, transcendental point, does not modernity itself as a tradition or set of traditions, one of which is deontological, institutionalize and incarnate a lived deontology as a part or aspect of our day-to-day life with others? The institutionalization of human rights around the world and in the U.N. Charter is an example. Third, I agree with Ricoeur's recourse to the prudential and to conviction as a complement to universality, but he may do that too quickly. Gunther has shown in a recent work how, up to a point, argumentation concerning application can arise that employs criteria. For example, if I have promised to meet somebody for dinner and a friend falls sick who needs my aid, then I may legitimately break my promise. Prudence comes in after such argumentation, which considers all relevant circumstances and moral norms, occurs.[4]

Fourth, it seems to me that Ricoeur's emphasis on the good adds a motivation that is lacking in Habermas's ethics and critical theory. Fifth, an example of such motivation is that liberation becomes the good we are seeking when we resist sexist, racist, heterosexist, and classist injustice. Justice is the right and liberation the good aimed at in the praxis of social movements. We resist and act not only because we are unjustly treated but because we are unhappy.[5]

Sixth, an implication of Ricoeur's analysis, which he develops in chapter 10, the last chapter, is that a Levinasian concern for the exploited, marginalized other needs to be complemented by ethical and moral reflection on the universal. Without the concrete experience of the marginalized other, moral and ethical reflection remains abstract and unconvincing. Without moral, ethical reflection on the universal, response to the marginalized other remains dogmatic and arbitrary; "Why should I respond?" becomes a legitimate question, for which moral, ethical reflection is legitimate and necessary.[6]

On a subway train in New York City, for example, people beg all the time, but often are denied any money. The reason is that, although they are perceived as "other," their requests are not taken as legitimate. They are perceived as welfare chiselers, lazy, and so on. If, however, they are perceived in the light of neo-Marxist hermeneutics as victims of social injustice, which is the way I am inclined to perceive them, then they have a legitimate claim on our compassion, on our solicitude.[7]

We see that "otherness is not added onto selfhood from the outside . . . but that it belongs instead to the tenor of meaning and ontological constitution of selfhood . . ." (317). Ricoeur insists that a Husserlian movement from the same toward the other apprehended from within my "sphere of ownness," my immediate lived body present in the world, and a Levinasian movement from the other toward the same complement each other. Otherwise, if interiority were not essentially open to and receptive toward the other, how could it hear a word addressed to it? Must there not be a capacity in me to recognize the legitimacy of the claim of the other on me? And does not such a capacity lead up to and presuppose the reciprocity of dialogue in which the exchange between question and answer presupposed a continual changing of roles? The other challenges me and brings me into question, and I in turn respond to and bring her into question (312–318, 338–391).[8]

In conclusion, Ricoeur, I think, has taken major steps in overcoming the antinomies mentioned at the beginning of this essay, at reconstructing the ethical Humpty Dumpty. Progress in this area lies in striding farther along the path he has staked out.

NOTES

1. Paul Ricoeur, OA. Hereafter references to this text will be made by indicating relevant page numbers in my text. For a statement of and reflection about the communicative ethics controversy, see *The Communicative Ethics Controversy*, ed. Seyla Benhabib and Fred Dalimayr (Cambridge: MIT Press, 1990).

I made my own attempt to reconstruct the ethical Humpty Dumpty in *Critique, Action, and Liberation* (Albany: State University of New York Press, 1995), especially chapters 7–9, pp. 113–176 (hereafter referred to as CAL). After I had finished the book, I read *Oneself as Another* and found myself much confirmed in my general line of argument. My interpretation and critique of Ricoeur, therefore, will flow from the hermeneutical-critical framework of CAL.

2. Jürgen Habermas, *The Past as Future*, ed. and trans. Max Pensky (Lincoln: The University of Nebraska Press, 1994), 5–31. Jacques Derrida, *The Other Heading*, trans. Pascal-Anne Brault and Michael Naas (Bloomington: Indiana University Press, 1992). Noam Chomsky, *Year 501: The Conquest Continues* (Boston: South End Press, 1993), 33–64.

3. Jürgen Habermas, *The Theory of Communicative Action, I: Reason and the Rationalization of Society*, trans. Thomas McCarthy (Boston: Beacon Press, 1984), 41–42.

4. Klaus Gunther, *The Sense of Appropriateness*, trans. John Farrell (Albany: State University of New York Press, 1993), 229–255.

5. CAL, 120–124.

6. CAL, 174–175, 180–183.

7. CAL, 267–274.

8. CAL, 180–183.

About the Contributors

Patrick L. Bourgeois is the William and Audrey Hutchinson Distinguished Professor of Philosophy, at Loyola University of New Orleans. He has published many articles and several books, including *Extension of Ricoeur's Hermeneutics* (1973), and edited numerous texts.

Richard A. Cohen is the Isaac Swift Distinguished Professor of Judaic Studies at the University of North Carolina at Charlotte. He is author of *Ethics, Exegesis and Philosophy: Interpretation After Levinas* (2001), and *Elevations: The Height of the Good in Rosenzweig and Levinas* (1994). He has edited and translated several books by and about Levinas.

Eric Crump is Associate Professor of Systematic Theology at the Lutheran Theological Seminary, Gettysburg, Pennsylvania. He received his M.A. (1977) and Ph.D. (1989) in Theology from the Divinity School of the University of Chicago. His dissertation, supervised by Paul Ricoeur and David Tracy, will be published in revised form as *Truth, Faith and the Figural Imagination*.

Bernard P. Dauenhauer is Professor Emeritus of Philosophy at the University of Georgia. His two most recent books are *Paul Ricoeur: The Promise and Risk of Politics* (1998), and *Citizenship in a Fragile World* (1996).

John van den Hengel is titular professor of Systematic Theology at Saint Paul University in Ottawa, Canada. He is the author of *The Home of Meaning* and has written extensively in the field of hermeneutics and religious education. He recently edited and contributed to a special issue of *Eglise et theologie* on Emmanuel Levinas.

Don Ihde is Distinguished Professor of Philosophy at the State University of New York at Stony Brook. He is the author of thirteen books, the most recent of which include *Bodies in Technology* (2001), *Expanding Hermeneutics*

(1998), and *Postphenomenology* (1993). He is also the author of *Hermeneutic Phenomenology: The Philosophy of Paul Ricoeur* (1971) and editor of Paul Ricoeur, *The Conflict of Interpretations* (1974).

Lenore Langsdorf is a Professor at Southern Illinois University. Her research and teaching is focused on the philosophy of communication, using resources from both the European (Husserl, Gadamer, Ricoeur) and the American pragmatic (Dewey, Mean) traditions. She has published many articles in books and professional journals.

James L. Marsh is Professor of Philosophy at Fordham University, Bronx, New York. Among other writings, he has written most recently *Process, Praxis and Transcendence* (1998), and *Critique, Action, and Liberation* (1994).

David Pellauer is Professor of Philosophy at DePaul University, Chicago, Illinois, and editor of the journal *Philosophy Today*. He has translated a number of works by Paul Ricoeur.

David Rasmussen is Professor of Philosophy at Boston College and editor of the journal *Philosophy and Social Criticism*. Among other writings, he is the author of *Mythic-Symbolic Language and Philosophical Anthropology: A Constructive Interpretation of the Thought of Paul Ricoeur* (1971).

Charles E. Reagan is Professor of Philosophy at Kansas State University, where he also serves as Associate to the President. He is author of *Paul Ricoeur: His Life and His Work* (1996), editor of *Studies in the Philosophy of Paul Ricoeur* (1979), and co-editor of *The Philosophy of Paul Ricoeur: An Anthology of His Work* (1978).

Index

Because this book is devoted to a single author and to a single book by a single author, the editors did not think it necessary to include entries under every letter in the alphabet. Readers should rest assured, however, that every major topic and subtopic, both in the book as a whole and in each individual chapter, are present in the index.

H

Human action
  aspects of Ricoeur's approach to, 74; epistemology of in relation to a science of, 86–88; historical, philosophical context for Ricoeur's account of, 72–74; limitations to questions about the possibility of science of, 79; ontological thrust of, 74–79; possibility of science of, 71–72; repercussions of analytic account of, 76–78; role of attestation in, 87; role of narrative in an account of, 76–78; Ricoeur's account of the self in relation to, 83–86; units of, 80–81; ways of expressing intentionality in analytic account of, 76; "who" as more than "what" in Ricoeur's account of, 74–79

Husserl
  dilemma of intersubjectivity in as bequeathed to the philosophy of language, 58

I

Identity
  as bound up with the other, ix; narrative version of in relation to subjectivity, 57; personal version of in relation to narrative version of, 61–65; process of identification as occurring in semantics and pragmatics, 5–61; relation of time and narrative to, 65–68; as sameness and ipseity, 83–84

Intentionality
  genesis of concept of in Husserl and Ricoeur, 42–46; Husserl's account of, 36–42; repressed aspect of in Husserl's account of, ix–x, 46–51; role of gnosis in, 38–40

L

Levinas, Emmanuel
  authority of alterity in as operative at a different, more fundamental

Levinas, Emmanuel (*continued*)
level than Ricoeur's sociality, 133–34, 141; differences between his thought and Ricoeur's, 129; greatness of his ethics as not putting a stop to morality, 152; his challenge to Parmenidean-Hegelian heritage of philosophy, 131–34, 138; his concept of the other as transcendent in the strong sense, 111–13; as missing Ricoeur's twofold sense of identity, 121–22; as not taking into account solicitude, 114; as overstressing the identity of the same, 114; Ricoeur's critique of him for missing the importance of solicitude, 130–31; similarities and differences from Ricoeur in response to Heidegger, 135–36; as too radically opposing the same to the other, 120

M

Mehl, Roger
his concept of reflective philosophy as influencing Ricoeur, 163–67; eschatology as horizon of reflective philosophy in, 163–71

Moral givenness
slavery as an example of, 194–95

O

Oneself as Another
account of ethics and morals in, 16–26; account of narrative identity in, 13–16; account of ontology of the self in, 26–30; account of personal identity in, 8–10; account of relation of action of agent to agent in, 10–13; brief summary of individual essays in, ix–xiii; importance of, vii, 30, 93–94; organization of, ix; relation of to earlier works, vii–ix; role of attestation in, 6–8; significance of, xiii–xiv; synopsis of, 4–30; threefold purpose of, 188–91; three themes of, 4–5

P

Parfit, Derek
his version of science fiction as leading to a concept of self, 93–97

R

Rawls, John
criticism of his view of constitutional provisions as clear and unalterable, 216–19; evaluation of Ricoeur's critique of his giving the right priority over the good, 215–19; his view of considered convictions as implying the golden rule, 213; priority of the right over the good in, 215–219; Ricoeur's critique of his priority of the right over the good, xii, 21–22, 203–16, 227–28

Ricoeur, Paul
autonomy of his philosophy in relation to theology, xii, 163; critique of his critique of Levinas in Chapter 7 of *Oneself as Another*, 135–59; critique of Levinas in, xi, 110–13, 232–33; critique of Ricoeur's critique of Levinas in Chapter 10 of *Oneself as Another*, 135–59; as hermeneutically transforming reflective philosophy, 163; illegitimacy of his critique of Levinas's use of hyperbole, 147–53; implications of using moral blindness as a test of his philosophy, 198–99; as missing the passivity of self in Levinas, 134; moral blindness as testing the limits of philosophy, 99, 187; as not recognizing a legitimate element of receptivity to the other in Levinas, 111, 115–17,

138–41; as providing a viable ethics, in contrast to deconstruction, 110–23; as recognizing the need for Levinas's "face to face," 110–11, 119; as sharing aims with Levinas, 127–28; as too severe in his critique of Levinas, 109

Ricoeur's ethics
account of conscience in, 152–57; Aristotle's contribution to, 224–26; as bringing together the self to other and the other to self, critique of Levinas, xii; contribution of Kant and critique of Kant in, 19–23, 25, 226–27; critique of his critique of Levinas, xi; definition of and as having three aspects, 210–12; evaluation of, 231–33; features of critical solicitude in, 229–30; goal of, 17; Habermasian universality as simultaneously criticized and retained in, 230–32; primacy of ethics over morality in, 224–33; as putting reciprocity and symmetry before asymmetry in ethics, 118–20; as putting the ethical humpty-dumpty back together again, ix, xiii, 223–24; role of friendship in, 16–19, 191–92; role of practical wisdom in, 228–32; role of self-esteem in, 17; solicitude in, 17–19; telling the truth and abortion as issues and instances of practical wisdom in, 24, 214–15, 229–30; validity of his critique, 232–33; weakness of his criticism of Levinas's account of conscience, 157–59

T

Technomyths
comparison of literary and science fiction in Ricoeur's account of, 94–97; constraint systems in analytical and hermeneutical accounts of, 102–104; different body technologies as present in, 95, 100–102; science fiction as identical with technology in Ricoeur's account of, 95, 97–100

Thévenaz, Pierre
his version of reflexive philosophy as an influence in Ricoeur, xii, 171–77

www.ingramcontent.com/pod-product-compliance
Lightning Source LLC
Chambersburg PA
CBHW020648230426
43665CB00008B/345